CENTRAL ASIA'S NEW STATES

CENTRAL ASIA'S NEW STATES

Independence, Foreign Policy, and Regional Security

Martha Brill Olcott

UNITED STATES INSTITUTE OF PEACE PRESS
Washington, D.C.

The views expressed in this book are those of the author alone. They do not necessarily reflect views of the United States Institute of Peace.

United States Institute of Peace
1550 M Street NW
Washington, DC 20005

First published 1996

Printed in the United States of America

The paper used in this publication meets the minimum requirements of American National Standard for Information Sciences—Permanence of Paper for Printed Library Materials, ANSI Z39.48-1984.

Library of Congress Cataloging-in-Publication Data
Olcott, Martha Brill, 1949–
    Central Asia's new states: independence, foreign policy, and regional security / Martha Brill Olcott.
       p. cm.
    Includes bibliographical references and index.
    ISBN 1-878379-51-8 (pbk.)
    1. Asia, Central—Politics and government—1991- I. Title.
DK859.5.043 1995
958—dc20   95-30153
                                          CIP

To Alison, Andrew, and Hillary

CONTENTS

FOREWORD

In her analysis of the new states of Central Asia, Martha Brill Olcott has produced a seminal study of the foreign policies of three former Soviet republics during their first years of independence. In so doing, she has provided us with unique insights on a region that is blessed with tremendous economic resources and yet has come to be defined largely by its potential for ethnic and political instability.

The future of the post-Soviet political milieu is one of distinct regions defined by ethnic and religious identities. While the Baltic states and the western republics seek the familiar embrace of Europe, the republics lying along the southern rim of the former Soviet Union are situated on an unpredictable confluence of past empires, current geopolitical competition, the spreading influence of Islam, and the continuing influence and intervention of their past colonial and Soviet master, Russia. Such a political landscape is bound to present daunting challenges to stability, and we have already seen several outbreaks of violence in the wake of the USSR's demise. In the Caucasus, post-Soviet Georgia has been rent by two major secessionist battles. In neighboring Central Asia, while Tajikistan's civil war has lessened in its intensity, the potential for other such conflicts across the region has by no means exhausted itself.

Central Asia was the arena where England and Russia, in the nineteenth century, played the "Great Game" of geopolitical competition. Now other new players have entered the contest for influence and control of the region, especially Turkey, Iran, and China. That Professor Olcott is able to integrate the region's variegated history into a comprehensive description of its contemporary political landscape shows her remarkable grasp of politics outside the realm of Russia's "near abroad."

At the same time, this book is no less an analysis of Russia than it is of the Central Asian states themselves. Indeed, Russia is a constant presence throughout the pages of this study, as its author plumbs the Russian leadership's views on a region that is exercising the rights and opportunities afforded by statehood but is still decidedly within Russia's sphere of influence. Besides the historical territorial buffer and the natural resource wealth, there is another essential element of Russia's national interest in the region: the millions of ethnic Russians who still reside in the Central Asian states. Their fate is of no less concern to Russian officialdom than it is to Russian nationalists, who view the increasing marginalization of ethnic Russians in lands their country once ruled as a national humiliation.

Most of Central Asia's leaders have thus far maintained the stability of their societies through a delicate balance of ethnic politics, catering to their Russian populations and assuaging Russia's concerns, particularly in Kazakhstan. Yet increasingly powerful nationalist forces among these countries' titular ethnic groups vie for the same economic and political resources. Russians are not the only ethnic minorities in these new states that concern their leaders. Many diaspora ethnic groups provide potential flashpoints for civil and political unrest.

Any serious discussion of Central Asia necessarily includes a detailed examination of Islam as a political force in the region. The present analysis is no exception. Yet Professor Olcott's analysis of political Islam departs from the more alarmist views of these former Soviet republics' "going Islamic," particularly in light of Iran's increasing influence in the region. While Islam is indeed heightening its influence throughout the region, Dr. Olcott puts this development into a relatively constructive context, arguing that Islam has been a force that has buoyed both the political fortunes of titular nationalist groups in the republics and the attractiveness of these new states as their leaders search for an identity—and for economic assistance from other predominantly Muslim states.

While Professor Olcott's investigation of this region provides us with a comprehensive look at the growing pains of these new independent countries' polities and economies, she goes one important step further by linking their domestic concerns to their foreign policies and their role in regional and international security. In particular, this book will provide context and insight to officials in the U.S. foreign policymaking establishment as they attempt to establish guidelines for how far Russia can and should exert its influence among the new, independent states of Central Asia. For Western nations searching for new foreign policy principles in light of post-Soviet realities, Professor Olcott provides some crucial and timely advice in the book's final chapters.

Dr. Olcott's book is the product of a recent grant from the United States Institute of Peace. The Institute's work in this region spans many years and an equal number of forums, from seminars and congressional briefings on Tajikistan's ongoing civil war, to former Jennings Randolph Peace Fellow Nancy Lubin's assessment of the region's reform course in *Central Asians Take Stock: Reform, Corruption, and Identity* (Peaceworks no. 2, February 1995).

As part of the Institute's continuing examination of the sources and causes of regional conflict and their outward manifestation in the international arena, Martha Brill Olcott has indeed delivered a significant contribution to our understanding of a very complex part of the world.

Richard H. Solomon
President
United States Institute of Peace

PREFACE

The original focus of this book was the struggle by several mineral- and energy-rich Soviet republics in the Caucasus and Central Asia to profit at least in part from the development of their natural resources. The project was conceived with the assistance of three Soviet colleagues from Azerbaijan, Uzbekistan, and Kazakhstan and was begun in 1990.

The world has changed a great deal in the past five years, and following the independence of their republics, these three men no longer had time for such a project, as each became deeply involved in helping his respective nation weather the transition to independence. New opportunities opened for me as well, including a brief stint of part-time consulting for Acting Secretary of State Lawrence Eagleberger.

Travel to the region became much easier, and with the introduction of international business and financial institutions there, my expertise became more valuable to a number of international organizations and Western firms doing business in these countries. These contacts and opportunities did a great deal to broaden my understanding of the nature of the changes that the various Central Asian states were undergoing.

My observations during that period led me to shift my focus somewhat and broaden my perspective from what I set out to do in the original project. What fascinated me at the time was the birth of new, independent states that I had devoted my academic and professional life to researching and writing about as pliant yet troubled Soviet republics. Not only were the Soviet Central Asian republics becoming republics in their own right, but they were setting about the soul-searching and somewhat arduous task of defining new roles for themselves as independent actors in a volatile region and in the international community at large. Yet their leaders had few guidelines that would enable them to craft urgently needed foreign policies.

This book is the result of my assessment of these enormous changes and the equally enormous challenges these new states have addressed—and continue to address—in making their transition to statehood. The creation of any new state poses special challenges, but the new, independent states emerging from Soviet Central Asia seemed to have some unique problems and promises on both the domestic and international fronts that warranted further investigation.

I have devoted my academic career to studying this region, but in this book I focus on three of the five Central Asian states—Uzbekistan, Kazakhstan, and Kyrgyzstan. My choice of these three does not reflect my lack of interest in the other two states in this distinct region. For largely pragmatic reasons, I have confined my discussion of Tajikistan and Turkmenistan to related sections within separate chapters. The challenge of doing research in Turkmenistan is truly daunting, and one of the impetuses for writing this book stemmed from the fact that most of the countries of Central Asia were considerably more hospitable places to do research than they had been prior to independence. Turkmenistan, though rich in natural resources, simply did not offer the same opportunities of access to and open exchange with policymakers that existed in Uzbekistan, Kyrgyzstan, and Kazakhstan. Nevertheless, I have devoted a portion of chapter 7 to Turkmenistan's place in the region. I did not devote a separate chapter to Tajikistan because, although the conditions are now somewhat more stable there, it is still a country at war with itself. Even today, the legitimacy of the Rahmonov government is still in question, and because of this it is still not possible to write meaningfully about Tajikistan's state policies. The civil war in Tajikistan, though, is an event that has had an enormous impact on political and economic developments throughout Central Asia. As such, it is an event that requires discussion in this volume, and I have provided in a section of chapter 6 what I hope will suffice as a thorough analysis of the war's origins and its political developments up to the present.

Let me add a special note here on usage. Two of the three states I selected for this study—Kazakhstan and Kyrgyzstan—have just very recently added some significant nuances to their official state names.

Nevertheless, I have chosen to stay with the names with which these countries arrived in the international community as sovereign, independent actors since they are still familiar and widely used among specialists and nonspecialists alike, and are also still widely used in the two countries themselves.

Regarding the adjectival forms of these republics' names, I have decided to rely on the terminology currently used by the U.S. Department of State, numerous media outlets, and various research institutes across the country. In this system, the common adjectival ending of "-stani" is appended to the titular ethnic group's name to denote state policies and institutions that pertain to the particular republic's entire citizenry, including its ethnic Russians and other diaspora minority ethnic communities. Without this ending, the adjective is meant to apply solely, in most cases, to the republic's titular ethnic group.

This book would never have come about without the financial support and professional guidance that I received from so many people. Key among them is the United States Institute of Peace, and especially David Smock and the Grant Program. Without their support, the research upon which this book depends could never have been done.

I am also grateful to the wise counsel of my colleagues at the Foreign Policy Research Institute in Philadelphia. Of particular benefit was the work on Central Asia that we did in concert for the Office of Net Assessment of the U.S. Department of Defense. Finally, I should thank the Dean's Office at Colgate University for their ongoing financial support of my research, which has served as the glue to hold the various larger bits together.

In addition, parts of the manuscript were presented in a number of scholarly forums and the project benefited from the comments received. I am particularly grateful to Professor Robert Legvold for including me in the November 1993 meeting of the Japanese-American Working Group on CIS affairs, and to Professor Michael Mandelbaum for my invitation to participate in the Council on Foreign Relations' June 1993 conference on Central Asia. The comments of the colleagues assembled on both these occasions proved especially valuable.

Finally, I would like to thank my husband, Anthony. As always, I am indebted to his advice and editorial assistance, as well as grateful for his willingness to put up with the disruption that my research trips inevitably brought.

CENTRAL ASIA'S NEW STATES

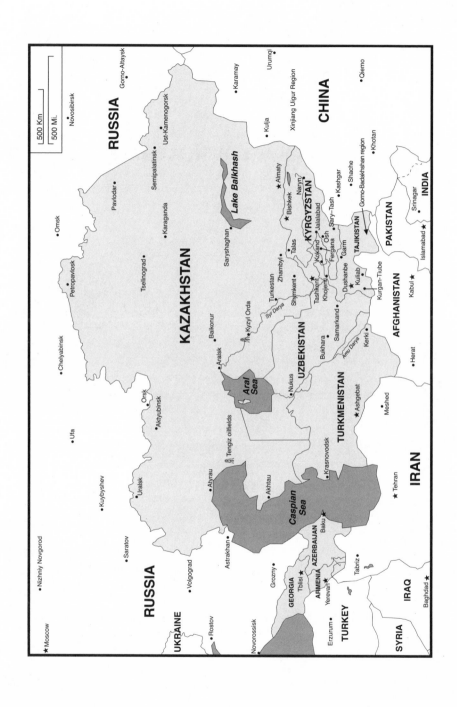

1

A Premature Birth

This book is an effort to describe how the five sub-national territories of what used to be known as Soviet Central Asia handled their transition to statehood. Within a span of weeks in late 1991, these republics went from being dependent appendages of the central Communist Party and state hierarchies in Moscow to being sovereign members of the international community. With their independence came the need to develop their own unique domestic and foreign policies, policies whose content had to reflect the "national interest," a concept that was not only alien but was also antithetical to the core values of the Soviet system.

The present study focuses on how the leaders of these newly independent states went about defining "national interest" in the formulation of foreign policy, and how their foreign policy priorities were in turn shaped by domestic policy concerns, as well as by the legacies of seventy years of Soviet rule. Finally, this study will consider whether the paths these various states have taken to advance their national interests are compatible with the interests of promoting regional as well as international peace and security.

Three states—Uzbekistan, Kazakhstan, and Kyrgyzstan—are examined in particular detail; events in the rest of the region are discussed more generally. In none of these states were initial policy decisions easily taken, nor were the initial challenges of state-building ever fully resolved. In the case of Tajikistan, the challenges of independence have torn the country apart and overwhelmed the former Soviet republic's political elite.

3

Still, four of the region's five new states—Kazakhstan, Kyrgyzstan, Turkmenistan, and Uzbekistan—have managed to get through almost four years of independence with no bloodshed or profound economic and political dislocations. Indeed, judged by the criteria of other former Soviet and Yugoslav republics, this early period of independence could even be called uneventful, despite the fact that the leaders of the Central Asian states did not anticipate their independence and had little preparation for it.

Very few states in the world have had as little advance warning prior to independence as did the five new states of Central Asia, which were effectively chucked out of the USSR when the Soviet republics of Russia, Ukraine, and Byelorussia reconstituted themselves as the Commonwealth of Independent States (CIS) on December 8, 1991. Even so, when de jure independence came to their countries in December 1991, all of Central Asia's leaders accepted it as something that could be to their republics' benefit. This was even true of President Nursultan Nazarbaev of Kazakhstan, who had been leery of independence because of his republic's apparently unseverable links to Russia—so leery, in fact, that he did not allow his republic's legislature to debate and pass Kazakhstan's declaration of independence until December 16, 1991, after Nazarbaev had spent a week in a furious but ultimately fruitless effort to get the USSR reconstituted.

Nazarbaev's nervousness about independence was a product of his wealthy republic's unique demographic situation, which was the most multinational of the Soviet republics. The Kazakhs make up slightly more than 40 percent of Kazakhstan's population, while Russians make up about 35 percent; moreover, most of the Russians live close to the three-thousand-mile-long border that Kazakhstan shares with their mother country. Nazarbaev was the most dubious of all the Soviet republics' leaders about what independence could mean for his republic, but none of the region's leaders—even those who were publicly endorsing independence—believed that their respective republics were prepared to "go it alone."

All of the region's leaders recognized that their new states were beginning life with considerable disadvantages, not the least of which was the lack of an experienced elite capable of developing domestic or international policies independent of Moscow. There were no institutionalized political decision-making structures either, since throughout the Soviet period the executive responsibility of republics had been limited for all intents and purposes to the enforcement of decisions. Rarely were republic-level executives able even to elaborate programs for specific local needs or to adapt policies to local conditions; responsibility for the formulation of policies that would be applied in the republics resided exclusively in Moscow. This began to change somewhat after the Gorbachev reforms of 1989 and 1990. However, the Central Asian republics had been the slowest in the union to begin to take effective advantage of the new rights that republics were being granted.

Still, Central Asia's five presidents all approached independence with a naive optimism. Though all had loyally served Moscow, each seems to have believed secretly all the while that Moscow had been systematically cheating his respective republic. Now, each president embraced the prospect of his republic's benefiting directly from the "real-world" value of the republic's natural resources, and that he and his personal associates would get the "cream" from the deals that Moscow used to skim off.

Now the outside world could be let in, and each of the leaders saw the arrival of the international community as his salvation. Foreigners would help generate the capital that economic development required, through the purchase of energy and other valuable raw materials, through international funding (in part through joint ventures) of Soviet-era plans for resource extraction as well as through the further expansion of these projects, and through the use of foreign aid, international credits, and joint ventures to reform agriculture and to modernize and expand the industrial base. This strategy was common to all of the Central Asian republics—even Tajikistan, where the leaders were distracted from the beginning by a still unresolved struggle for power.

However, none of the republic leaders understood that the end of the USSR and the old order meant the end of the old economic ties, including the Soviet-era interrepublican linkages that had benefited their particular republics by supplying, among other things, cheap grain and energy. Now each republic, and most prominently Russia, would attempt to redefine these links to maximize its own national interests. Furthermore, the Central Asian leaders did not understand that the arrival of the international community would further imperil these ties, for the projects foreign investors wanted to help develop involved precisely those resources that had previously made the region of value to economic decision makers in Moscow.

In general, these first four years of independence have been very disappointing for the leaders of these new states, and extremely difficult for the majority of people living within Central Asia. Optimism has yielded to pessimism, as the Central Asian leaders no longer assume that independence will create easy solutions to their economic development problems. No longer do these regimes expect that the attentions of their brother Turks, Persians, or Muslims generally will begin to turn the magic wheel of folktales that can spin their straw into gold. Nor do they expect any more that unconditional international financial credits will rain down upon them in the manna-like way that the unused rations from the Persian Gulf War and the European Community's "butter mountain" and other agricultural surpluses had so magically appeared on their streets as "humanitarian assistance" at the end of the Gorbachev era.

These lessons are all the more bitter since another part of the leaders' newfound wisdom includes the realization that there is no going back to the past. Everyone now knows that the old USSR is unrevivable, yet Moscow remains the center of the geopolitical universe that the Central Asian leaders inhabit. In many ways, though, Moscow's new rulers treat the Central Asians more harshly than did Soviet rulers of the recent past. Any hopes that these states might rely on Russian generosity to help alleviate their current economic crises were dashed during the failed "ruble zone" negotiations of autumn 1993, when the terms that Russia offered other former Soviet republics for continuing to use the ruble were tantamount to surrendering all economic autonomy to Moscow. Since then, Moscow has defined relations with the Central Asian states in ways designed almost exclusively to Russia's own advantage.

This has left the Central Asian leaders with very few options, fewer even than they seem to have realized at first. New states entering into the international community rarely are able to reshape the existing rules of the game. Despite their enormous potential natural resource wealth, none of the Central Asian states has entered the community of nations from any sort of commanding position. This is true even of Kazakhstan, whose Soviet legacy of nuclear weapons gained President Nazarbaev an invitation to the White House, but the Americans still seated Russian negotiators alongside the Kazakhs at the president's table.[1]

Though certainly they have been a useful bargaining chip in international negotiations, Kazakhstan's nuclear weapons seem to have remained under exclusive Russian control. As Western firms bidding for exploitation rights are discovering, even Kazakhstan's oil, gas, and mineral wealth cannot be exported without Russia's cooperation. This cooperation does not come cheaply, and the transit costs of shipping through Russia may be so expensive as to bring the financial viability of the development of these resources into question.

Kazakhstan's problems are not unique. Although it has more transit options than does Kazakhstan, fossil fuel-rich Turkmenistan also is discovering that development projects take longer to realize than originally assumed, and—worse yet—that as a small country, it lacks the clout to collect payment for the gas it has already delivered. Kyrgyzstan has learned that democratic inclinations alone cannot turn a remote former Soviet republic into an "Asian Switzerland," and that no matter how enthusiastic Western countries are to aid a new nation, foreign assistance is governed by annual budget cycles and is allocated in accordance with strict procedures for project authorization and development.

Uzbekistan, too, is finding that there are subtle subtexts in international relations, and that not all states are accorded the same stature by the international community. President Islam Karimov is learning that some states can commit human rights violations with impunity while others cannot, and that neither Uzbekistan's wealth nor its market potential is large enough for the international community to be willing to bend the rules of the game to Uzbekistan's benefit. At the same time, Karimov has gotten lessons in Russia's fickleness and has seen how strategic alliances do not always transform themselves into economic partnerships.

Tajikistan's learning experience has of course been the most painful of all. The civil war in this republic is a frightening reminder to all the region's leaders of the cost of independence. Moreover, as armed populations have begun to spill over existing boundaries, the leaders have seen that the interconnectedness of independent states is not significantly less than that of dependent republics. However, the threats posed by Tajikistan, as well as by various failures within each of these republics, are far greater than they previously were. Central Asia's presidents are now held directly responsible for the well-being of their respective nations. Ouster by an angry mob is no longer merely a nightmare for Central Asia's rulers; it is also a real possibility. It has occurred once, in Tajikistan, and could occur again.

The Central Asians' new geopolitical world is not so different from their old one. Russia remains in the neighborhood, which it claims as its own "near abroad." Russia remains committed to the preservation of order in the region to keep trouble from spilling over into Russia and to ensure that Central Asia's twelve million Russians should have no cause to flee "home." Though Russia remains poised to intervene in the region, the cost of any Russian "international" assistance would be quite high. Unable to finance a social welfare safety net for their own population, Russia's rulers are unlikely to offer many carrots to the Central Asians, nor will they be shy about deploying their arsenal of sticks if the behavior of their new neighbors is not to their liking.

FORESTALLING INDEPENDENCE

For all these problems—and in spite of the fact that the Central Asian republics obtained their independence not only abruptly, but also with virtually no direct public or even elite involvement in their "liberation"— the Central Asian states still began their "sovereign" lives under more auspicious conditions than do most new members of the international community. The boundaries of the Soviet republics had not been drawn with an eye to possible future independence, but rather to impede secession by any of the USSR's various national communities, yet seven decades of living with roughly the same borders had nevertheless given each of the five republics a certain internal cohesion.

While local, Russian, and Western scholars may debate ad infinitum the "naturalness" of any of Central Asia's five peoples, the Kazakhs, Kyrgyz, Tajiks, Turkmens, and Uzbeks of the 1990s are no longer the loose ethnic formulations which Stalin-era social engineers transformed into nationalities. These are now five sovereign states, each of which—save Kazakhstan—is dominated demographically by the titular ethnic group.

Equally important is the Soviet bureaucratic legacy. The Soviet Union was divided into republics, and each of these was further subdivided into provinces (*oblasts*) and districts (*rayons*). These divisions have provided the former Soviet republics with a bureaucratic structure that has needed only some modification since independence. Moreover, although the current office-holders may lack extensive executive decision-making experience, Soviet rule led to the development of an extensive bureaucratic elite in each of these republics, almost all of whom have had specialized post-secondary or advanced education. Each republic also began independence with a complete education and social service network. It was no doubt for these reasons that the republics were able to act so quickly after independence to set up the basic appurtenances of statehood.

The Central Asian leaders did not, however, regard these advantages as sufficient, and rather than encouraging independence they became the most stalwart supporters of the Soviet Union's perpetuation. In fact, in the March 1991 Soviet referendum, it was only in the Central Asian republics that the population was turned out en masse to vote for the continuation of the USSR. This was not simply because all the leaders (save Kyrgyzstan's Askar Akaev) were Moscow appointees who had come to power with briefs that included the containment of sepa-ratist sentiment in their respective republics; there was no shortage of communists-turned-nationalists in the other republics either. The Central Asian leaders, however, seem to have been genuinely fearful of what independence would mean for their republics.

In Central Asia the collapse of the Soviet Union was more than just a blow to their part of an interdependent, all-USSR economy. All five republics faced serious economic problems well before the Soviet Union's economic crises of the late 1980s. But independence also brought an abrupt end to subsidies from Moscow, including cash sent as compensation for the costs of the region's economy based on cotton monoculture and mineral extraction, as well as the direct grants-in-aid that were paid to individual citizens to ease the burdens of the region's high birth rates. These two sources of financing allowed the Central Asian republics to provide a minimum standard of living for a fast-growing and largely unskilled rural-based population for whom unemployment and underemployment was a growing problem.[2] Even before the Soviet collapse, the regional leaders knew that independence was also likely to mean the exodus of hundreds of thousands of technologically skilled Russians, since they were already unhappy over the growing national-ism in these republics.[3] Unfortunately, it was precisely during indepen-dence that these skilled workers would be most sorely needed, since independence would mean that the Central Asian countries would now be on their own to deal not only with their immediate economic prob-lems, but also with the neglected long-term ones, such as an acute water shortage[4] and the more pervasive ecological crises that fifty years of Soviet economic planning had created.

Up until the very last minute, almost all of Central Asia's leaders maintained hope that the union could be saved. To that end they were willing to compromise continually with Moscow, and so they watched with particular dismay as events seemed to slip from Gorbachev's con-trol in 1991. Several of the leaders were so frightened over Gorbachev's apparent failures and the Communist Party's own growing loss of power that they even saw the abortive August 1991 coup as a possible solution to their problem.[5] Tajikistan's Makhkamov even publicly supported the coup attempt, while Karimov's pronouncements in Uzbekistan fell just short of endorsement. When the coup failed, and it was clear that the "union" would have to be redefined if it were to survive, each of the Central Asian republics except Kazakhstan declared independence. But even then, the region's leaders were all willing to accept a form of state-hood which was more symbolic than real and to share control of their republic's natural resources with a smaller and more benevolent Soviet central authority structure.[6]

President Nursultan Nazarbaev of Kazakhstan was the most enthusi-astic defender of a revitalization of the USSR; it was his plea for a rede-fined union that was endorsed by the emergency session of the Supreme Soviet following the failed coup. Nazarbaev also spearheaded the unsuc-cessful effort to get a new Union Treaty drafted and fully ratified.[7] All of the Central Asian leaders strongly supported the idea of a coordinated economic reform program complete with a currency union and tariff-free trade zone to encompass all of the republics.[8] Even as late as 1995, several of the region's leaders still remain committed to some version of this idea.

On the other hand, by 1991 the Central Asian leaders were no longer content to be mere puppets of Moscow. Public shows of independence grew after the August coup attempt. Within days, Karimov went from tacitly supporting the return of an iron hand in Moscow to ardently endorsing full independence, while the Tajiks ousted their party leader and toppled the statue of Lenin that had long presided over their capital's main square.

Throughout the region, Central Asia's rulers sensed Moscow's grow-ing weariness with the "burdens of empire," and all recognized that the responsibility for feeding their region's growing Muslim population would be among the first responsibilities that Moscow would shuck.[9] These leaders also recognized that if they were to meet these obliga-tions, more money would have to remain within the republics than had been the case under Soviet economic practice. Until 1990, the republic administrations functioned as little more than clearinghouses for Moscow, which allocated to republic enterprises the funds it deemed necessary for them to operate, while viewing whatever was produced in the republics to be part of the all-Union profit. Because of this, although republics had limited rights of taxation, it had traditionally been considered Moscow's responsibility to supplement public funds to ensure that each republic could meet its social service needs.

However, even in Central Asia a pro-autonomy stance had been slowly developing, even though such a posture was really antithetical to the background and training of the region's leaders. Saparmurad Niyazov of Turkmenistan, Kakhar Makhkamov of Tajikistan, and Absamat Masaliev of Kyrgyzstan (who was deposed by his legislature in October 1990) all came to power as part of Gorbachev's 1985 campaign to reassert more control over the republics. These three men had all been chosen and prepared for office by Egor Ligachev, a staunch proponent of the idea that republics had to be subordinated to the center. Even Nursultan Nazarbaev and Islam Karimov (who were appointed as republic party heads in June 1989, when Moscow had already recognized that republic interests had to be responded to somehow) were advocates of the Gorbachev formulation of "a strong center and strong republics." By contrast, their colleagues in the Baltic republics were by this time already demanding complete autonomy.

By June 1990, however, all five Central Asian leaders recognized that it was inevitable that power would be devolved to the republics. All participated in the drafting of the new, and ultimately ill-fated, Union Treaty, part of Gorbachev's fruitless efforts to forestall the dismemberment of his country. For the first time, some of the hard currency earnings from the sale of energy and precious metals began to be credited to republic budgets, making clear that the tendency toward economic reform was irreversible. Greater autonomy at the enterprise level would mean greater autonomy for the republic as well; this was advocated by a succession of economists who in turn rose to prominence in Gorbachev's court, each arguing that this would increase economic efficiency and improve economic performance. In fact, by mid-1990, Gorbachev was no longer resisting the premise that the republics were sovereign; the battle now was to delineate the respective authority of center and periphery.

This situation made the Central Asian leaders profoundly nervous, because until fall 1991, none of Central Asia's presidents—not even those who previously had worked in the ministerial side of their republic's government—had ever had responsibility for managing his republic's entire economy; neither had anyone on their staffs had much direct experience in this area. USSR ministries and their Moscow-appointed representatives in the republics controlled all of the nation's key industries and natural resources without regard for the republic in which these industries and resources were located. Republic ministries had partial decision-making authority only for those sectors of the economy that were both nonstrategic and confined to a specific region.

However, Central Asia's leaders understood that if economic reform were to have any possibility of success in their republics, they had to gain control of precisely those sectors of the republic economies that had always been exclusively Moscow's responsibility. Central Asia's sole chance of achieving economic solvency was to profit directly from the development of its natural resources. In contrast to the Baltic republics, Central Asia produced very few finished goods for either all-Union use or foreign export, so without at least partial control over the sale of their natural resources they were doomed to remain Moscow's dependents.

The leadership in Moscow was also eyeing these same resources. As part of his economic reform program, Soviet president Mikhail Gorbachev was making a major effort to bring foreign investment and technology to the USSR, and the Central Asian republics contained a number of very attractive investment possibilities, especially in the energy sector and, more generally, in the mineral-extraction sector. It was on this issue that Gorbachev and the republic leaders did clash, albeit quietly. As Moscow began to sell off rights to Central Asia's resources, the republic leaders began to hatch their own plans. From mid-1990 on, the republic leaders tried to take advantage of their status as leaders of sovereign—not independent—entities to carve out some sort of international posture of their own. When the three Baltic republics created the Baltic Council and began to develop some of their plans in concert, formal efforts at regional cooperation were begun in Central Asia as well.

Gorbachev showed no signs of displeasure with this situation, and at points may well have encouraged it. The Central Asian leaders were merely demanding a "piece of the action" at a time when many other republic leaders were trying to exclude Moscow entirely. The various foreign investment schemes that were being discussed were all in their early stages, so Moscow's priority was to get the investments in place and start the revenue flowing, and then the republics and Moscow, through which payment would be directed, could come to terms.

Moreover, Gorbachev accurately sensed the real advantages that would accrue from encouraging the Central Asian leaders to make their own way in the international community. For one thing, the prospects for foreign investment were increased through these new emissaries who could go forth seeking support from Turkish, Iranian, or Asian "brothers." The threat to Gorbachev or to the security of the USSR that any of these efforts posed was virtually nonexistent. Ten-year-old fears of an Islamic revolution in Central Asia paled in comparison to the realities of Baltic secession. Moreover, it was clear that an international community that was reluctant to encourage or endorse Baltic separatism after forty years of refusing to recognize Soviet rule over these republics was hardly likely to greet Central Asian independence with enthusiasm. Thus Gorbachev was able to point to his treatment of the leaders of these republics as evidence of his sensitivity to the "national needs" of non-Russians.

First International Moves

Central Asia's leaders were very enthusiastic about the prospect of developing direct foreign economic relations with potential trade partners, although they had even less experience in international relations than they had in managing the economies of their republics. As substate entities, these republics were initially restricted from forming direct diplomatic relations with foreign countries. Thus the various republics concentrated on developing or expanding ministries for foreign economic relations. Long confined to traveling as part of larger, official Soviet delegations on trips planned by the USSR's Ministry of Foreign Affairs, Central Asia's presidents seemed particularly eager to take advantage of the new opportunities to propose and execute their own international travel.

Initially, the transition to international actor was easiest for Kazakhstan's Nursultan Nazarbaev. Alone among the Central Asian leaders, Nazarbaev had attained the stature of a major political figure for the general Soviet populace, and he was regularly rumored to be on the verge of becoming Gorbachev's "number two" in Moscow. Kazakhstan's vast natural reserves figured prominently in Moscow's plans even before Nazarbaev was named to head his republic, as the output from the republic's Tengiz oil field (in western Kazakhstan) was to provide enough profit to interest a consortium of eight major U.S. investors, headed by Chevron. Plans for this project were developed in 1987 and 1988, but representatives from the Kazakh government were not brought into the negotiations until May 1991, a year after the principle of republic sovereignty was recognized, and well after the main terms of the contract were already worked out between Chevron and Gorbachev's representatives in the USSR's Ministry of Oil and Ministry of Foreign Economic Relations. The project, which initially called for a sixty-forty split between the Soviet side and Chevron, immediately became a hot political issue within Kazakhstan.[10] Environmentalists in Moscow and Nazarbaev's critics in Kazakhstan all argued that the Kazakhs had been "taken" in the deal, even before the terms of the profit-sharing relationship between Kazakhstan and Chevron had been made public.

In the end, Kazakhstan extracted more favorable terms from Chevron than the USSR had achieved. After Kazakhstan attained independence, the deal was renegotiated to provide the republic with a substantial signing bonus and some 80 percent of the profits. The Tengiz deal, which is discussed at greater length in chapter 4, was an early learning experience for Nazarbaev, who quickly became convinced that as head of a large and wealthy republic he had need for independent advice and expertise.

However, in the period just prior to independence, Nazarbaev seems to have had little idea of where to turn to get such advice. Eventually (in 1992) the J.P. Morgan firm was brought in to consult with Kazakhstan in some of these negotiations, and in 1993 and 1994, a host of Western firms opened offices in Almaty.

All of Central Asia's leaders have faced this dilemma; and as demonstrated by the scolding that Kyrgyzstan's legislature gave President Akaev in 1993 for having temporarily turned over the management of Kyrgyzstan's gold reserves and mines to Boris Birshtein, few of the leaders have resolved the dilemma easily or well. Birshtein was a former communist functionary from Lithuania who emigrated first to Israel and then to Canada, along the way setting up an international trading company (Seabeco) in Switzerland that relied heavily on his former communist connections to identify lucrative investment opportunities for Western businessmen. After Birshtein was named a presidential adviser in Kyrgyzstan, Seabeco (and its local partner, Seabeco-Kyrgyzstan) collected "finder's fees" for the sale of exploitation rights to Kyrgyzstan's gold and was compensated for helping the republic arrange its first international transfers of gold reserves. Perhaps not surprisingly, several of the country's prominent politicians were directly tied to the Seabeco-Kyrgyzstan embezzlement scandal.

Nazarbaev's early mistakes proved to be less embarrassing. In early 1991, Nazarbaev turned for help to Chan Young Bang, a Korean-American professor from the University of San Francisco who is rumored to have close ties to South Korea's major industrial families. Professor Bang was made vice chairman of Kazakhstan's Council of Economic Experts for the salary of $1 per year. Nazarbaev is reported to have been introduced to Professor Bang in a Gold Star factory in Seoul, where Nazarbaev was traveling as part of a fact-finding trip to East Asia. The Kazakh president was already attracted to the "Four Tigers" of East Asia because of the speed with which they had achieved economic development, as well as the fact that they had done so without also ceding too much control from the state to the private sector. Nazarbaev saw this chance encounter as a stroke of fortune. Nazarbaev also sought counsel from Singapore's former prime minister Lee Kuan Yew, who was also named a special advisor.[11] Lee did not take up residence in Kazakhstan, but he is said to have made suggestions for some of its first independently produced economic planning documents.

Bang wound up staying in Kazakhstan for more than two years, but was quickly shunted out of the political decision-making loop and assigned instead to develop Kazakhstan's first institute of management, which took over the republic's Higher Party School (probably the best-equipped educational facility and dormitory complex in the Kazakh capital of Almaty). Much of Bang's time, however, was said to have been spent scouting for business prospects for Korean investors, while Lee's interest in the republic is said to have overlapped heavily with those of Singapore's major industrialists.

The East Asians were not the only ones to come scouting in Central Asia. Turkey's late president, Turgut Ozal, was probably the one international actor most involved in marketing himself and his country in the region. He made a state visit to Kazakhstan (as well as to Azerbaijan) in March 1991, during which he signed some preliminary agreements on economic, cultural, and scientific cooperation.[12] In fall 1991, Ozal hosted a return state visit by Nazarbaev, during which a number of bilateral "memoranda of intent" on economic and scientific cooperation between Turkey and Kazakhstan were signed.[13]

Turkish leaders also laid the foundations for direct state-to-state relations with the heads of the other Turkic republics, and visits were exchanged between Ozal or then-prime minister Suleiman Demirel and the Central Asian leaders. In the end, though, the Central Asian leaders overestimated the importance of these early visits and the resulting bilateral agreements, which they understood as precursors of major investment or assistance programs rather than as the diplomatic fishing trips they really were.

Though slightly slower than the Turks to become involved in these early days, the Iranians also made repeated efforts to assess the potential advantage that could be gained from the increasing sovereignty of Central Asia's republics. Iranian foreign minister Ali Akbar Velayati spent a substantial part of his November 1991 trip to the USSR in this region, traveling to the Turkic republics as well as to Tajikistan, the region's sole Persian-speaking republic. While Iran showed more interest in resource-poor Tajikistan than did any other foreign power—bruiting plans well before independence for direct air links, telephone and television service, as well as banking assistance, and opening the first embassy in Dushanbe in January 1992, when the local Iranian consulate became an embassy—Iran did not pursue a Tajik-centered policy in the region.[14]

By December 1991 it was already clear that Turkmenistan would be a republic of equal, and possibly even greater, interest to Iran. Iran and Turkmenistan share a common border, and there is an irredentist Turkmen population in Iran. Moreover, close ties with Turkmenistan are imperative in any Iranian plan to become an international transport center for the Central Asian region. During Velayati's winter 1991 trip, Iran pledged funds for the completion of the railroad line between Turkmenistan and Meshed, the last spur in a rail system designed to provide direct service from Urumqi in western China, across all of Central Asia, through Iran, and on to Istanbul.[15] Set to open in mid-1994, this railroad line was completed one year behind schedule.

Already by this early date, Iran was offering Turkmenistan assistance in developing its oil industry and was promising to both purchase and help develop Turkmenistan's natural gas resources.[16] Iran further hoped that involvement in the development of Turkmenistan's fossil-fuel industries would help open up a path toward Kazakhstan, since Teheran believed that the logical pipeline route for fuel originating in western Kazakhstan was through Iran via Turkmenistan. However, at this point, both Iran and Turkmenistan were more concerned about preserving good relations with Moscow than with each other. Although discussions over foreign development of Turkmenistan's fossil-fuel industry preceded independence, Niyazov's policies in this sector were still set in close coordination with the old Soviet energy ministries in Moscow. Nevertheless, the Turkmen president already understood the importance of maintaining close ties with Iran; he too had an ambitious travel schedule for December 1991—even before the USSR collapsed—with trips to Pakistan and Turkey on his itinerary.[17]

Pakistan was even slower to respond to the possibilities offered in Central Asia than was either Turkey or Iran, but it was also interested in involving itself in the region. All three states recognized that regional security relations would be changed as a result of events in Central Asia, and within days of gaining international recognition as independent states, all five republics were invited to join the Economic Cooperation Organization—run by Turkey, Iran, and Pakistan—which, up to that point, had been largely moribund. Tajikistan, Turkmenistan, and Uzbekistan accepted this invitation immediately, while Kyrgyzstan and Kazakhstan joined later on. Pakistani interest in Central Asia also further stimulated India's interest in the region. Ties between Uzbekistan and India had begun to develop in the 1970s, when Tashkent was made the Asian hub for the Soviet airline Aeroflot.

However, sharing borders as it did with three Central Asian republics (Tajikistan, Kyrgyzstan, and Kazakhstan), Chinese leaders understood better than any others how events in Central Asia had potential consequences for their own country's security concerns. Throughout the late 1980s, trade between western China and Central Asia (particularly Kazakhstan and Kyrgyzstan) was increasing and was expected to grow faster following the opening of direct rail links between China and Kazakhstan in 1991, which broadened the access of these republics to Chinese factories and new sources of raw materials.[18] At the same time, as the USSR was coming apart, officials in Beijing were concerned about the prospect of these five republics' bypassing Beijing and developing direct economic ties with Chinese border provinces. It is rumored that Nursultan Nazarbaev was even given a firm scolding on this score by his Chinese hosts when, on his first trip to the People's Republic, the Kazakh leader visited Urumqi prior to traveling to Beijing for an official welcome.[19] Uzbekistan's Islam Karimov also traveled to China, a month after Nazarbaev, and came away very impressed by what the Chinese had achieved. Indeed, his admiration resulted in a considerable public relations disaster soon after his return, when he announced at a press conference held days after the August 1991 coup attempt that the Uzbeks should emulate the "Chinese model" of development.[20]

By comparison, perhaps because he had lived more than two decades in an academic milieu in Leningrad, Askar Akaev (who came to power in Kyrgyzstan in October 1990) seems to have had more awareness of what diplomacy entails, just as he appears to have appreciated that Kyrgyzstan's economic recovery would inevitably depend upon foreign investment in his republic's mineral extraction industries, especially gold. Moreover, Akaev seems to have been more attuned to the imminent breakup of the USSR than were his fellow leaders; in September 1991, he banned the shipment of Kyrgyzstan's gold to Russia for refinement.[21]

Akaev was also the first of Central Asia's leaders to understand the West's agenda in the former Soviet Union, grasping the preoccupation of Western leaders with the linkage between political and economic reform. Akaev also took great pains to familiarize himself with Western political thinking, going so far as to hire a well-read local university professor, Leonid Levitan, as his paid advisor and part-time speech writer. Akaev used his newfound knowledge of Jefferson and John Stuart Mill to make a strong impression on both U.S. President George Bush and Secretary of State James Baker during his fall 1991 trip to Washington.[22] This positive impression, further strengthened during Baker's December 1991 "fact-finding" trip to Bishkek, led to Kyrgyzstan's inclusion on the list of six ex-Soviet republics that gained immediate and full U.S. diplomatic recognition after the collapse of the USSR.[23] Even then, Akaev was laying the foundations for developing a "balanced" foreign policy, and tried to pursue ties to the West as well as investment from Asia and trade with China in equal measures.[24]

This does not mean that the other Central Asian leaders created a bad impression when they traveled abroad. Some, especially Nursultan Nazarbaev, made strong favorable impressions. However, all were said to have traveled without any sort of briefing as to what they might expect to find at their destinations, since none of these republics had any sort of diplomatic representation and few of their citizens had even served in the Soviet diplomatic corps.

Generally speaking, during the period prior to independence, the Central Asian republics were more acted upon than active in their international relations, and only a few leaders seem to have had an inkling of how international relations might be used to advance their domestic purposes. Each of Central Asia's leaders understood the importance of developing good ties with both neighboring states and the world's leading economic powers, but few had much idea of how to go about it, or of how to define their republics' priorities in the process. In the months just prior to independence, the concept of "national interest" was alien to the republics' leaders. Those who headed the Central Asian republics were now called presidents, but their states were not independent, and it was wholly unclear how much discretionary authority Moscow might cede—or the republics might grab.

Further, it was even more unclear by what criteria a republic was to define its national interests. During the Soviet period, a republic leader who claimed a distinct identity for his republic, to say nothing of a national interest, was considered politically deviant, and to err in this way was considered grounds for dismissal. Ethnic groups were recognized to have cultural, but not political, rights. In spite of the fact that every Soviet republic bore the name of its principal ethnic group, Soviet leaders steadfastly maintained that the republics were political entities but not *national* political entities. For the leaders of the Central Asian republics, the question of whose interests they were to advance was undoubtedly a troubling one, which grew no less complex after independence. The USSR disintegrated in large part because the various national communities it comprised demanded recognition as sovereign peoples, yet independence was awarded to republics without any recognition of the right to national self-determination for the peoples who lived in these republics.

Of course, all of the Soviet successor states faced the same fundamental problem. The collapse of the USSR and its interrepublic economic links dramatically exacerbated the economic crisis in each individual republic, simply adding the new burden of political institution-building to the burdens of economic restructuring that had driven the USSR towards reform in the first place. Previously, republic leaders had fought with Moscow to gain the right to structure economic reform in ways that would benefit their own republics rather than the USSR as a whole. Independence granted all the republics this right, which some had struggled so hard to obtain.

However, as we will see in subsequent chapters, it soon became clear that for all the volumes of advice that legions of people came forward to offer (most of it conflicting), deciding how to reform a republic is not a simple task. It was not long before Central Asia's leaders realized that defining a republic's interest was really no easier than the old problem of deciding what the USSR's interest was. Different constituencies within each republic, only some of which coincided with ethnic divisions, had very different ideas about whom reform should benefit, and frequently a decision to benefit one group was a de facto decision to punish another.

As we will see in the next chapter, in the first months after independence, the republic leaders looked to the international community to provide them with easy answers. However, within a year they realized that such answers were not to be had. The remainder of this book is devoted to their individual efforts to define the separate identities of their various states, and the impact this is likely to have on regional as well as broader international security concerns.

2

FAILED ETHNIC CARDS

The suddenness of the USSR's collapse pushed the new Central Asian states into the international arena before they had thought out what they wanted to do when they got there. Over a matter of months, certainly no more than a year, Central Asia passed from being an international backwater to being an obligatory stop for diplomats and the investment-minded, while the Central Asian leaders themselves became sought-after international guests.

The leaders of these new states could ill afford to ignore the opportunities with which they were being presented, for the collapse of the Soviet Union dramatically deepened the economic crises in their region. The Russian government quickly made clear that its international claims to be the USSR's heir did not mean that it was agreeing to make good on old Soviet contracts within the USSR. Trade relations between Russia and the other Soviet successor states were to be based on new bilateral treaties, while Moscow demanded that they promptly repay their Russian partners for goods received.

Although it would be nearly two years before this policy was fully enforced, the republics got a fast lesson in what independence would mean. In December 1991, Russia cut off oil and coal to Kyrgyzstan and completely closed the border for trade with Kazakhstan. Uzbekistan and Russia had already clashed on Uzbek cotton prices, so this Central Asian republic went into the winter of 1992 short of fuel and grain. New bilateral agreements were quickly negotiated, which eased these crises somewhat, but throughout the region there was an understanding that the former Soviet republics would soon have to make their own way in the world, feeding and providing for their own populations as they did so.

At the same time, there was real uncertainty about how to achieve this, let alone pay for it. None of the Central Asian states had any foreign legations—indeed any foreign property at all—since Russia had seized the USSR's foreign assets, saying that the price of receiving a share of them was to accept a share of the USSR's foreign hard-currency debts. This was something that none of the Central Asian states felt able to do, so one by one (the last of them in 1993) the republics signed treaties with Russia in which they renounced claims to the USSR's legacy.

Yet, there was an even more serious question: Who could plan and execute foreign policy for these new states? Throughout the region there was an acute shortage of qualified, trained personnel who had international experience of any sort, to say nothing of diplomatic experience. Few Central Asians had even managed to travel abroad, and if they had, it was rarely to the sorts of countries to which they were now all turning for international aid and technical assistance. As one Kyrgyz official bitterly put it, "In the old days, for us—if we were lucky—travel abroad meant a trip to Bulgaria."

New Rules and New Games[1]

Only a few dozen Central Asians had any sort of formal preparation for diplomatic service. A few non-Russians had trained at Soviet diplomatic academies, serving in the USSR Ministry of Foreign Affairs and in Soviet embassies and missions abroad. However, most of these worked as translators or served in junior-level positions. Those who rose to visible positions of responsibility were obvious and deliberate exceptions who tended to play very tightly defined roles, usually as examples of how tolerant the Russians (who dominated the Soviet bureaucracy) were of their various ethnic "brothers."

Of course, as was true of so much of the Soviet experience, this "brotherhood" was more appearance than reality; not all nationalities were treated equally. Ukrainians and Byelorussians—especially those who spoke Russian as their first language—were allowed access to diplomatic service on an almost equal basis with Russians, while both Armenians and Jews were "overrepresented" in terms of their percentage in the overall population of the Soviet Union. Central Asians, though, were dramatically underrepresented. Although discrimination against them eased somewhat when Georgia's Eduard Shevardnadze took over the USSR Ministry of Foreign Affairs in 1985, no Central Asians ever made it to the highest levels of foreign-policy decision making.

By the late Gorbachev years, when Moscow was straining to demonstrate the multinational character of the USSR, a few Central Asians did receive senior diplomatic postings: the noted Kyrgyz writer Chingis Aitmatov was made USSR ambassador to Luxembourg; Roza Otunbaeva (now Kyrgyzstan's minister of foreign affairs and formerly the republic's ambassador to the United States and Canada) was named USSR ambassador to Malaysia; and Kazakhstan's then-minister of culture, Kanat Saudabaev, was named USSR ambassador to Turkey. (He was Kazakhstan's first ambassador to Turkey and then returned to that post after briefly serving as the republic's minister of foreign affairs.)

These people were all quickly pressed into service for their new nations, as were Central Asians who had worked at less senior positions in the Soviet diplomatic corps. The latter group included T. Suleimenov and R. Abdurazakov, who were named ministers of foreign affairs of independent Kazakhstan and Uzbekistan respectively. Suleimenov then served as Kazakhstan's ambassador to the United States

In the end, though, it was finances even more than expertise that restricted the first efforts of these new states to develop an international presence. The Central Asians joined just about every international body that offered them membership. All of the Central Asian nations joined the United Nations and the Conference on (now Organization for) Security and Cooperation in Europe (and, in the process of joining the latter, extended the geography of "Europe" right up to the borders of Afghanistan and China), applied for membership in the World Bank and the International Monetary Fund (IMF), and began to talk of applying for membership in the European Union and NATO.[2] They also joined two "Eastern" groups, the Economic Cooperation Organization (ECO)[3] and the Organization of the Islamic Conference (excluding Kazakhstan, which accepted observer status).[4] However, rarely were these new Central Asian states able to take advantage of the various opportunities that membership in international bodies theoretically offered them, since they were able to pay for only a minimal presence abroad. All of the states were slow to set up embassies, even where an "exchange of quarters" with a foreign power could be arranged, since most lacked the money to fund and staff missions.

Their acute economic need, combined with the limited nature of their international diplomatic presence, provided an even greater incentive for the region's presidents to take advantage of all the foreign travel opportunities being offered them. Presidents Nazarbaev and Karimov were particularly active travelers, both of them visiting Europe and Asia extensively as well as journeying to the Middle East. Nazarbaev also came to the United States in May 1992.[5] Though far more strapped for hard currency, President Akaev left his country nearly as often as Karimov and Nazarbaev did theirs. Senior officials from the Central Asian republics also made the rounds in the major industrial nations.

Here again, limited funds and poor staff work often proved embarrassing for the Central Asian leaders, since most felt obliged to accept whatever international invitations were offered to them, no matter how inappropriate they might be to the offices they held. Thus, early impressions of Nazarbaev were tainted when a dubious Kazakh-American joint venture charged prominent U.S. industrialists $50,000 a plate for a dinner with Kazakhstan's president, while the Kyrgyz were left unable to refute charges that corporate sponsors had benefited from the international travel they had underwritten for the republic's prime minister, foreign minister, and vice president.

PLAYING THEIR ETHNIC CARDS

Still, in the midst of considerable confusion, the Central Asian states did begin to sort out their priorities. Each now understood that a state's foreign policy was a give-and-take proposition. While the Central Asians were trying to figure out what to ask of the international community, many of the members of that community were simultaneously trying to decide how to redefine their own foreign policies to take advantage of the new opportunities that the independence of the Central Asian nations might afford them.

One element of a successful foreign policy that the Central Asian leaders soon understood was how to make use of strategic advantage to strike the best deal possible in the trade-off between one's own national interests and those of a partner. Prominent among the strategic advantages that each Central Asian state enjoyed was its ethnicity.

This was truly ironic. During all the decades of Soviet rule, Moscow was nothing short of vigilant in restricting ethnicity and combating its politicized form, nationalism. With the republics' independence, the leaders of Central Asia's new states hoped to use their ethnic or national composition to attract international investment and support. Broadly speaking, there were three ethnic "cards" that the Central Asians could put into play in the international arena: their Turkic or Persian nationality, their Islamic religion, and their "Asianness."

THE TURKISH AND PERSIAN NATIONAL CARDS

Most immediately obvious was nationality. All of the Central Asian nationalities can claim cultural affinity with either Turkey or Iran. The Turkmen, Uzbeks, Kazakhs, and Kyrgyz speak Turkic languages and share many cultural attributes with the people of Turkey, while the Tajiks have similar connections to Iran. For their part, both the Turks and the Iranians were eager to reciprocate the new nations' interest.

In fact, the interest of the Turks and the Iranians in Central Asia, in the beginning, exceeded Central Asian interest in developing ties with either of these two states. Central Asians play a role in the founding myths of both modern Turkey and modern Iran. In the Turkish case, nationhood is based on the migration of Oguz Turks (the ancestors of the modern Turkmen) to Anatolia. Anatolian Turks, however, never ruled Central Asia, while up until the eighteenth century various parts of Central Asia had come under Persian rule. Earlier still, parts of Persia had come under the domination of Central Asia's khans.

Central Asia has a dual Turkic and Persian heritage; before the revolution the region's educated population generally had a knowledge of several languages. However, fifty years of Russian rule, followed by seventy years of Soviet domination, decisively isolated the Central Asians from Turkey and Persia. The collapse of the Soviet Union came at an auspicious time for both Turkey and Iran, and both became eager to use the independence of the Central Asian states to advance their national interests more generally. In fact, both were so eager that the international press began to write of Central Asia as the site of a new "Great Game," played this time by Turkey and Iran, rather than by Russia and Great Britain.

Since 1989, two years before the collapse of the USSR, Turkey's government has made improved ties with the Caucasian and Central Asian republics a stated goal of its foreign policy.[6] Pro-Western, Muslim, and democratic, with an expanding market economy, Turkey was, in President Ozal's opinion, a natural model for the four Turkic republics of Central Asia as well as for Azerbaijan. After Ozal's death, this belief was restated by President Demirel.[7] Ozal's goal of turning Turkey into the West's bridge to Central Asia fit very well with Turkey's rapid economic development and industrial growth, and would help compensate for the Turks' rejection by the European Community.

For the leaders of the Turkic republics, Turkey was an obvious and, at first glance, attractive model for emulation—much like an "older brother," in President Karimov's words,[8] as it seemed to incorporate features of both East and West. Turkey was the first nation to recognize Uzbekistan and Kazakhstan, and was among the first to open embassies everywhere in Central Asia, save Tajikistan. In mid-1992, Karimov, Niyazov, Akaev, and Nazarbaev all went to Ankara to be present at the celebrations of the Turkish state's sixty-ninth anniversary, and numerous high-level Turkish delegations have visited the various Central Asian capitals.[9] Both private businessmen in Turkey and the Turkish government have aggressively pursued business and cultural contacts in the region, creating scholarships for Central Asian students (initially two thousand per republic), hiring Central Asians skilled in traditional crafts like leatherwork, and opening or assisting in the creation of banks, telecommunications systems, and food-processing plants. In early 1992, Turkey also began independent television programming, via satellite, with the capacity to cover the entire area.[10]

However, by mid-1992, Turkish politicians and businessmen, although often loath to admit it in public settings, were becoming frustrated with the situation in Central Asia, which they were finding more inaccessible and harder to do business in than they had expected. Moreover, their strategy of becoming a "bridge" was faltering because of a general lack of interest on the part of Western investors.[11]

In addition, the Turks found these regimes to be far weaker than they had anticipated, while the varieties of interplay between secular and clerical Islam in Central Asia also affected the tensions between secularists and clericalists in Turkey, bringing into question the wisdom of embracing Central Asia more tightly.

Most importantly, Turkey had to face the realities of its own national self-interest. The development of good relations in Central Asia could not come at the expense of Turkey's trade with Russia, the volume of which was then about ten times that of trade with Central Asia. Moreover, it is Russia and not Central Asia that is central to Turkey's security interests. Economic collapse and political disorder in the new Central Asian states pose no direct threat to Turkey, whereas it is possible to imagine any number of scenarios in which developments in Russia would have a direct impact on policymakers in Ankara.

Similarly, the Central Asians had also grown somewhat disenchanted with the Turks, although bilateral relations with Turkey remained good throughout the region. After seventy years of Soviet domination of their region, Central Asia's leaders are eager to avoid constructing deliberate or inadvertent dependency relationships with foreign partners; after the first few months, Turkey's talk of being Central Asia's elder brother made many of the region's leaders nervous.

Furthermore, the cultural and linguistic similarities between most of the Central Asians and the Turks have turned out to be much fewer in practice than people had assumed would be the case. Save Turkmen, most of the Central Asian languages have not really proven to be mutually intelligible with Turkish in any immediate sense. Russian was, and for the time being remains, the business and scientific language for the great majority of the Central Asian elite, especially when outside of their own country. Those members of the economic and political elite who speak their "native" languages fluently generally have a "kitchen" vocabulary, one that is ill suited for the purposes of international negotiation.

At the same time, the greatly increased access to the world at large which the first year of independence brought the Central Asians showed them how far the "Turkish model" lagged behind that of other economies. Turkey's domestic economy did not prove to be as robust as Central Asia had supposed, and there were disappointing limits to the amount of unsecured investment money that Turkish businessmen were willing to direct to the region. While considering it an achievement if they could reach Turkey's economic levels immediately, the Central Asians were no longer inclined to view the Turkish standard of living as a long-term final goal. Moreover, all of Central Asia's leaders are committed to building secular or quasi-secular states, and to some of the region's leaders, nominally secular Turkey appeared at a closer distance to be more Islamic than they believed desirable for their multinational societies.

Obviously, the concern of Central Asia's leaders to build secular states was an even greater impediment to the Iranian government's goal of establishing good relations with these new nations. This is an issue to which both Iranian President Rafsanjani and Foreign Minister Ali Akbar Velayati were sensitive. While traveling to and receiving guests from the region, both men generally offered their hands in the name of national Iranian interests, not in the name of Islam, although both tended to stress in their appeals the greater reliability of Muslim allies (compared to Western—especially American—ones) for Central Asia.

However, it is precisely Iran's clash with the West, and the Islamic republic's status as a virtual pariah in the international community, that made it difficult for the leaders in Teheran to take the additional step beyond their offers of transportation and communication links to the Central Asians, even with the added blandishment of preferential terms that were justified by consanguinity.

International pressure did little to deter the Central Asian nations from developing friendly relations with Iran, but international constraints did cause economic connections between Iran and Central Asia to develop far more slowly than the Iranians had thought would be the case. The one exception to this is Turkmenistan.[12]

Most problematic to Iran, though, has been the question of relations with Tajikistan, the one Central Asian country where Iran can make a direct national appeal. With a population of just over five million, Tajikistan is the most economically disadvantaged of all of the ex-Soviet republics. In addition to being the most mineral-poor of the Central Asian states (although as a processor of nuclear and other defense-related materials, Tajikistan has some strategic economic importance), the republic is overpopulated and short of arable land. It was only natural, then, for the Tajiks to have initially seized on their Persian origins as an asset, coveting the support this could bring from Iran. In practice, however, the extremely unsettled political climate in Tajikistan has largely confounded early Iranian efforts to advance its interests there in any sort of permanent fashion.

Politically unstable even before the collapse of the USSR, Tajikistan was quickly preoccupied with internal problems at its independence, and those problems rapidly degenerated into a full-fledged civil war. President Kakhar Makhkamov was removed from office in September 1991 by a temporary coalition of ousted communists, Islamic activists, and democrats, led by former Tajik Communist Party First Secretary Rahmon Nabiev, whom Gorbachev had removed from power in 1985. In 1992, Nabiev honored the Iranians by making Teheran the destination of his first foreign visit as president, to attend the Economic Cooperation Organization meeting convened on February 16.[13]

However, domestic politics quickly overshadowed international relations when Nabiev broke with the Islamic activists and democrats. Angered at being shut out of the republic's political life, these groups in turn resorted to force in May 1992 to make Nabiev share power with them. By September 1992, their demands included Nabiev's ouster, while the Islamic activists and democrats who forced Nabiev out were themselves forced out in November 1992 and were replaced by the pro-communist regime of Emomali Rahmonov.

Iran's diplomatic presence in the republic was substantial during this turbulent period, but the seizure of power by Tajikistan's "Islamic-Democratic" coalition indirectly served to dampen Iran's prospects in the region in 1992 and 1993, in part because of the greater affinity that was perceived between Iran and the Tajik coalition than between Iran and the communist or former communist rulers.[14]

The Tajik civil war also complicated the situation within Iran itself, as it seemed to strengthen the position of Iranian clerics who had argued that Iran's policies must be formulated to advance the cause of Islam at the expense of the government's more moderate position, which prefers to capitalize on new opportunities to strengthen Iran's economy and its geopolitical position. Each group within Iran has been able to advance its interests simultaneously; although the Iranian government has remained on good terms with the Rahmonov government, Iranian-Tajik relations have become complicated by the fact that thousands of anti-Rahmonov opposition figures have fled to Afghanistan, where they are assumed to be receiving aid and comfort from pro-Iranian *mujahideen*.

More importantly, the civil war in Tajikistan thoroughly traumatized Central Asia's leaders, who were inclined to accept the statements of the Nabiev supporters, and now of the Rahmonov government, that the opposition was inspired and armed by "Islamic fundamentalists," described variously as being Afghan or Iranian in origin. The region's leaders did not so much blame Iran for "causing" Tajikistan as much as they considered Iran's existence as an Islamic state to be a dangerous precedent which could disrupt the precarious political balance in their own republics. In this way, the Tajik civil war heightened the perception that Iranian influence was, by its very nature, threatening to the secular nature of Central Asian societies.

As we will see later, improved diplomatic relations over time between the various Central Asian states and Iran, as well as Teheran's role in the Tajik peace process, have helped modify this view. By contrast, many of the Iranians' early actions helped strengthen the initial biases of the Central Asian rulers: Iranian diplomats behaved differently from most others. They drank no alcohol, did not wear ties, and would not shake a woman's hand. In addition, a mandatory part of any Iranian's trip to Central Asia is a visit to the local mosque, just as Iranian promises of aid almost invariably include offers of assistance with religious education. Moreover, from the onset of their diplomatic overtures, the Iranian leaders have stated that one of their interests in the region is to counter Turkey, which they claim is seeking influence in Central Asia in order to defeat Islamic revivalism.[15]

For their part, the Iranians also became more wary of involvement in Central Asia. To the Iranian leadership, the failed Tajik revolution demonstrated the basic instability of political life in Central Asia; Iran's attempts merely to be a regional "good neighbor" had been compromised by a civil war that managed to discredit not only Islam but Iran as well. Furthermore, the instability in Tajikistan also served to reinforce the Iranian predisposition to see relations with Russia as more important than ties to any of the Central Asian states. In many ways, the new Russian rulers had a far less complex agenda toward Islam than did their Soviet predecessors; if Russia wished to try to restore stability to the region, the Iranians would certainly not be likely to try to stop them.

Thus by the end of the first year of independence, it was already clear that neither the Turks nor the Persians were much inclined to replay the "Great Game" in Central Asia. There was certainly competition between the two states, and after the pro-Turkish Abulfaz Ali Elchibey came to power in Azerbaijan in 1992, the relationship between the two became quite tense on the question of Armenian "aggression" in Azerbaijan. However, it was also clear that there was a great deal of overlap in the interests of both states, particularly on issues such as the development of a Turkish-Iranian oil pipeline and, more generally, the advantages of a "southern" transport route. More importantly, though, both states at this point also shared the conviction that Russia was still, and was likely to remain, the dominant "foreign" power in the region.

Still, it was not the Russians who pushed the Turks and Iranians off to the sidelines as much as it was the Central Asians themselves. Ultimately, and perhaps in part because of their Soviet-era experience, Central Asia's rulers shied away from playing their ethnic cards too frequently, recognizing that to put nationalism into play brings as much potential for adversity as it does for reward. The elevation of one national community creates the risk of a backlash from all the others, and even the "purest" of the Central Asian states is decidedly multinational.

As risky as the playing of "ethnic/national cards" was beginning to appear, the outbreak of the Tajik civil war made reliance upon religion as a strategic asset look even riskier.

THE ISLAMIC CARD

Though all of Central Asia's leaders are committed to the development of secular societies, a second "ethnic card" that they hoped to use was that of Islam. This was conceived of as an ethnic rather than a religious "card," since their Soviet-era experience had shaped the consciousness of Central Asia's leaders to think of religion primarily in ethnic terms. All five of the Central Asian republics are historically and culturally Muslim, although the primacy of religion before the revolution, and the extent to which the observance of religious rituals had survived the state atheism of the Soviet period, varied among the former Soviet republics of Central Asia: from the thorough Islamicization of Tajikistan, Turkmenistan, and Uzbekistan, to the generally more superficial observance of the faith in Kazakhstan and Kyrgyzstan.

There is little doubt that Central Asia's leaders were all primarily interested in Islam for financial reasons, since Saudi Arabia and other oil-rich Persian Gulf states were obvious potential sources of aid and investment. However, the way in which the "Islamic card" has been "played" also varies among the Central Asian states, even more so than the use of ethnicity.

Turkmenistan and Uzbekistan, in which the population is more devout and more homogeneous, have both had a strong motivation to pursue contacts with the Muslim states aggressively. The leaders of both former Soviet republics made highly publicized pilgrimages to Mecca soon after independence,[16] and both have traveled widely throughout the Arab states, where they encouraged commercial representatives and Muslim religious leaders to expand activities in their respective republics.[17] Though remaining a strong advocate of a secular state, Turkmenistan's Niyazov has embraced the role of leader of a Muslim people with great enthusiasm, going so far as to replace the large statue of Lenin in Ashgebat's main square with a statue of himself as a *hajji*.

Karimov also initially played this role with gusto, swearing his presidential oath on a Koran and telling interviewers that in the Karimov home only *halal* meat was served.[18] However, following the ouster of Nabiev in neighboring Tajikistan, Karimov became more nervous about the potential volatility of religiously inspired political activism, termed "Islamic extremism," which was his public characterization of the nature of the Tajik opposition from 1992 through 1994. Accordingly, he cracked down on suspected religious activists within his republic for most of this period and became more hesitant about advancing Uzbekistan's "Islamic" interests abroad.

The constraints on "using" Islam have been stronger in Kyrgyzstan and Kazakhstan from the outset. The former has a small but important Russian population which constitutes a strong bloc of support for President Akaev, while the latter's population is at least half non-Muslim. Both Akaev and Nazarbaev have been reluctant to identify their states too closely with "Islamic" causes, which delayed both states' entry in the ECO and the Organization of the Islamic Conference.

Of the two leaders, President Akaev has capitalized the most on his Muslim heritage in the foreign policy realm. In October 1992, he made light of a trip to Saudi Arabia, joking that he would be happy to become a *hajji* if that would help bring Saudi money into his republic. While he did not make that pilgrimage, Akaev did make sure to visit other holy sites while in Saudi Arabia; Kyrgyzstan has also declared two traditional Muslim observances as state holidays.

Nazarbaev prefers to cast his nation as a bridge between the Islamic East and the Christian West. As such, he is the only Central Asian leader to have been wary of direct association with Islam from the beginning of independence. Alone among the Central Asian republics, Kazakhstan recognizes no Muslim holidays and does not mention Islam in its constitution. All religion-based political parties have been refused registration in Kazakhstan, including Alash, an Islamic-nationalist party. Ever since Kazakhstan's independence, Nazarbaev has defined Islamic "fundamentalism" as one of the gravest threats that his young state might face. Nevertheless, anxious to develop his republic's economy to the fullest extent, President Nazarbaev has been willing to take up offers from Oman, Saudi Arabia, and Iran for assistance in the oil and financial sectors, even when these "gifts" have been linked to funds for the construction of new mosques and religious centers.

Demography has conspired against Central Asian leaders' ability to use Islam for foreign policy purposes in yet another way. Kazakhstan, Kyrgyzstan, and Uzbekistan have all witnessed a large exodus of Russian Jews from their republics to Israel. From the beginning of independence it was hoped that the expertise, and even more important, the capital investment of these expatriates might somehow be lured back into the new Central Asian states.[19] Thus, although leaders of all of the Central Asian states have on various occasions expressed their solidarity with the Palestinian people, none—even prior to the Israeli-Palestinian accords—was willing to accept the guiding premise for so much of the Muslim world: that relations with Israel must remain hostile in order to demonstrate commitment to the Palestinian cause.

For their part, though, the world's Muslims have also been in no great hurry to embrace their brethren in Central Asia. Saudi Arabia was quick to ship millions of Korans to the region, and has given large sums of money for the construction of religious establishments. Some humanitarian assistance has also been provided, but it is nothing like the sums provided by the Western nations or by Turkey. As for commercial investment, the Arab states have been very cautious about entering the Central Asian market.[20] The Saudis and the Omanis have both floated suggestions for some ambitious development schemes in the region, but even by the end of the first year of independence it was obvious that such schemes would be straightforward traditional investments, meaning that their realization would remain in doubt as long as their profitability seemed less than certain.

In general, though, the Muslim world seems content to keep a certain distance from these states, at least while ex-communists dominate Central Asia. The leaders of the Central Asian states may espouse or applaud selected Muslim ideals, and some may even don traditional dress if the occasion merits, but at heart they remain adherents to a concept of a secular world that is nearly as alien to a Muslim believer as it was to an old Soviet one.

There is one great change from the Soviet period, however. It is now reasonable to expect that the next generation of Central Asian leaders might embrace Islamic ideals, and if not, then the generation after that. If the Central Asians become observant Muslims, inevitably their leaders will as well. For many in the Muslim world, it is enough to invest in helping to bring about the first condition, since the second will come as a consequence.

"Asianness"

The third ethnic bond that the new republics of Central Asia tried to use to attract international investment was a broadly defined appeal to the economic powerhouses of Asia. Not fully articulated, and having only the most general ethnic overtones, there was nevertheless a wide recognition throughout Central Asia that the development models of Europe and America are more remote to the experience of these five nations than the various Asian success stories—Japan, Singapore, Korea, Malaysia, Taiwan, Hong Kong, and China's coastal provinces. The rapid economic gains that each of these Asian countries has achieved have captured the interest of the Central Asian states as appropriate models for their own economic development.

It is not just the levels of material enrichment these states have attained that makes the Central Asian states long to repeat their economic miracles, but also the fact that the state played a significant role in these countries' rapid economic growth while maintaining tight social controls. These are preconditions of development that Central Asia's leaders find familiar and fathomable, while the diffuse democracies of the West offer a model of development that leaves most of these leaders profoundly uncomfortable.[21] Missions and delegations have been sent to each of these Asian nations, and a number of investment and joint-venture possibilities have opened up, as the Central Asian republics attempt to tap into the technical expertise underlying the Asian "economic miracles."

The appeal to Asianness was most important in Kazakhstan and Kyrgyzstan, where the leadership was able to claim almost a racial connection, since Kazakhs and Kyrgyz traveling overseas are frequently mistaken for Japanese, Koreans, or Chinese. In this sense, Nazarbaev's claim that his country is a bridge between Europe and Asia was intended to mean as much a cultural bridge as a physical one, across which goods and ideas may travel.

The appeal of Kazakhstan for Asian investors is clear, even without the ethnic factor; the former Soviet republic is obviously a source of enormous potential wealth. Kyrgyzstan has much less with which to sustain Asians' economic attention, so Akaev has invoked direct appeals to ethnicity in his quest to turn his land into an "Asian Switzerland." Sometimes these appeals have been successful, especially in Kyrgyz-Japanese relations, where the Akaev government quickly managed to get a $60 million technical assistance package—the first such Japanese program in Central Asia—as well as subsequent lines of credit and help with the republic's currency stabilization program. One result is that Japan was the first Asian country (other than neighboring China) in which the Kyrgyz have established a diplomatic representation.

Still, vague appeals to "fellow Asian" ethnicity have generally proven the least successful of the three ethnic "cards." In their dealings with the new Central Asian states, the various Asian nations have demonstrated the unsentimental business behavior that made them economic powers in the first place. All of the Asian nations have been happy to do business with the Central Asians, but generally only on the principle of maximum return on investment. In cases where they see little or no potential profit, Asian investors have not been reluctant to refuse to invest.[22] Even Japanese generosity in Kyrgyzstan should not be viewed as a significant exception, since the sums given are minuscule in comparison to the size of Japan's economy. After the first two years of independence, Japanese attention in the region switched from Kyrgyzstan to Kazakhstan and Uzbekistan because of the greater investment opportunities these economies offered.

In fact, the Asian nation that has profited the most from the emergence of the new Central Asian republics is China. For Kazakhstan, Kyrgyzstan, and Uzbekistan, China was initially each republic's largest non-CIS trading partner as well as a principal funder for numerous joint projects throughout the region.[23] Unlike most other states, China is especially enthusiastic about barter commerce, and a considerable portion of its trade with the region has involved cash-free exchanges of Chinese goods for Central Asian raw materials.

This is ironic, because China is the one Asian state that the Central Asian leaders have traditionally deeply feared, making their collective attitude toward the PRC almost schizophrenic. They are attracted to China's economic miracle of achieving rapid modernization without sacrificing political control. Although he was widely criticized for having said so publicly, Karimov was only articulating common sentiment when he praised China's development model as something to be emulated in his postcommunist Asian environment.

At the same time, though, the Central Asians fear any appeal the Chinese make in the spirit of "kinship," since the region's precolonial history is punctuated by invasions from the East. Help given in the name of Asian ethnic solidarity is attractive only if it carries no accompanying threat of conquest or neo-imperialist control. Far removed from the region, the Japanese and Koreans obviously pose no direct imperial threat to Central Asia. The same cannot be said of China, which shares borders with Tajikistan, Kyrgyzstan, and Kazakhstan. Moreover, on its side of the borders, China has its own potentially nationalist-minded

Kazakh, Kyrgyz, and Uighur enclaves, which makes China's initial refusal to recognize the existing borders with Kyrgyzstan profoundly unsettling, as were the implications of its demand for "clarification" of twelve specific border points. Schooled in the days of the Sino-Soviet conflict, the Central Asian leaders fear retaliation if the Chinese take offense, and have tried hard to offer no cause for such. Thus the Kyrgyz government has refused to register a Uighur nationalist political party, while Kazakhstan has been unwilling even to discuss the idea of permitting an autonomous Uighur region.[24]

In the eighteenth century, Kazakh leaders turned to the Russians in order to save themselves from the Kalmyk Mongols, invaders who came across what is now the Chinese border. This historical precedent is not lost on any of Central Asia's current leaders, but Kazakhstan and Kyrgyzstan are the most aware of being situated between two great powers. Given the background and training of the region's current leadership, it seems inevitable that they would turn again to the Russians to protect them from the Chinese rather than vice versa, should the need to make such a choice arise again.

That fact suggests Central Asia's fourth "identity," of a common Soviet/Russian heritage, which may well be the strongest "ethnic card" of all. Not only did Russia shape the intellectual world and supply the technical training for all of the Central Asian elites, but it continues to remain a presence, even after the fall of the USSR. Ties formed over long decades of shared existence do not disappear overnight, even if it took many of Central Asia's leaders the better part of a year to realize the fact.

A year after independence, the economies of the Central Asian nations were still tightly tied to Russia, which continued to provide them with currency, food, spare parts, and even uniforms for their newborn armies. Russia was the supplier of all or part of the energy used in the new states, as well as their primary port of access for international transportation and communication; Russia also met most of the new states' security needs. An equally constant reminder of Russia's continued influence was the more than twelve million ethnic Russians whom independence had "stranded" in the Central Asian republics.

Over the course of that first year of independence, the Central Asian nations were reluctantly coming to the realization that Russia was the only predictable ally that any of them were likely to find in the region. Moreover, the importance of having some sort of security guarantees was brought home vividly when the Tajik government began to crumble in April and May 1992, with some semblance of civil order restored to the country only after Russia finally intervened in October 1992.

As aware as they are of the potential threats Russia poses for them, the governments of Central Asia are equally aware of both the problems they potentially pose for one another and the problems various Central Asian irredentist populations might pose within each state. Violence in any one state in the region has the capacity to spill over into neighboring countries. After the outbreak of fighting in Tajikistan, it is not surprising that the current Central Asian leaders would begin to see Russia increasingly as the only regional force able to guarantee stability, enforce existing borders, and perpetuate the current elite's continued rule. Indeed, the leaders sometimes even seem to find comfort in leaving intact the physical and psychological dependencies that have traditionally bound their states to Russia.

3

FALSE HOPES OF COOPERATION

The USSR collapsed so suddenly that the leaders of the Central Asian states did not believe that the dissolution had really happened. In the months immediately following independence, most expected that some form of collective decision making would be retained, with responsibility shared between Moscow and the former Soviet republics. This is not surprising, especially since the Soviet Union had always been a country where words and reality frequently bore little relation to each other.

It was one thing to proclaim the independence of all the republics; it was quite another to expect that they would actually exercise the powers that were now juridically bestowed upon them. One point did seem intuitively obvious to everyone: The transformation of the Soviet republics into functional, independent states would require a transition period. At the very beginning, though, no one was sure how long that transition would be, or what powers the new states might expect to exercise freely during such a transition.

Since the fall of the USSR and the birth of the CIS occurred almost simultaneously, it was logical to assume that the latter would take on some—perhaps even most—of the powers of the former. All of the republic leaders recognized that the political universe they had lived in for so many years was now being reshaped, and they could also sense that a power vacuum now existed. Their new political universe had yet to take shape since so many actors—the individual republics, the new state of Russia, and the CIS—were all rushing in at the same time to fill the political void. In the very beginning, it was not even universally acknowledged and understood whether the USSR had truly broken up or had merely undergone some sort of administrative renaming. Gorbachev was now definitely out of power, as were the USSR's legislative bodies. But everybody else was still in place, in the republics and in Moscow as well, where Yeltsin and the Russian Federation's legion of legislators and bureaucrats easily shouldered the responsibilities they had sought control over in their seemingly endless struggle with the "Gorbachevites."

It was true that the republics now had de jure sovereignty, but this was a status they had been pressing for since 1990, and one which they believed could have been achieved within the legal framework of the USSR. During November–December 1991, Kazakhstan's Nazarbaev campaigned for popular election as president of his republic with the catchy slogan of "Want a flag for Kazakhstan? Cast your vote for Nursultan!" Yet at the same time, he was actively working to keep the Soviet Union intact and saw no contradiction between the two programs.

At the same time, the leaders of the other Central Asian republics, most prominent among them Uzbekistan's Islam Karimov, were agitating for international recognition of their republics, including UN membership. In fact, the demand for a seat in the UN had been a part of Azat's program since 1990, despite the fact that this Kazakh nationalist organization did not advocate independence for Kazakhstan. The demands for membership in such international organizations were not in and of themselves destabilizing for the USSR, as Ukraine and Byelorussia had enjoyed UN membership since the body's founding. More recently, under Gorbachev, Moscow had begun to allow republics to participate as constituent members in appropriate regional councils, such as the Black Sea Economic Cooperation Council and the Caspian Sea Littoral Consultative Group.

Sovereignty, though, must be exercised to have meaning. Initially, it was unclear whether the republics had simply been given expanded responsibilities, or whether they would now have to chart their own course in the international arena. It was certainly true that in December 1991 all of Central Asia's leaders wanted increased control over their republics and the right to exploit all of the resources contained therein. It is far from clear, however, that any of them were eager to be left fully to their own devices, as would be true of genuinely independent states.

A NEED TO COOPERATE

Two different structures offered the prospect of institutionalizing cooperation for the Central Asian states. The first was the CIS, which many thought at the time of its founding would develop into something resembling the confederative system Nazarbaev had proposed during the emergency sessions of the Supreme Soviet and the Congress of People's Deputies that were convened following the failed August 1991 coup. The second structure was a proposal for some type of regional organization of the Central Asian states.

The Central Asian leaders recognized that the two structures could exist alongside each other. Indeed, the development of a workable CIS structure might stimulate greater regional cooperation and aid in creating the second organization. While the eventual success of the CIS was far from certain, that institution did build upon the decades-old tradition of consultations between the republics and Moscow. Moreover, these consultations had been greatly expanded during Gorbachev's last two years in office, when Communist Party organs began to give way to more representative governmental structures. Gorbachev transformed the Politburo into a consultative body of the republics' leaders, and introduced a cabinet-style council of republic presidents.

By contrast, there was little in past Soviet experience to give anyone confidence that attempts to institutionalize cooperative mechanisms among the leaders of the Central Asian region might succeed. Such efforts were very much at odds with the Central Asian presidents' competing ambitions for regional leadership, the conflicting historical claims of the area's various peoples, and the increasing impoverishment of the population throughout the region. Of these, the last is probably most important, for it appeared inevitable that Central Asia was headed for hard economic times, and hard times stimulate greater competition over dwindling resources.

Certainly this is what Soviet precedent portended. Throughout most of the Soviet period, Moscow had tried to stimulate competition among the republics by creating the impression that republic politics was a zero-sum game in which one republic's gain was usually understood to be another republic's loss. As the period of economic difficulties approached, this history of distrust and competition only increased regional unease about the prospects for stable interstate relations.

Central Asia's borders had also been designed to diminish the likelihood of regional cooperation. The five republics had been carved from the feudal states of Khiva and Bukhara and the colonial provinces of Turkestan and Kazakhstan in such a way as to create irredentist populations throughout the entire region. There are more than a million each of "stranded" Tajiks and Uzbeks living in each other's republics, and there are irredentist Kyrgyz and Tajik populations in Tajikistan and Kyrgyzstan respectively. There are some Turkmen in Kazakhstan and some Kazakhs in Turkmenistan, but the Turkmens' main pretension is to Uzbekistan, which now contains their ancient capital of Khwarazm (which the Uzbeks renamed Khiva). For their part, the Uzbeks claim as their ancestral soil all of Khiva's lands, including those now in Turkmenistan. The Uzbeks also lament their loss of southern Kazakhstan and southern Kyrgyzstan, which in the early nineteenth century were part of Kokand; Kazakhs respond that in the previous century, Uzbekistan's present capital of Tashkent was on the lands of the Kazakh Great Horde.

Central Asia's biggest territorial losers were the Tajiks, since the region's two main Persian centers, Samarkand and Bukhara, were included in Uzbekistan, while the Tajiks were left with the backwater town of Dushanbe as their republic's capital. Central Asia's main zone of potential unrest lies not among the region's ancient capitals, but in the Fergana Valley, which was divided up among Tajikistan, Uzbekistan, and Kyrgyzstan. Small, irredentist Kyrgyz and Tajik populations were left in each other's republics, and tension exists between the two communities over land and water rights. Even more tension exists between Uzbekistan and Kyrgyzstan over similar issues; several districts in Uzbekistan are predominantly Kyrgyz, while nearly half of southern Kyrgyzstan is Uzbek.

The Fergana Valley was the scene of violence twice during the last two years of Soviet rule. In June 1989 some Uzbek youths turned on local Meshket Turks, who had lived in the region ever since Stalin relocated them from the North Caucasus in the 1940s. These clashes led to a rampage of several days' duration, which resulted in more than one hundred deaths. A year later there was a second, even bloodier clash that started as a dispute over housing between Uzbeks and Kyrgyz in Kyrgyzstan's border city of Osh; according to unofficial accounts, the result may have been nearly one thousand deaths.

Such clashes served as a frightening warning of what terrible things might occur if the Central Asians were left to mediate their own quarrels. To this day, rumors still circulate in the region that the "warning" at Osh may have been deliberately provoked, that the riots were too politically convenient, and so they must have been instigated by "dark forces," referring to security and intelligence agents from Moscow.

The fact is, though, that regardless of who was responsible for beginning the violence in Osh, it was the locals who continued it, and the trail of blood they left behind made prospects for regional cooperation that much more ambiguous. The disturbances also left the Central Asians convinced that their regional security interests would be best protected if Moscow or, even better, a group of disinterested states were to participate in the process of resolving common problems.

COMMONWEALTH OF INDEPENDENT STATES

Of all the post-Soviet republic rulers, the heads of the various Central Asian states were the most eager for the CIS to succeed. It was precisely to ensure their continued ties with Russia and the other industrialized republics that they had forced their way into this organization in the first place, following their unceremonious exclusion at the time of the first meeting to dissolve the USSR, on December 8, 1991, in Minsk. The leaders were also willing to surrender substantial amounts of sovereignty to the new organization.

At the time of its formation, there was a great deal of confusion about the sort of organization the CIS should become. Some of its founding members, particularly Ukraine, saw the CIS as a temporary, transitional organization that had come into being to adjudicate the various issues the collapse of the USSR had left unresolved, and that it would either disband or become a largely ceremonial organization following the completion of this task.

Other founding members, including the Central Asian republics, saw the CIS as a more enduring structure. Of course, the immediate task of the organization was to negotiate the terms of the transition period, but the hope of these members was that the CIS would evolve into something more lasting, a "supra-government" of the type that the European Community (EC) was preparing to transform itself into. At that time, the EC was planning to tighten the economic integration of its members by ushering in the Single Market Act, complete with a common currency to use throughout the community. However, even the most integrative model of the EC assumed the continued existence of sovereign nation-states and their own governmental structures, including presidents, parliaments, and legal systems. Each of the member states would also retain its own educational system, leaving linguistic and cultural policies unaffected, while also continuing to preserve a large measure of control over its economy. By contrast, the CIS was only beginning to develop institutions similar to those that had evolved over decades in the European Community and that allowed the preservation of statehood and national identities within an integrated economic and political framework.

The Russian government, though, was attracted to an entirely different concept of the CIS. Such an organization seemed to be an ideal way for policymakers in Moscow to supervise, if not control outright, economic and security policies in former Soviet territories that they still deemed as vital Russian interests. Yet, while Russia was still clearly in favor of member-states preserving their juridical independence in the new organization, its early designs for the CIS were too all-encompassing for several of the new post-Soviet states. By early 1992, when it became clear that the CIS was going to become a sort of post-Soviet EC, several republic parliaments—in Azerbaijan, Georgia, and Moldova—refused to ratify the founding CIS accords.

, The dispute among the republics over the nature of this organization crippled the CIS within months of its formation, leaving it a virtual shell. Its capital was established in Minsk, but the member-nations had neither sufficient funds to set up the new organization nor a surplus of skilled officials to staff it. This meant that the real center of power for the CIS remained in Moscow, with its technical staff composed of Soviet-turned-Russian government advisors.

Thus the CIS, especially in its first years, was simply another device for Russian policymakers to use in advancing their own goals, which they could do since the constituent member-states of the CIS were still unaccustomed to exercising their new sovereignty. As a result, they were able to do little to limit or shape Moscow's continuing control of their economic and political existence. Russia's leaders had inherited that control upon the USSR's dissolution, and they now exercised it in the name of the CIS.

The old Soviet borders, save those in the Baltics, became the CIS borders. While the Ukrainians raised strenuous objections from the very beginning, the rest of the CIS members agreed that the boundaries of these member-states were to be governed by a single set of conventions and a common border guard. The old communication systems remained intact, including the private *nachalstvo* telephones which continued to link the inner offices of the old USSR elite, who now were the new elite of CIS member-states. This high-quality, well-secured communication system, which was still controlled in Moscow, made it particularly easy for leaders in the new states to continue their old habits of Soviet-style policy coordination through private and frequent communication. While these communications links began to break down in the second and third years of independence, Russia's commitment to a common Russian-dominated border regime only strengthened over time.

Among the most pressing problems the CIS had to address were regulation of the military and other security concerns. At its first meetings, a CIS military command was established under General Yevgeni Shaposhnikov (a Russian), along with protocols for ensuring control of the Soviet nuclear arsenal, which effectively remained in Russian hands.[1] This CIS command also claimed control of all strategic forces (including, of course, nuclear forces) wherever they were stationed in the former USSR. These forces remained under CIS command until June 1993, when Russia formally asserted its control over them. Though each state could now claim control of the armies on its territories, these "national armies" were still led by officers trained in the Soviet command and control system; as such, their loyalties were still unclear.

Meetings of the CIS ministers of defense became a regular feature of the organization, with the intention that these functionaries would elaborate and enforce a common security policy. Yet it soon became clear that, by themselves, CIS institutions were incapable of answering the "nuclear question."

The official rhetoric of the CIS leaders was that the USSR's nuclear arsenal would be used for common defense. At the same time, however, Russia, Ukraine, Belarus, and Kazakhstan—the four republics where Soviet nuclear forces had been stationed—all maintained that they had proprietary rights over the weapons systems on their territory. Even if those claims were largely intended only to gain the new states some bargaining advantage before dismantling the weapons or turning them over to Russia, the international community—particularly the United States—preferred to recognize the claims of only one post-Soviet nuclear state, Russia. However, U.S. policymakers also realized that it would be advantageous to the general cause of arms control if the nuclear issue were subject to international negotiation, rather than defined as an internal CIS matter.

Even without the "nuclear question," the CIS had a wide range of military issues to tackle and few mechanisms by which to do so. One important issue concerned military secrets still lurking within the republics. Top military officials from the old Soviet national security establishment in Moscow still jealously guarded these secrets. For example, in late 1993, Kazakhstan's Nursultan Nazarbaev admitted that while he was head of Soviet Kazakhstan, he had been denied access to statistics about the secret military cities in the republic. He further implied that even after his country had become independent, he still had difficulty gaining access to this information.

Similarly, KGB records had never been fully duplicated in republic capitals, so that even after the KGB was broken up into separate national units, no one could be absolutely certain about which spies in the former Soviet republics were still active, who they were, or how great a capacity Moscow still retained for spying on its new neighbors. Those serving in the republic organizations of the KGB were themselves suspect, as these organizations had traditionally been used by Moscow to spy on republic leaders and governmental bodies. There were shakeups in all the republic security organizations after independence, but many with dual loyalties must have remained in place, a point that was driven home in 1994 when a state security official in Osh resigned in order to take up a posting in Moscow. There was also the question of clandestine agents. While unable to determine its dimensions, no one doubted that such intelligence activity was continuing. When a search of Lithuanian KGB files unearthed a KGB agent among President Landsbergis's close associates, this "dual loyalty" was presumed to be the rule, not the exception. Indeed, fears over uncovering the extent of KGB infiltration through similar searches in other capitals of former Soviet republics kept the enthusiasm for pursuing such questions very low throughout the CIS.

There was also another kind of "infiltration" of the new states by Moscow. The USSR had a system of "rotating" officials, in which Moscow sent top-level state and party bureaucrats (usually ethnic Russians) from central ministries and party organizations to serve in the various Soviet republics. When the USSR collapsed, many of these officials became the ministers and civil servants of the newly formed "foreign" states. In one sense their presence was a considerable advantage to the new states, since many of these officials were competent administrators with an understanding of how modern economies should be administered. This cadre proved to be a valuable asset to the CIS states by coordinating the interrepublic linkages that were a feature of both formal CIS policy and informal post-Soviet reality.

At the same time, though, it was unclear to whom these administrators were loyal, and doubtful whether they could be trusted to protect the interests of their new "homelands" if those interests conflicted with Russia's. After independence was declared, all of the non-Russian republics tried to lure home from Moscow their nationals who had been serving in central Soviet institutions that were now transformed into Russian institutions. This was a very different scenario from the "career change" of Oleg Soskovets, an ethnic Russian who served for a year as a deputy prime minister of *independent* Kazakhstan. He resigned his job on a Friday, only to start work the following Monday as a deputy prime minister of Russia. Now, as first deputy prime minister in charge of Russian industry, Soskovets regularly faces off against the Kazakhs on economic issues. Several months after Soskovets's departure from Kazakhstan, German Kuznetsov, a deputy prime minister in Kyrgyzstan, also quit his position. Within weeks, he was named to a senior post representing Russia in interrepublic economic relations.

RUSSIA'S ADVANTAGE

Even without such defections, it was clear that policymakers in Moscow generally had more knowledge about the republic economies than the leaders of these states did themselves, knowledge that Russia was skilled in using to its own advantage. During this first year of independence it became clear that Moscow would remain the economic center for all of the member-states of the CIS for an indefinite period. The commonwealth members all shared, and were likely to continue to share, a single "economic space" with open borders, an interlocking energy network, and a common currency. At least for a while, that currency would also have a single source of emission, a single exchange rate, and a single clearinghouse for both international currency transactions and interrepublic transactions—all functions still executed by the Central Bank in Moscow.

Still, the question of currency and banking reform was a constant agenda item at CIS meetings and at the economic planning sessions held in between. Paralleling the debate about the nature of the CIS, there were two distinct positions emerging about the nature of CIS eco-nomic policy. Countries that viewed the CIS as simply a transitional body (as did Ukraine and, at least for a time, Belarus) wanted the CIS to help facilitate the shift from a ruble zone to a multicurrency free-trade union. On the other hand, as was stated energetically by Nazarbaev and, some-what later, Karimov, the Central Asian states wanted the CIS to maintain a single currency and customs union, but wanted the responsibility for currency regulation to be shared among the CIS member-states.

The new Russian government was unwilling to give up either control of the ruble or the idea of a single CIS currency bloc until it had worked out the details of its own economic reform program. Russian officials were also laboring under what proved to be a misconception: that preservation of a single monetary system would slow the rapid decline in levels of industrial production in Russia and the other Soviet succes-sor states.

That this was a misconception was demonstrated when the Russian Central Bank ignored the tight-fisted monetary program of the Russian reformers and responded to rising prices and a growing budget deficit by continuing to print new currency. The result was skyrocketing inflation that sank the ruble's value—from about 60/U.S.$1 in December 1991 to more than 1,000/U.S.$1 in June 1993. Later, the Russian government blamed the ruble's drop partly on the other Soviet successor states, whose governments also were demanding, and for a time receiving, shipments of rubles to cover the rising prices of Russian goods.

Even when they were receiving ruble transfers, the republics felt abused by the currency situation. Denied any voice in the formulation of the financial policies that governed their economies, they also fell victim to currency transfer and debt-clearing mechanisms, which could take six months or more to execute fund transfers between republics. Trade with Russia put the other former Soviet republics at a disadvantage as well, since they frequently found themselves having to sell resources to Russia at old, preinflationary prices, while simultaneously having to buy goods and services from Russia at the new, inflated prices. It is no surprise that under these conditions the republics' trade deficits with Russia began to grow, with some of them (including Kazakhstan) piling up astronomical debts, particularly to Russia's energy sector.

The former Soviet republics had few options to impose even a mod-icum of order in their economies. The one option they could exercise both angered Russia and further weakened the CIS. Unable to print money, the republics sought to reduce inflation in their economies by controlling prices on basic commodities, keeping them artificially low, while protecting against cross-border "runs" on cheap goods by setting up trade barriers. Not only were such barriers a violation of the founding principles of the CIS, but they also effectively stopped most inter-republic trade. All of the Central Asian states instituted such trade barriers. Fully dependent on trade with Russia, Kazakhstan introduced only a moderate trade barrier with Russia, and Kyrgyzstan only a slightly more severe one. Uzbekistan and Turkmenistan introduced elaborate price controls and strict cross-border trade restrictions.

These moves were part of an effort by the former Soviet republics to carve out economic development strategies for themselves, separate from those designed in Moscow. Yet, as they did so, they discovered one of the basic paradoxes of the CIS: The newly independent states that had banded together to help preserve a common economic space now began to realize that they were all potential competitors with each other. Still bound together by the old network of interrepublic trade links, the new states obviously would have found all-out competition destructive, but they also began to see that cooperation was impossible unless each state was able to define economic advantage for itself.

Prying loose the former Soviet republics from Moscow's control caused great dissatisfaction on all sides. Russia believed that, as the USSR's heir, it should be compensated for Soviet-era infrastructural investments made in what have now become exportable commodities for these republics, while the republics saw themselves as the victims of Russian and Soviet colonization and wanted compensation for the wealth Moscow had accrued by selling resources taken from their territory. The dispute continues to this day. Moscow continues to demand part ownership in the form of equity shares in foreign joint venture projects for the development of oil and gas fields in Kazakhstan, Turkmenistan, and Azerbaijan, while the republics argue that they should still be entitled to buy energy from Moscow at the old Soviet-era prices, which were a fraction of world prices.

At their core, these issues involved conflicting understandings about how to balance the rights of the former Soviet republics with the proprietary interests of Russia. As such, the CIS was not prepared to resolve these disputes. Instead, solutions have been reached through bilateral, behind-the-scenes negotiations, and sometimes even through under-the-table arrangements, rather than through CIS-sponsored forums. In fact, most of these issues were so controversial that one president could not talk about them in front of the others without risking embarrassment.

Still, much of the blame for failing to reach a consensus on these issues resides in the nature of the CIS itself. In its first years of existence, the organization failed to establish a mechanism of decision making that focused on the *process* of making decisions rather than on the *product* of the decision. A process-oriented model of decision making permits all participants to feel as if their needs are being addressed as part of the give-and-take that occurs as a decision is being reached. Instead, the CIS regularly focused on outcomes, adopting policy recommendations that had been elaborated by Russian-dominated interrepublic working groups. These recommendations were ratified at large ceremonial meetings, hosted by each member-state on a rotating basis, at which the host-presidents were generally more interested in the photo opportunities than in the meeting's outcome.

The deficiencies of the CIS in this regard were mirrored in many of its member-states. It is easy to claim to be a "rule of law" nation, but much harder to adhere to the laws legislatures pass. Like the CIS itself, in the two years following independence, many of these new nations passed new laws faster than they could print them. Yet, most of the legislatures lacked the authority to enforce the laws they were passing; contempt for the law grew. The rulings of the CIS were no exception, as President Karimov made plain at the April 1993 meeting of republic presidents, when he said that the CIS had adopted 270 "inefficient" measures that were unacceptable to his country, so he did not recognize them.[2]

As willing as the leaders of the new states were to express contempt for or impatience with the CIS, most remained fearful of what would happen if the organization disappeared. This was particularly true of Kazakhstan's Nursultan Nazarbaev, who in speech after speech spoke of the importance of not simply *preserving* the CIS, but of *strengthening* it as well. While they chafed at what they perceived to be Russia's abusive behavior in their common economic space, the leaders of the former Soviet republics all continued to see Russia as the sole competent political arbiter in the CIS and the only guarantor of interrepublic security accords. Additionally, Russia served as a potential quarter to which appeals could be made in *intra*republic disputes, especially those involving autonomous political entities.

This last point was a concern of growing importance, because by mid-1992 security was no longer an abstract question in many parts of the former Soviet Union. Azerbaijan (then outside of the CIS) and Armenia were at war. Georgia (also not a CIS member-state at the time) was being split apart by the secessionist regions of Abkhazia and Ossetia, both of which did not recognize Georgia's rule and looked for support from the bordering Russian state that they hoped to join. Moldovans were fighting with secessionist Russians in the Transdniestr region. Then, after a winter of skirmishes, full-fledged civil war came to Tajikistan in May 1992, and Central Asia's leaders began to fear that if this violence continued unchecked, the stability of their entire region would be at risk.

In each of these cases, the state or states involved appealed to Russia directly to try to arrange suitable terms for their protection, which resulted in a host of bilateral security accords. As we will see in the next several chapters, some of these cases involved agreements that touched on the foundation of the signatory state's foreign policy strategy. This was particularly true of Kazakhstan, which shares almost three thousand miles of border with Russia, and whose leaders negotiated their first bilateral agreement with the Russians as early as August 1991. Similarly, bilateral security guarantees with Russia became a key feature in Uzbekistan's security policy after May 1993.

Such bilateral arrangements, however, did not dim the appeal of CIS-wide security agreements or military initiatives. Multilateral actions seemed to offer the republics assurances of the continued recognition of state sovereignty while simultaneously allowing Russia to protect its own interests in a less clearly hegemonic way. The military operation that brought Emomali Rahmonov to power in Tajikistan in November 1992, and which has sustained his rule since, exemplifies the role the CIS has acquired as an instrument of security policy implementation, rather than simply an arena of security policy decision making. The decision to intervene was ultimately made in Moscow, with some firm pressure from Uzbekistan. As a result, the Tajik government of Akbarsho Iskandarov was ousted on the basis of a bilateral Uzbekistan-Russia security agreement that had been adopted to secure these states' internal and external borders. A CIS peace mission led by Kyrgyzstan had been active in Tajikistan until just weeks before the invasion, and it was only after Rahmonov had replaced Iskandarov that a CIS mandate for the action was sought.[3]

Certainly all of the CIS leaders recognized from the beginning that it would be extremely difficult to elaborate Russia's proper role within the geopolitical space of the former USSR. Whatever they said in public notwithstanding, each of the CIS leaders realized that the organization would never become a forum of equals; Russia's dominance was tacitly acknowledged by the organization's member-states. This made it all the more important to develop formal and informal constraints on Russia. However, after a year of confronting the problems of independence and the increasing security risks associated with it, Central Asia's leaders were no longer confident that the CIS, as then structured, could balance Russia's security concerns with their own desires to survive as independent states. This was all the more disturbing since the regional initiatives the Central Asians had set in place in part to attenuate their dependence on Russia were failing to take hold.

A CENTRAL ASIAN COMMON MARKET

It was not until 1990, when the republics began to exercise greater sovereignty, that Moscow reversed its long-standing policy of refusing to carve up the USSR into discrete regional subunits for fear that this would threaten the effectiveness of Moscow's unilateral control. Over the course of Soviet history, a number of efforts were made to divide the USSR into regional economic units, but such divisions were almost always done in a way that reduced rather than enhanced republic autonomy.

As a result of this legacy, the Central Asian leaders did not meet as a group to discuss common interests until June 23, 1990, when Nursultan Nazarbaev, then First Secretary of the Kazakh Communist Party, hosted fellow First Secretaries Niyazov (Turkmenistan), Makhkamov (Tajikistan), Karimov (Uzbekistan), and Masaliev (Kyrgyzstan) at a meeting in the Kazakh capital of Alma-Ata (renamed Almaty shortly after independence).[4] Although these leaders had of course met in other, larger groupings, this was the first gathering at which they assembled both without senior representatives from Moscow and as leaders of semiautonomous political entities, with the power and authority to initiate an agenda and execute the decisions that it produced. The impetus for this new and significant accretion of regional power revealed how much the central leadership's relations with the Soviet republics had changed: Moscow no longer felt able to or interested in responding to the Central Asian region's problems, so that local initiatives were imbued with real importance for the first time in the Soviet experience.

Kazakhstan's decision to join—let alone originate—a Central Asian group represented a policy departure of equal significance for the former Soviet republic. Traditionally, Kazakhstan's leadership, which was responsible for a republic that was equal parts Asian and European, had been loath to identify the republic as Central Asian. For most of the Soviet period, planners in Moscow also did not consider Kazakhstan entirely within Central Asia. The economy of Kazakhstan's northern region had generally been administratively joined with Siberia, while southern Kazakhstan's economy was delegated to the planners who concerned themselves with the rest of Central Asia. In fact, the Soviet term for the region, *Srednaia Aziia* (Middle Asia), excluded the Kazakh republic and referred only to the Kyrgyz, Tajik, Turkmen, and Uzbek republics. Where all five were concerned, the term *Srednaia Aziia i Kazakhstan* (Central Asia and Kazakhstan) was used. Not until their January 1993 meeting did Central Asian leaders make the decision to refer to the entire region as *Tsentralnaia Aziia* (Central Asia), which for the first time included Kazakhstan.

Little of importance came from that first meeting of Central Asian leaders in 1990. The cause of greater regional economic cooperation was repeatedly championed, but there was no elaboration on how it might be achieved. While the region's economies were at the top of the meeting's agenda, the most definitive proposal in this issue-area resulting from the discussions was a commitment to meet again in a year to discuss the same questions more concretely. The June 1990 gathering also mandated the creation of regional councils to address common problems in the areas of culture, science, and the preservation of the environment.[5]

The region's leaders gathered in Tashkent for their second annual meeting on August 15, 1991, passing resolutions calling for the gradual activation of these regional councils; one noteworthy resolution also sought to include Azerbaijan in their group.[6] Azerbaijan's prime minister, Hasan Hasanov, was an observer at the meeting, but the collapse of the USSR and the subsequent ouster of the Azerbaijani government led to the abandonment of tentative plans to add Azerbaijan to the Central Asian grouping. The Central Asian leadership had also changed somewhat since the first meeting. Kyrgyzstan had undergone its "Silk Revolution" in October 1990, which replaced former Communist Party boss Absamat Masaliev with party outsider Askar Akaev. Akaev took office with a mandate to further distance his republic from Moscow. However, the fighting between Uzbeks and Kyrgyz in Osh during June–July 1990 had not only helped bring about Masaliev's downfall but had also drastically reduced trust on both the Uzbek and Kyrgyz sides, diminishing prospects for regional unity. Of course, the political outlook changed even more markedly with the Moscow coup attempt, which happened just four days after this meeting. Those gathered at the Tashkent meeting *seemed* to have had no warning of the coup attempt, which unquestionably wreaked havoc with their plans.

The fate of the Central Asians had once again been shaped without any involvement on their part, when Russia, Ukraine, and Belarus met to dissolve the USSR, on December 8, 1991. The year-end events forced the Central Asian leaders to hold an extraordinary meeting on December 12 in Ashgebat. The sense of purpose made this gathering quite different than their previous sessions, which had been largely symbolic. Central Asia's leaders were now orphans; their common "fatherland" had died at the hands of their Slavic brothers. For the first time ever, Central Asia's leaders themselves had to make some hard decisions with little or no guidance from Moscow.

At the end of 1991, the Central Asian leaders had three crucial choices before them: press for inclusion in the CIS; form a regional grouping of their own, such as a Central Asian Community or Turkestan Confederation; or work out their terms of independence individually. Their decision is, of course, well known. While opting to join the CIS, however, Central Asia's leaders also sought to preserve some sort of expanded regional structure that would be both less formal than, and obviously subsidiary to, CIS decision-making bodies.[7]

Each of Central Asia's leaders had his own priorities, although in the end it seems to have been Nursultan Nazarbaev's arguments that carried the day. For Nazarbaev, the creation of a new union that included all the former Soviet Central Asian republics was the highest priority, and he believed that a united stance by the five Central Asian republics would help achieve this.[8] To this end, Nazarbaev even resorted to some hardball tactics by calling publicly for the creation of a Central Asian organization to parallel the new union of the three Slavic republics. The specter of a revived Slavic-Turkic rivalry was at least part of the reason why the Russia-Belarus-Ukraine troika soon felt it prudent to widen the membership of the new union they had named the Commonwealth of Independent States.[9]

However, the ability of the Central Asian states to forge a common position, as witnessed at the Ashgebat meeting, was not a harbinger of future unity. All those present seemed cognizant of the fact that their collective agreement was based more on the fear of worse alternatives than on a sense of a shared purpose for the future. Now that their states were independent, Central Asia's leaders were free to go their separate ways, which was a viable option with their new opportunities. Both Kazakhstan and Kyrgyzstan had petitioned to join the CIS even before the Ashgebat meeting, and Nazarbaev and Akaev were clearly more oriented toward Russia than were the other three leaders. The Kyrgyz and Kazakh leaders were interested in adopting integrated strategies of economic and political reform similar to those being debated in Moscow. By contrast, Uzbekistan's Islam Karimov believed that a "strong hand" was necessary to maintain order and so advocated a lengthy period of economic transition, as did Tajikistan's Nabiev, who was already facing stiff political opposition in his own republic precisely because he endorsed such views. Saparmurad Niyazov had little interest in pursuing "democracy" in Turkmenistan, believing that the oil and gas wealth of his sparsely populated republic would be sufficient to purchase popular allegiance to his own heavy-handed and highly personalistic style of rule.[10]

Despite the growing differences among them, Central Asia's leaders believed it important that they continue to meet, if only to discuss common problems. However, events in Tajikistan again disrupted their good intentions. Indeed, at the next Central Asian meeting, held in Bishkek on April 23, 1992, Tajikistan was absent.[11] Just as significantly, discussions of greater economic cooperation and coordination among the remaining four new states were given added importance by the presence of Russia's foreign minister, Andrei Kozyrev, whose very attendance underscored Russia's continuing role in determining interrepublic relations.

Such subtle reminders of Russia's continuing interest were no longer necessary once Russian troops were sent to bolster the Soviet Army's 201st Motorized Division, which had already been stationed in Tajikistan before the USSR broke up. Efforts at regional cooperation continued, but they began to take on a surreal quality. This was especially true of the January 1993 meeting in Tashkent, when they formally adopted the name *Tsentralnaia Aziia* and announced the inauguration of a common "Asian" market. The new common market was based on the European model: unfettered movement of goods across borders, standardization of tariffs on foreign imports, elimination of customs duties and tariffs within the union, and the establishment of a common currency.[12] Their declarations and pronouncements notwithstanding, there is not a shred of evidence to suggest that any of the leaders gathered in Tashkent thought that these goals would be attainable anytime in the near future. In fact, a few days later, all of them gathered again for a CIS meeting in

Minsk, where they signed a quite different and generally contradictory set of resolutions.

In the unlikely event that anyone at that Tashkent meeting might have required a lesson about how closely the new geopolitical realities of Central Asia resembled the old ones, the presence of Emomali Rahmonov at the table as head of Tajikistan was a vivid reminder of Central Asia's continued dependence on Russia. Once the mushrooming military operation in Tajikistan came under CIS command, the Central Asian leaders had fewer and fewer issues that would justify their meeting together. Rahmonov was never accepted as an equal by his fellow Central Asian leaders, and Niyazov, who had declined to send troops to Tajikistan in support of the effort to install Rahmonov, now became less enthusiastic about participating in regional meetings as well.

As 1993 wore on, meetings of the Central Asian "five" increasingly became gatherings of a regional "troika." Subsequent regional meetings took the form of consultations among Nazarbaev, Akaev, and Karimov, meeting jointly and separately, while the idea of a full-fledged Central Asian regional organization disappeared from most people's minds.

The first year or so of independence brought some real disappointments to Central Asia's leaders. First, they learned that independence carried with it no magic formula for economic development and that prominent members of the international community were just as adept at making empty promises as were members of the old Communist Party Politburo. They also learned that more home-grown efforts at mutual assistance, such as the CIS or some new Central Asian regional organization, offered only limited help in solving pressing local problems.

The Central Asian Common Market was at best a wistful fantasy, while the CIS had proved to be neither multinational nor supranational, but simply a structure that Moscow used to advance Russian geopolitical interests. Yet Russia, too, proved to be erratic in both giving assistance and in applying its will. In truth, Central Asia's leaders were probably just as disturbed by Russia's frequent inability to follow through on its threats as they were by Russia's strong-arm tactics themselves.

4

KAZAKHSTAN

Living with a Hegemon

By summer 1993, the optimism that independence had stimulated eighteen months before had wilted throughout most of Central Asia. Tajikistan's civil war, nearly a year old, now seemed a threat to regional stability. Maintaining a regime dominated by members of the old Communist Party *nomenklatura* in Tajikistan required a constant CIS military presence. While the ethnic makeup of this "multinational" force was overwhelmingly Russian, it also included a large contingent from Uzbekistan and smaller ones from Kazakhstan and Kyrgyzstan. By summer 1993, all of these groups in the CIS military force were deployed on the increasingly porous Afghan-Tajik border.

By this time, Central Asia's leaders also had a better sense of both the value of their natural resources, which was in most cases quite high, and the pace at which these resources could realistically be developed, which was invariably far slower than the leaders had originally envisioned. Moreover, all had discovered that, like it or not, they were still tied to the decaying remnants of the old Soviet economic system. Moscow's *diktat* had disappeared, but the economies of the various post-Soviet republics remained interconnected.

This was especially true in the case of Kazakhstan, whose economy was still fully interconnected with Russia's. In fact, Russia accounted for approximately 70 percent of Kazakhstan's total trade. While it was coming to be seen as a "new Saudi Arabia," Kazakhstan still shipped its oil to Russia for refining and was dependent upon Russia to ship it back if it was to have energy supplies. Moreover, with no port of its own, Kazakhstan was unable to capitalize on its vast oil and gas reserves without Russia's cooperation and access to its pipelines and port facilities. Bypassing Russia meant shipping oil south, through Iran, which would jeopardize the international financing Kazakhstan needed to see its various development projects through to completion.

From the very moment the republic's sovereignty was first raised in 1990, Nazarbaev understood that Kazakhstan's challenge would be to develop the republic's natural resources in a way that did not threaten Russian interests. Unique among the Central Asian states, Kazakhstan shares a border with Russia. Any new state sharing a long border with a more powerful neighbor would be vulnerable, but Kazakhstan's problems with Russia are also exacerbated by having more than six million ethnic Russians living in the former Soviet republic.

Independence only compounded the challenge of keeping relations with Russia on an even keel. Although statehood gave Nazarbaev a great deal of discretionary authority he had previously lacked, he also acquired new responsibilities, which included keeping public order; this often meant finding ways to appease Kazakh nationalists without offending the Russian nationalists living in the former Soviet republic. This was an almost impossible task, as the Kazakhs saw in the collapse of the USSR the birth of Kazakh nationhood, while the Russians understood independent Kazakhstan to be a multinational state which would preserve the same rights and privileges they had enjoyed under Soviet rule.

Although the Russian government has assumed the role of protector of all Russians living throughout the former Soviet Union, it has embraced the issue of protecting Kazakhstan's ethnic Russian population with particular enthusiasm, and it closely monitors Nazarbaev's performance in this regard.

To a certain degree, Nazarbaev has met Russia's expectations, working hard to promote the idea that Kazakhstan is a unique and multinational state. However, this does not mean that Nazarbaev is reluctant to carve out some sort of independent posture for himself and for the republic. As a Kazakh himself, and as a politician whose views are still shaped in part by the Kazakh-dominated republic Communist Party elite, Nazarbaev has allowed a Kazakh view of statehood to predominate over the Russian position on several key questions. Every time he has done so, though, the Russian government has been quick to present a "bill" for the cost of his independent line.

DOOMED BY DEMOGRAPHY

Nazarbaev's efforts to create an independent foreign policy posture for Kazakhstan have been shaped more by the republic's demographic situation than by any other factor. Although nearly half of its Slavic population came to Kazakhstan in the years since World War II, Russians have for several hundred years looked upon Kazakhstan as their frontier, and could not contemplate a future in which the two territories were not somehow joined. Thus while both countries are now officially sovereign and independent, it would be unthinkable for Nazarbaev to pursue a foreign policy that was anti-Russian, or even substantially at odds with Russia's interests.

Russians initially came to the area in the first half of the seventeenth century, when the Cossacks set up posts on the banks of the Yaik (Ural) River, and at Gurev (Atyrau) and Uralsk, at the western edge of the Kazakh lands. Prior to this, Kazakh herds had grazed on both sides of the river, and the Kazakhs came to accept the Ural River as their western boundary. The Russians, though, did not see this as their eastern boundary. In the first part of the eighteenth century, again relying on Cossacks, the Russians set up a line of defensive fortifications in the northernmost part of present-day Kazakhstan, in Orsk, Omsk, Pavlodar, Petropavlovsk, and Ust-Kamenogorsk. Although these too were placed on what had earlier been traditional Kazakh grazing lands, from that time on these garrison cities have been almost exclusively Russian settlements.

At the time these forts were being established, the Kazakhs were being driven from their lands by Kalmyks (Mongols), who were invading from the east. In 1731 and 1740 respectively, the khans of the Small and Middle Hordes turned to Russia for protection, swearing loyalty to the Russian tsar. From the Russian viewpoint, this gave them license for the conquest of the Kazakh lands. The Kazakhs, of course, did not concur, and took up arms in the middle of the nineteenth century, when the Cossacks and Russians began to erect another string of forts from Fort Shevchenko, on the Caspian, to Verny (Almaty) and Pishkek (Bishkek) in the east. The Russians prevailed, later marching southward to conquer the territory of the Kazakh Small Horde, and then on to "Turkestan," the name given to the lands of Khiva, Bukhara, and Kokand.

Other than the Cossacks and the staffs of Russia's governors-general, whose job it was to ensure control of this newly acquired territory, few Europeans lived in either the Kazakh Steppe or Turkestan in the first decades following conquest. As Russia increased its administrative presence, the numbers of Cossacks and other imperial servants grew. By 1917, there were more than a half-million Cossacks in Kazakhstan. Russian and Ukrainian homesteaders did not begin to arrive in the region en masse until the first decade of the twentieth century, when more than a million families were settled in northern Kazakhstan and on both sides of the Chu River, in present-day Kazakhstan and Kyrgyzstan. The next mass wave of Russians came to the area in the 1920s and early 1930s as *kulaks*, peasants dispossessed of their land by Stalin's collectivization. Evacuees came to the republic in large numbers during World War II, while a million settlers and their families came during Khrushchev's Virgin Lands drive of the 1950s, their numbers further augmented by the arrival of tens of thousands of technicians during the industrialization drives of the 1960s and 1970s.[1]

These various migrations left Russians in every one of Kazakhstan's nineteen oblasts, as well as in the republic's capital, Almaty, where they still account for some 80 percent of the population. Even more significant was the fact that at the time of independence Russians also made up more than 50 percent of the population in the nine northern oblasts of the republic. The threat of secession is so obvious that it does not need to be stated, and it is viewed as so calamitous that no serious politician in Kazakhstan dares speak of it in public. When anyone does mention changing Kazakhstan's borders, as did Vladimir Zhirinovsky obliquely in the 1993 parliamentary campaign and Aleksandr Solzhenitsyn directly in a 1990 *Komsomol'skaia pravda* article[2] and once again in May 1994,[3] the political climate in the republic becomes almost hysterical.

The Kazakhs regard the shifting of borders as unacceptable, and respond to claims that such moves might be historically justified by demanding reparations for the three genocides the republic suffered at Russian hands, the first in the 1890s, the second at the time of the revolution, and the third during collectivization. Kazakh demographers estimate that some three million Kazakhs died or were forced to emigrate as a result of Russian and Soviet policies during these three periods, leaving Kazakhstan with the distinction of being the only Soviet successor state where the titular nationality makes up less than half the population. Kazakhstan's government now claims that as of January 1, 1995, ethnic

Kazakhs accounted for 44 percent of the population, up from 38 percent in the Soviet census in 1989. During this same period the percentage of Russians dropped by 1 percent, to 36 percent. The latter figure is somewhat deceptive since Kazakhstan has lost an average of 150,000 Russians per year since 1990, while more than 75,000 Russians per year have made their way into the republic (generally from even less desirable parts of Central Asia). Though technically illegal, there has been no effort to stop the Russian in-migration.

Demographically, time is on the side of the Kazakhs. Their population is much younger than the Russians'. The Kazakh baby-boomers of the 1960s and 1970s are just now reaching their prime reproductive age. Kazakhs continue to have much larger families than Russians—more than three more children per family on average—which has led some local demographers to predict that by the year 2015 Kazakhs will make up more than 60 percent of the population.[4] For now, however, the European influence continues to predominate in the republic; together, Ukrainians, Germans, and Russians form a plurality of Kazakhstan's population.[5]

The Kazakhs do not want to wait until they reach majority status to turn Kazakhstan into a Kazakh national state. As a result, ethnicity remains a question of pressing national concern, affecting all aspects of domestic and foreign policymaking. Kazakh nationalists are far less eager to court Russian approval than the Nazarbaev government, and are not embarrassed to have Kazakhstan identified as an Asian or Islamic state.

The displeasure of Kazakhstan's Russians, however, is not so much with the foreign policy agenda of the Kazakh nationalists as with their domestic goals; it is here, of course, that they hope Russia will serve as an advocate of their interests. Kazakhstan's Russians view Russia's intervention in the republic's affairs as wholly legitimate. Although many strongly identify with Kazakhstan, Russia is still viewed as their homeland; therefore, Kazakhstan's Russians—with strong backing from Russia—have pressed hard for dual citizenship, a status denied them by Kazakhstan's constitution.

Kazakhstan's Russians also complain of second-class treatment by a Kazakh-dominated legislature which not only affirmed Kazakh as the sole state language but has also encouraged the "Kazakhification" of the non-Kazakh population; the legislature has also passed laws designed to draw diaspora Kazakhs back into the republic. Interestingly, the number of such "returned" Kazakhs is less than the number of new Russian settlers; according to official Kazakhstani government statistics, the latter were more than 100,000 in 1992, while the former were about 70,000,[6] and actually may have been only about half that.[7] Moreover, Kazakh in-migration dropped off in 1993 and 1994, as did the enthusiasm of Kazakhstan's government to assume the burdens of resettling these people. It should also be noted that according to the most recent constitution, those who cannot speak Kazakh will still be able to serve in official national posts until the year 2010. Nevertheless, local Russians have grown increasingly more nervous since independence, as they confront a society becoming increasingly dominated by Kazakhs and the Kazakh language. This presumably is a major reason why a poll conducted in the northern city of Petropavlovsk in early 1994 found that 14 percent of the population planned to emigrate to Russia "soon."[8]

However much Kazakhs may mutter that Russians who are unhappy should leave the republic, neither the Kazakhstani nor the Russian government wants them to leave. Kazakhstan can ill afford to have many of the Russians depart, since Soviet employment practices left Russians and other Europeans almost in exclusive control of the important industrial and extraction sectors of Kazakhstan's economy. For its part, the Russian government does not welcome the prospect of having to reabsorb a large expatriate population. In this regard, as in many other issues, the policies of Kazakhstan's rulers are strongly affected by Russia's preferences.

COMING TO TERMS WITH RUSSIA

From the beginning, Kazakhstan's survival as an independent nation required Russia's tolerance of Kazakh statehood. Good sense as well as good politics meant that Kazakhstan had to, and must still, maintain close ties with Russia. Close relations with Russia were an explicit, fundamental part of Kazakhstan's strategic doctrine.[9] What this means in practice, however, has proven difficult for Kazakhstan's government to work out.

Nazarbaev has never seemed as awed by Yeltsin as he was by Gorbachev. The Kazakh leader's administrative experience was at least equal to that of the Russian president when their states became independent. Still, during the first year or so of independence, Nazarbaev continued to display a reflexive tendency to obey Moscow, generally following its lead in formulating his country's policies. Over time, though, state policies in both Russia and Kazakhstan have made these former Soviet republics appear to be ever more distinct, independent states.

President Nazarbaev's goal in relations with Russia has been to achieve the eventual integration of the two states without the subordination of Kazakhstan's sovereignty. An important breaking point for Nazarbaev was the 1993 negotiations over the continuation of the ruble zone. Believing that economic and political stability were thoroughly intertwined, Nazarbaev continued to argue until November 1993 that preserving economic linkages with Russia would stimulate a rapid economic recovery for his republic. Such a belief led Nazarbaev to submit to a series of humiliating conditions imposed by Kazakhstan's giant northern neighbor during the lengthy, and ultimately futile, negotiations over the creation of a new "ruble zone."

Over the months during which these negotiations were conducted, there was considerable debate in Kazakhstan about the wisdom of joining the new ruble zone. Critics of the proposal, who included many of the former *nomenklatura* members as well as the Kazakh nationalist lobby, argued that by keeping the ruble as its currency, Kazakhstan was ceding its sovereignty to Russia. Such criticism was not without merit, since one condition for membership in the ruble zone was to surrender virtually total control of the republic's economy to Russia, which was to be the sole emission source for new currency.[10]

As a number of critics inside and outside of Kazakhstan pointed out, signing over the right to make policies on questions of budget, tax, customs, and investment policy would have effectively turned Kazakhstan into a Russian confederate, bound together even tighter by Nazarbaev's recent agreement to accept Russia's claim that Kazakhstan owed 547.6 billion rubles for goods and services supplied since independence.[11]

Even Kazakhstan's submission to Russia's demands was not enough to give the republic access to the new rubles issued in 1993, even though Moscow planned to remove all the earlier emissions from circulation within the Russian Federation. Still part of the ruble zone but denied the new currency issue, Kazakhstan was forced to continue circulating Soviet-era rubles. Since it was the only large Soviet successor state still accepting the old currency, Kazakhstan all but drowned in the flood of bills shipped in from other former Soviet republics where they were now worthless.[12] As a result of the economic policies Russia imposed, inflation in Kazakhstan shot up to more than 2,500 percent for 1993.

In spite of all these problems, Nazarbaev expended considerable political capital in October 1993 to secure parliamentary ratification of an agreement designed to keep Kazakhstan within the ruble zone. As is usually the case with affairs of state, Kazakhstan's press was required to play up the ruble-zone accord as an event of great significance for both the republic's future economic development and its diplomatic posture. Less than a month later, however, Russian leaders changed the terms of ruble-zone participation, now requiring that all zone members surrender their gold reserves to Moscow. Nazarbaev was furious. He thought Yeltsin had sought to embarrass him deliberately by initially demanding submission and then imposing terms that the leader of any state with sizable gold reserves would find impossible to accept. Thus, a month after persuading Kazakhstan's legislature to submit to Russian-imposed terms for remaining in the ruble zone, Nazarbaev announced the introduction of a national currency, the tenge. The International Monetary Fund, which had been a strong supporter of the ruble zone's continuation, now supported Kazakhstan's action and provided a stabilization fund for the new Kazakhstani currency.

However, the introduction of the tenge merely complicated further Kazakhstan's economic relations with Russia. Although more stable than some of the other Soviet successor states' new currencies, the tenge lost half its value in the first six months of its issue, and by May 1995 it was worth less than 10 percent of its original value. Should the current stabilization effort falter, Kazakhstan will reach the point where its money costs more to print than to exchange.

Although by now no one expects the tenge to be completely abandoned, President Nazarbaev continues to hope that the economic union agreement of October 1993, or some of his own subsequent proposals, may eventually lead to the introduction of a CIS-wide currency, if only for use in intra-bloc trade. For now, this seems unlikely, since the coordination of economic policies of member states and the creation of a tariff-free trading bloc (the original conditions of the union) have yet to be implemented; eighteen months after the economic accord was signed, the Interstate Economic Council remains only a skeletal organization. Largely because of this, Kazakhstan chose in January 1995 to enter a customs union with Russia and Belarus. The goal of the union is to remove trade barriers between the member-states, to stabilize their exchange rates, and to develop a clearinghouse for intra-union debt. Unlike the largely stillborn economic union, the newer tripartite union does show signs of developing into a functional body, which may expand to include Kyrgyzstan, Uzbekistan, and possibly even Ukraine.

Certainly, from Kazakhstan's point of view it is imperative that some mechanism be found to stimulate the region's interstate trade, since Kazakhstan's departure from the ruble zone has been a further blow to its already beleaguered industries, which are concentrated in the northern part of the republic and are largely staffed by Russians. Kazakhstan is the most industrialized of the Central Asian states. In 1989, it had a work force of 6.5 million; of these, 21.4 percent were engaged in manufacturing, including the staffs of some fifty defense-related plants that together accounted for some 11 percent of the USSR's total military production. All of these plants require component parts from outside Kazakhstan, principally from Russia and some from Ukraine.

At the time of the Soviet Union's demise, Kazakhstan was sending about 70 percent of its industrial production and mined products to Russia, as well as just over one-fourth of its agricultural production. In addition, Russia received all of Kazakhstan's exports of iron ore, chrome, and aluminum; it also received 95 percent of the republic's lead and phosphate fertilizer; 80 percent each of its exported oil, rolled metal, radio cables, aircraft wires, train bearings, tractors, and bulldozers; 75 percent of its cotton and silk; and 65 percent of its zinc and tin. In return, Russia was Kazakhstan's primary supplier of refined oil, gasoline, and diesel fuel (at the world price equivalent of $1.2 billion in 1991), paper ($466 million in 1991), cars ($240 million in 1991), trucks ($576 million in 1991), as well as soda ash, sodium hydroxide, rolled ferrous metal, steel pipes, tires, timber, and most agricultural equipment.

However, very little of this trade was on a cash basis, and almost none of it was for hard currency. In the Soviet past, such transactions were paid for in paper transfers of rubles, but that system broke down completely in 1993. Even within the republic, interbank transfers of funds required an average of forty-five days, and all such transfers had virtually ceased between republics, with differential ruble valuations from republic to republic further complicating the few such transfers that did occur. Throughout much of 1992 the system was maintained either through barter or by informal loans between enterprises, which shipped goods to one another more or less on good faith. By 1993, all parties in these transactions began demanding real payment, usually in hard currency.

Trade with Russia was severely disrupted even before Kazakhstan's departure from the ruble zone. In 1992, delivery was refused on some 1.2 billion rubles worth of goods previously ordered by the Russian defense industry. As a result, by the end of 1992, Kazakhstan's military-industrial output dropped by more than 40 percent, which was far larger than the overall drop in the republic's economic performance. Accordingly, 80 percent of the 150 large enterprises in Kazakhstan's military-industrial sector effectively went bankrupt by the end of 1992. The Petropavlovsk Factory for Heavy-Machine Building, for example, had fired 20 percent of its work force by the end of 1992, while in 1993, between 30 and 70 percent of all skilled workers in all of the factory's major departments were put on leave, forcing them to live on meager stipends of rapidly depreciating rubles. Similarly, in mid-1993, the Zenit factory in Uralsk made personnel cuts of 10 percent, and the Omega factory cut its work force by 14 percent; the Alateu industrial plant in Almaty slashed its employment rolls by almost half.[13]

Because of Kazakhstan's trade deficit, Russian goods ordered by Kazakhs went unpurchased; but Russia has a greater choice of potential customers than does Kazakhstan. Thus in 1992, Russia crippled many of Kazakhstan's already flagging industries when it purchased slightly more than one-third of the orders it placed with Kazakh firms before the USSR's dissolution. While the scale of trade is much smaller, essentially the same picture obtains in Kazakhstan's trade with other CIS members, all of which have bilateral trade agreements with Kazakhstan. Similar agreements have also been reached with Russia's autonomous republics, such as Bashkortostan and Tatarstan.

Kazakhstan's economic managers know that, in the long run, most of the disrupted trade ties will be restored; yet, year by year, the stagnation of Kazakhstan's economy has grown more profound. In 1992, Kazakhstan's gross domestic product (GDP) dropped by 13 percent; in 1993, it dropped by 12 percent in relative terms; and in 1994, it registered a similar decline of 25 percent.[14] Thus, the value of the republic's GDP in 1994 was roughly 60 percent of the 1991 figure.

Some industrial plants have sought foreign investment to prop up their operations, usually on the individual initiative of their factory heads. Yet it is obvious that only massive investment from Russia would be sufficient to reverse this situation on a national scale; prior to 1995, neither the Russian government nor Russian private investors were willing to leap into the Kazakhstani market. A few of Kazakhstan's factories did come under a 1993 Kazakhstan-Russia agreement on cooperation in military production and conversion, and so continue to receive goods from Russian suppliers.

In the short term, though, the consequences of these trade disruptions could serve to increase Kazakhstan's political instability and exacerbate interethnic tensions within the country. It is largely because of the government's concerns over popular impatience with the country's economic plight that Kazakhstan entered into a series of new economic agreements with the Russian government in early 1995, which call for the joint development of some strategic resources (including energy) and defense-related industries.

In general, by May 1994 the government of Kazakhstan recognized that it was reaching a "make or break" point in its economic policymaking. Although the government introduced a new eighteen-month crisis-management plan at that point, Kazakhstan's basic economic dilemma remains unresolved: how to encourage privatization of the economy while holding the line on both unemployment and inflation. While economic recovery is not possible in the absence of a successful privatization program, the republic will not survive if it is faced with massive unemployment, discontent, and mass flight of its predominantly Slavic work force.

In 1993, when Kazakhstan was still a part of the ruble zone, the government sacrificed the goals of privatization in favor of using state orders to keep virtually all state-owned plants running on at least part-time schedules. Until June 1993, most factories had enough rubles on hand at least to meet their payrolls. However, currency shortages became commonplace in the last half of 1993, forcing some enterprises to pay their employees in scrip, while others simply issued IOUs or paid in kind.

These practices became more difficult to sustain, as they ran directly counter to both the government's privatization goals and the stabilization of the new currency. Thus in 1994, state orders were sharply cut back, and plant closings or "enforced vacations" became commonplace, especially in northern Kazakhstan. At the same time, energy shortages and the lack of spare parts were squeezing Kazakhstan's metallurgy industry, compounding the dissatisfaction of workers, many of whom had gone without pay since the end of 1993. These conditions have led to escalating calls for local and national strikes, especially among miners, as well as increasing numbers of public demonstrations. Simultaneously, the government faced staggering inflation rates, which reached a high of 45.9 percent in June 1994 before they began to drop. The monthly inflation rate for December 1994 was 10.0 percent; in March 1995, it had dropped to 5.1 percent. Also in March 1995, industrial production had begun to rise, up 5.6 percent from the previous month.

Kazakhstan's new prime minister, Akezhan Kazhegeldin, has been quick to take credit for the republic's improving economic situation. Kazhegeldin came to power in October 1994, when, after having been caught in an economic vise for nearly a year, the by then highly unpopular government of Prime Minister Sergei Tereshchenko was forced to resign.

It would probably be a mistake to overestimate the success of Kazakhstan's economic policy. Kazakhstan's population seems to be growing weary of economic hardship. Without question, they are becoming poorer; in an April 1995 public opinion poll, 75 percent of those surveyed stated that they had purchased no consumer goods at all in the previous year.[15]

Kazakhstan's economic difficulties have stimulated the growth of political opposition within the republic, including Kazakh nationalists (and their organizations Azat and Alash), disaffected members of the old *nomenklatura*, and politically estranged new entrepreneurs.

Most disturbing from the point of view of the Nazarbaev regime is that disrupted trade ties with Russia have also further stimulated the rise of a variety of Russian nationalist groups, including the legally sanctioned LAD and Slava groups, as well as the unsanctioned Edinstvo movement. All three enjoy wide support in northern Kazakhstan, where they have mobilized large public demonstrations in favor of dual citizenship and more funding for Russian schools, and against Kazakh remaining the sole official language. Kazakhstan's departure from the ruble zone gave these groups a new set of grievances, for Kazakhstan's Russian community can no longer easily trade with Siberia, nor can its members easily receive alimony, pensions, or other regular cash remittances from Russia. Moreover, Kazakhstan's trade deficit with Russia has substantially reduced access to the Russian books, magazines, newspapers, and television they previously depended on for information and entertainment.

How much political clout can Kazakhstan's Russians wield? Underrepresented in Kazakhstan's Soviet-era parliament, they were further disadvantaged after the March 1994 elections, which resulted in a new parliament composed of about 60 percent Kazakh and just under 30 percent Russian members. This left Russian nationalists few places to vent their anger other than in the streets, which they did regularly. Just one year after the elections for the new parliament, it was disbanded. No new elections were scheduled until December, according to a constitutional referendum that was ratified in August 1995. The referendum also mandated the creation of a smaller and far weaker bicameral legislature, which is likely to leave political opposition groups of all stripes even more underrepresented following the new elections. The new constitution does, however, increase the status of the Russian language in the republic, but not to the level of the Kazakh language. Similarly, the 1995 constitution is more assertive in defending the country's multiethnic character, and downplays somewhat the idea that Kazakhstan is the homeland of the Kazakhs.

Kazakhstan's Russians do have a powerful political patron just across the border, however. During 1993, Russia's policies went from quiet endorsement of its conationals' goals to a strong defense of the rights of all Russians living in what Moscow has come to call "the near abroad." Yet Russia's patronage has been erratic. While it was rumored to have made veiled references to the discontent in this large Russian community during its economic discussions with Kazakhstan, Moscow made no formal protest when the 1994 national elections, conducted along less than democratic lines, caused the Russian nationalist groups to do very poorly.

Similarly, the Russian government declined to comment when that same parliament was dissolved because of a March 1995 Constitutional Court decision that confirmed the legislature's election to be undemocratic. Russia has also muted its protests about Kazakhstan's treatment of the Cossacks. The Kazakhs view these descendants of Kazakhstan's early Slavic settlers to be a subgroup of the Russians, while the Cossacks claim to be a distinct ethnic group. Their demand to be treated as a national minority has cost Kazakhstan's Cossacks legal registration in the republic, while Russia has granted its own Cossacks the right of self-rule, including the right to form armed militias; this obviously does little to assuage Kazakh fears about Cossacks in their country.

The Russian media catalog the difficulties facing Kazakhstan's Russians on an almost daily basis. Such coverage is a constant reminder that the plight of these "foreign Russians" is certain to shape election platforms in Russia for years to come. For the moment, however, the public posturing of Russia's politicians has little direct impact on political developments in Kazakhstan.

President Nazarbaev remains wary of antagonizing Russia; indeed, he would be reckless and irresponsible to behave otherwise. However, as he becomes more accustomed to Kazakhstan's independence, and as Russia itself continues to flounder, he has become more willing to stand up to his

Russian colleagues. Thus, by 1994 he was willing to demonstrate public pique with Russian officials who presumed to permit themselves *lèse majesté*. When Russian Foreign Minister Andrei Kozyrev came to Almaty to lecture Nazarbaev on the treatment of local Russians, Kazakhstan's president simply refused to meet him, though softening the snub by claiming to be ill. At about the same time, Nazarbaev also stopped responding automatically to Yeltsin's summonses. In February 1994, Nazarbaev flew to the United States via Moscow, but then returned home directly, without providing the traditional debriefing for the Russian leader.

Nevertheless, Nazarbaev remains committed to finding some sort of institutional solution that would satisfy both Kazakhstan's concern to protect its sovereignty and Russia's need to control the geopolitical expanse of the former USSR. It was immediately after his U.S. trip, in March 1994, that Nazarbaev proposed the formation of a Euro-Asian Union. The prospects for this union are fading as time goes on. As they do, President Nazarbaev and the Kazhegeldin government are striving to develop closer bilateral relations with Russia. As already noted, this is especially true in the area of economics, where Kazakhstan has made a number of concessions, including the appointment of ethnic Russians to head economic ministries or to serve as deputy prime ministers in charge of economic relations.

IN DEFENSE OF THE REPUBLIC

In no area are ties between Kazakhstan and Russia better than in the realm of defense. From the outset, the key element of Kazakhstan's military doctrine has been close cooperation with Russia; in January 1995, such cooperation was expanded to include plans for the unification of their armed forces. Given its proximity to Russia's industrial heartland in Siberia and its long border with China, Kazakhstan's strategic facilities were crucial to the defense of the Soviet Union. After the USSR's collapse, Kazakhstan inherited the most sophisticated military equipment in the Central Asian region, while the thousand-plus nuclear warheads "orphaned" on the republic's territory transformed Kazakhstan overnight into a member of the "nuclear club." These weapons made Kazakhstan an object of international attention, although they remained under the control of Russian officers loyal to Moscow.

In spring 1995, more than three years after independence, the last of these weapons had been dismantled or shipped back to Russia, but not before President Nazarbaev managed to use them for the benefit of his country and himself. Many of the same Kazakh nationalists who before independence had demanded that the republic become "nuclear free" were demanding after independence that Kazakhstan now keep the nuclear weapons as defense against potential Russian and Chinese aggression. Yet Kazakhstan signed both START and the Nuclear Non-Proliferation Treaty, and agreed to the gradual dismantling of its portion of the Soviet nuclear arsenal. In return, the United States agreed to give Kazakhstan an initial $85 million in assistance to compensate for the value of the fissile material in the warheads and for defense industry conversion. Nazarbaev was also able to use the negotiation process to increase his international stature, since he managed to appear both statesmanlike and in full control of his government and his country, in sharp contrast to President Kravchuk in Ukraine, who appeared unable to harness the sharply divided public opinion on this very same question in his country. As a result, discussions over the future of Kazakhstan's nuclear arsenal left the Kazakhs, the United States, and the Russians all satisfied.

Such has not been the case with Kazakhstan's Baikonur Spaceport, the launch site for all of the Soviet Union's manned space missions as well as for Soviet geostationary satellites. This same facility also houses testing facilities for liquid-fueled ballistic missiles. Initially, both Kazakhstan and Russia claimed ownership of the spaceport site. It is on Kazakh soil, but Moscow built it, and both countries wanted to be able to lease the site for lucrative commercial space launches, yet neither side wants to pay for the facility's maintenance.

In early 1992, Baikonur's work force included more than eight thousand highly trained Russians and only thirty-eight Kazakhs, fewer than half of the latter in any technical or managerial capacity. It was obvious at independence that the Kazakhstani government could not nationalize the facility, so it sought instead to strike an agreement with Russia for comanagement. Initially, Russia pledged to pay 94 percent of the maintenance costs, but with the facility's ownership still unresolved, neither side was eager to meet these obligations. The very severe climate at the site makes it imperative that basic maintenance work not be delayed for long; otherwise deterioration quickly becomes irreversible, as suggested by reports of a serious fire at the facility in March 1994.[16]

Twenty-two thousand Russians are reported to have already left the nearby city of Leninsk, which was basically a support town for Baikonur.

By the summer of 1993, there were more than twenty-five hundred job vacancies among the original eight thousand positions at Baikonur. Russian soldiers (most of whom were said to be in convict labor brigades) rioted there in June 1993, killing several Kazakhs. Kazakh militiamen near the area are even more disgruntled, in part because a Kazakh colonel earns a lower salary than does a Russian enlisted man. By early 1994, mass disorder and indifference had overtaken the Kazakh construction and maintenance teams at Baikonur, and it was clear that by the end of 1994, Baikonur and Leninsk would effectively cease to exist if no one intervened.

Neither side wanted this to occur, so both agreed to let the United States act as a third party to assist in the search for a mutually agreeable solution; in the end, though, the two sides worked out an agreement without U.S. participation. Russia's strong preference was to receive a long-term lease, ninety-nine years if possible, and to have only Russian troops guard the facility. The Kazakhs demanded the right to guard the facility themselves and were also demanding, at least through the first part of 1994, as much as $3 billion annually in rent. At the end of March 1994, however, the two sides reached agreement on a twenty-year lease, with Russia's initial one-time payment of more than $1 billion and an annual rent of $115 million, with an option to extend. In fact, Kazakhstan will receive no cash for a while at least, since the initial payment is to be deducted from the republic's indebtedness to Russia; in addition, the Russian military and civilian personnel serving at the site are subject to the laws of Russia, not Kazakhstan.

Even before this agreement, Kazakh public opinion was being prepared for the Russians to receive control of Baikonur, but given the low monthly rent, the settlement of this dispute is unlikely to be viewed as a Nazarbaev victory. President Nazarbaev faces an even greater public opinion problem concerning Russia's continued leasing of several nuclear weapons testing facilities in Kazakhstan, including the Semipalatinsk Nuclear Weapons Proving Grounds, which was the more important of the two major testing facilities in the former Soviet Union.[17] About 40 percent of the total territory used as weapons testing sites by the USSR Ministry of Defense was in Kazakhstan,[18] helping to explain why Kazakhstan's first and only truly mass "informal" organization was the Nevada–Semipalatinsk Antinuclear Movement, formed in 1989 to stop nuclear testing in the republic and to seek redress for the devastating human and ecological damage caused by the Soviet testing program. Nazarbaev will face extraordinary opposition in the event of any resumption of nuclear testing in the republic.

Despite the relative mildness of the eventual terms reached, the long and difficult negotiations over Baikonur have managed to convince the Russians that the Kazakhs are not simply going to "roll over" when their more powerful neighbor tells them to. Kazakhstan's security doctrine presumes a special relationship with Russia, and the republic remains committed to trying to put into effect the bilateral defense agreements for creating a common defense posture, common training, and interlocking command structures. The military relationship between the two countries is so close that Kazakhstan initially considered it redundant to be party to the NATO-style defense treaty drawn up between Russia and five former Soviet republics (Armenia, Kyrgyzstan, Tajikistan, Uzbekistan, and Turkmenistan); indeed, the provisions of that treaty are far less inclusive than the existing security pacts between Kazakhstan and Russia.

At the same time, though, Nazarbaev and the Kazakhstani leadership are unwilling to cede full control of their security arrangements to Russia. In September 1992, representatives from Kazakhstan met with their counterparts from Turkmenistan, Pakistan, Uzbekistan, Turkey, Kyrgyzstan, and Iran to discuss creation of a new Asian collective security agreement; although this idea is currently dormant, it is not dead. More significantly, Kazakhstan has been unenthusiastic about meeting CIS obligations imposed by Russia. Kazakhstani "peacemakers" took nearly nine months to arrive in Tajikistan, and the government has been no quicker about sending replacement troops to take up its assigned responsibilities on the Tajik border.

Kazakhstan's commitment to the creation of national armed forces has increased over time. Immediately after independence, republic officials spoke of creating only a national guard of fewer than twenty thousand; other security needs would be met by CIS combined forces. Continued erosion of the CIS, culminating in Russia's dissolution of a combined command in spring 1993, led Kazakhstan to amend its earlier preference for only a token military capability; efforts are now underway to create a full-fledged military, with army, air force, and even navy (for service in the Caspian) branches under the direction of Minister of Defense Colonel-General Sagadat Nurgamambetov (a Kazakh).

The obstacles to creating such a military are so formidable that in January 1995 Kazakhstan's government edged back from this goal by signing a new security agreement with Russia that called for the gradual unification of their armies through joint training, an integrated command structure, and rights of access to each other's bases and other military facilities.

Some of the causes of Kazakhstan's partial retreat on the military question simply had to do with matériel; in late 1992, Kazakhstan had to appeal to the Yeltsin government for help in outfitting its troops, since Russian factories were no longer filling orders for equipment, including uniforms.

However, the single largest problem Kazakhstan faces in its attempt to create an independent military centers on the national composition of its armed forces. Questions of national loyalty, which run through virtually every issue in Kazakhstan's daily life, will obviously be magnified in the country's military service. An all-Kazakh military is politically unthinkable (and probably numerically impossible in terms of adequate force levels), but the reliability of ethnic Russian troops serving under a Kazakh-dominated command, or their willingness to accept Kazakh command, would be a constant, nagging question. At present, the officer corps of the country's military is overwhelmingly Slavic, while the ranks are mixed. Kazakhstan retains the two-year compulsory service requirement of the Soviet era, but has experienced great difficulty in getting draftees to respond to call-ups; in 1992, as many as one-third of those receiving notice refused to show up for induction. Desertion also remains a serious problem. The predominantly Russian Pavlodar district, for example, reported that there had been 1,112 desertions between January and September 1992. Other districts were said to have had even more deserters. The situation is said to have grown even worse in 1993, but by then Kazakhstan's government stopped publishing precise statistics.

A more profound problem concerns the departure of officers, most of whom are Slavic. In 1992, 1,517 officers left the republic permanently, and another 836 were said to be preparing to do so, while only 621 officers arrived in the republic for their tours of duty. The result of this outflow has been serious understaffing of the command structure, which makes it unclear whether Kazakhstan can muster an effective military in the immediate future. By early 1994, these problems were so severe that senior Russian military officials began to argue that the border duties assigned to Kazakhstan's border troops (former KGB border guards) should be turned over to either the Russians or a joint Kazakhstani-Russian force. In spring 1994, Kazakhstan's military chose the latter option.

PRIVATIZATION AND FOREIGN ECONOMIC RELATIONS

Loyalty to the state (or, rather, its absence) posed further challenges to Kazakhstan's economic reform efforts. The country's economic resources are considerable, and the government has offered the most attractive conditions for foreign investment in the region. Kazakhstan was also the first of the CIS states to pass laws on foreign investment, including laws permitting the repatriation of profits.

Kazakhstan has three distinct economic zones. Most of its manufacturing, refining, and metallurgy are concentrated in the country's north and northeast. Significant products include heavy machinery, ball bearings, and some refined petroleum products. The north-central and southern parts of Kazakhstan are primarily agricultural; grain production is especially important in the north-central region, while cotton and rice predominate in the south. Kazakhstan is also a major producer of meat and milk. The western littoral region along the Aral Sea was until recently an important fishing area, but the dual environmental tragedies of desiccation and sharply increased salination have rendered this once-thriving body of water lifeless. Of greater significance in the country's western region, especially for the future, is oil production.

Then there is the country's vast mineral wealth. Soviet geologists used to boast that Kazakhstan was capable of exporting the entire Periodic Table of the Elements. At independence, Kazakhstan produced five tons of gold annually, with proven reserves of at least 100 tons. In 1989, Kazakhstan mined 23.8 million tons of iron ore and 151,900 tons of manganese. That year, the country produced 6.8 million tons of steel and 5 million tons of ferrous metals. In addition to its well-publicized, vast fossil-fuel reserves, the country also possesses substantial deposits of uranium, chrome, titanium, nickel, wolfram, molybdenum, bauxite, and copper. In addition, Kazakhstan is known to be rich in deposits of heavy oil, which is not now commercially viable but could become valuable in the future.[19]

The combination of vast natural resources and a relatively secure legal and political environment has made Kazakhstan the most attractive of the Soviet successor states for foreign investment; by early 1994, some 39.6 percent of all investment in these countries had been pledged to Kazakhstan, compared to Russia's 31 percent. There is no question that Kazakhstan has the natural resource wealth to provide not only an adequate standard of living for its entire population, but also substantial wealth for those who are able to gain exclusive or nearly exclusive control over these sectors of the economy. This makes the challenge of determining ownership and economic control of the country's natural resources particularly controversial. As was the case with other Soviet successor states, Kazakhstan was tightly integrated into the Soviet centrally planned economy directed from Moscow. Even at the time of the 1991 coup—when the USSR's central planning system was rapidly collapsing—43 percent of the republic's industrial capacity was under Moscow's direct control, 48 percent was under joint republic and central control, and only 8 percent was entirely under republic control. As a result, there has been considerable jockeying since independence for effective control of enterprises, accompanied by plummeting productivity and pervasive corruption, as commodities are sold, materials exported, and concessions granted to people who lack clear legal rights to the goods or services they are receiving.

Further complicating the question of ownership is an ambitious three-stage privatization program that was approved by Kazakhstan's government in 1992.[20] The first stage addressed privatization of housing and small enterprises. The second stage, which is currently underway, calls for the privatization of virtually everything short of the country's mineral wealth and the industrial "mega-enterprises" (including most of its military-related industry), which are slated for the third stage of privatization, beginning in 1995. Until then, these enterprises are to be run as self-managing "stock companies" in which the government is the largest stockholder.

However, as President Nazarbaev and others have noted, Kazakhstan's potential wealth is largely based on the classic Third World formula of supplying relatively cheap raw materials to other countries, which process them and sell the finished products back to the raw material suppliers at a handsome profit. The three-stage economic program to which Nazarbaev has committed his nation specifies that Kazakhstan will make the move toward establishing its own processing and manufacturing base for its raw materials within fifteen years, but multiple impediments stand in the way of realizing this goal. To date, Kazakhstan is still fully preoccupied with getting projects underway for the international development of its natural resources but, for a variety of reasons, has taken few steps toward working on an integrated plan for the development of a secondary processing industry for the country.

First, Kazakhstan's economy must be privatized. Like everything else in this young nation, ethnicity affects attitudes toward the privatization of the economy, which falls almost exclusively under the authority of the government. The country's overwhelmingly Russian industrial managerial class strongly favors informal *nomenklatura* privatization, in which management exercises the privileges of ownership over enterprises that are still technically owned by the state. This runs counter to the government's policy, since it would leave these managers, who generally have little loyalty to Almaty, in de facto control of Kazakhstan's industrial economy.

The existing privatization program, which issues vouchers to all citizens to use in auctions of enterprises, is said to allow Kazakhs (again, mostly members of the old *nomenklatura* or their children) to buy up most of the state assets on the auction block using capital accumulated from both privileged access to the country's raw materials (mostly copper and aluminum) and control of informal trade networks. Throughout Central Asia, large amounts of strategic resources have disappeared in such a way—sold by enterprise heads aided by members of the *nomenklatura* with international business contacts. Much of Kazakhstan's store of aluminum and copper disappeared this way, as did Kyrgyzstan's metal "futures" (from Russia and Kazakhstan). These metals were generally purchased at deflated ruble prices (based on old contracts) and were either sold at world prices for hard currency or were bartered for resalable goods. Virtually all of Kazakhstan's new and increasingly more powerful holding companies are said to have started out this way, and charges of favoritism have sullied the reputations of a number of the country's leading politicians, including several former members of the Tereshchenko government.[21] Such entrepreneurial machinations mean that Kazakhstan's new rich will be primarily those who were politically well connected in the Soviet era. As with so much else in Kazakhstan's public life, the country's new business and financial elites will be disproportionately Kazakh, leaving a substantially smaller share of Russians involved in Kazakhstan's capitalist transition.

Such practices also disrupt government plans for investment and reduce potential sources of capital. There is no shortage of potential foreign partners to help develop Kazakhstan's oil reserves; and however much graft and corruption may skim off, oil revenue should give the country ample income by 1996 or 1997 to meet the state's social service and defense needs—providing, of course, the issue of a pipeline for Tengiz oil is successfully resolved. Both Kazakhstan's development officials and the international financial community expected that such

projects would become profitable by 1995, but neither group had anticipated the transportation problems that have plagued the development
of this sector.

The Tengiz oil fields of Mangyshlak, which Chevron is attempting to
codevelop, alone are believed to contain reserves of twenty-five billion
barrels, or about twice as much as the Alaskan North Slope. The French
firm Elf-Acquitaine has leased nineteen thousand square kilometers of
land in the Emba region, where there are known to be large quantities of
sulfur-free oil as well as natural gas. Other oil deposits, with paraffin,
asphalt, or tar (all of which make refining more difficult), have been
found in the Novy Uzen area and in Buzachi; an international consortium has been formed for the exploration and exploitation of Kazakhstan's offshore Caspian oil reserves.

Initially developed under the Soviet regime, the Tengiz oil project has
come under regular and repeated criticism by Moscow as part of the
Russian government's growing effort to exert a strong proprietary interest over the development of the fossil-fuel industry throughout the entire
CIS. Initially, the Russian government sought to do this through fairly
subtle means, attacking projects such as Tengiz as violating a USSR-
Iranian agreement on the Caspian Sea that requires development projects affecting this international body of water to be approved by all relevant littoral states (which have grown to five from the original two
signatory countries). Exactly what kind of collective regime would control the Caspian Sea has come under formal examination only in 1995,
when international discussions began over whether the Caspian is an
inland sea or a lake. Yet, it is clear that Russia views itself at the center
of any and all Caspian Sea initiatives.

Next, Russia tried to assert its control over the fossil-fuel industry
through the development of new CIS-based institutions. The hope here
was that CIS member-states could develop their own mini-OPEC. The
basis of this initiative was the Surgut Agreement, signed on March 2,
1993 by prime ministers or other senior officials of eleven former Soviet
republics (only Estonia, Latvia, Kyrgyzstan, and Turkmenistan were
absent), as well as by delegates from Tatarstan, Bashkortostan, and
Komi.[22] This document called for Russia, Kazakhstan, Uzbekistan, and
Turkmenistan to band together in an OPEC-style cartel to control CIS oil
production and pricing through the creation of multinational corpora-
tions, which would eventually dominate the region's oil and gas industry. The architect of the agreement was Russian Prime Minister Viktor

Chernomyrdin, who had spent most of his career prior to becoming prime minister in the Soviet and Russian petroleum industry.

By October 1993, however, as it became clear that the idea of a CIS oil cartel was stillborn, Russia began to press the various CIS oil-producing states for a share of their oil and gas fields.[23] After coming to power in war-ravaged Azerbaijan, President Heidar Aliev (who, like Chernomyrdin, had long-standing, high-level ties to the old Soviet oil and natural gas industries) agreed to give Lukoil, Russia's politically powerful and partially privatized oil giant, a 10 percent share in an oil field that British Petroleum was developing, as well as a vague promise to give Lukoil shares in future projects. Yet even this was not enough to keep the Russian government from objecting to Azerbaijan's consortium agreement that was signed in September 1994; Russia now claimed that the development of all Caspian Sea oil resources required some form of common consent among all relevant littoral states.

Azerbaijan's concession on this point left Kazakhstan in a more difficult position regarding its own claims to exclusive control of its Caspian offshore oil reserves, while the economic troubles in Kazakhstan made it even more difficult to resist Russia's pressure for partial ownership of Kazakhstan's vast gas reserves. While the problems of developing the Tengiz oil field still remain partly unresolved, in autumn 1994 Kazakhstan decided to formally recognize Russia's claim to residual equity interest in the Karachaganak gas fields, requiring British Gas and Agip to renegotiate their participation in the development of these fields. In the new accord, announced in March 1995, the shares of Russia's Gazprom (which Chernomyrdin used to head and in which, it is now rumored, he is a major shareholder) will come from foreign contractors.[24] In addition, the gas from Karachaganak will be sold to Gazprom refineries in Russia at discounted rates.

In spring 1995, the government also entered into an agreement with Russia's Lukoil for joint development of the Kumkol oil field in Kyzyl Orda; in return, Lukoil will supply oil to Kazakh refineries in Shymkent and Pavlodar.

Chevron's development of the Tengiz oil field remains plagued with problems, many of which have been the result of Russian pressure. After years of negotiating and renegotiating, a "final" agreement was signed between Chevron and Kazakhstan's government in October 1993 which divided the profits in an approximately 80–20 percent split, with Chevron carrying much of the financing burden as well.

The process of reaching this agreement is said to have been highly frustrating, especially for Chevron, which had to negotiate with a government that not only changed the conditions of the deal as it learned more about the world oil market, but also rotated the occupants of ministerial-level positions with great regularity and unpredictability. Since the Tengiz-Chevron project was Kazakhstan's first large international deal, many Kazakh officials tried to get a piece of the proceeds, including the *hakim* (governor) of Atyrau, who at one point completely stalled the negotiations by demanding a large extracontractual grant for his region, on the grounds that the sands of Tengiz belonged to Atyrau, whose local citizens should receive a direct benefit from the project.

In fact, according to Kazakhstan's constitution, the hakim had a point. Kazakhstan's basic law, adopted in early 1993, provides for a unitary state, with a strong president (who appoints the cabinet) and a weak legislature. The country's nineteen oblasts all have their own legislatures, but their discretionary authority is mostly limited to the execution of state laws and regulations. Nonetheless, the oblasts do preserve some rights to the development of local (nonstrategic) resources, and though all foreign economic investments require Almaty's approval, local authorities do get to keep nearly 40 percent of the profits from projects that they originate. The oblasts' share of strategic projects initiated by the state cannot exceed 20 percent, and their share can be negotiated away by the government in order to make the deal more acceptable to a foreign partner.

While the 1993 constitution also gave the power of taxation to the Kenges (Kazakhstan's parliament) and the president, cash-poor and power-hungry local administrators frequently exceed their authority. The case of the Atyrau hakim is far from unique; oblast officials frequently press prospective investors for cash grants for the locality, or simply slap unsanctioned "export taxes" on goods leaving their territory.

In the end, though, the most paralyzing problem surrounding the Tengiz project is transport. Getting the oil to the surface is one thing, but getting it to market is quite another. A joint Russian-Kazakhstani-Omani company (registered in Bermuda) was given the exclusive right to construct a pipeline, but the first major problem the company faced was deciding on an appropriate route. A number of routes were initially proposed, each replete with potential problems. One would have taken the pipeline through Russia, including Chechnya, into Azerbaijan, with spurs through Georgia (and Abkhazia) to the Black Sea; through Iran to Rotas,

Turkey; and through Iran to Kharg. Another proposed route went through Turkmenistan and across the Caspian to Baku, from where the spurs would divide as in the first route. The third proposal would cross Turkmenistan and Iran, and end at the Kharg terminal. The route that has been chosen parallels an existing pipeline across southern Russia to ports at Novorossisk, on the Black Sea. Turkey, which is proposing construction of a joint Turkish-Azerbaijani pipeline to the Mediterranean, has expressed doubts whether the Bosporus passage out of the Black Sea is capable of handling the tanker traffic such an arrangement would entail.

The lingering problem of financing the pipeline's construction was still unresolved by mid-1995, preventing the start of the pipeline's construction. The members of the pipeline consortium believe financing is Chevron's duty, while Chevron considers this to be the responsibility of the pipeline's owners.[25] In May 1994, Chevron announced that it was cutting back operations in Kazakhstan, since the country's limited access to existing facilities allowed shipment of only one-fifth of the oil that was being produced at Tengiz. In March 1995, Chevron announced a second set of production cutbacks, effectively halving the projected oil sales from Tengiz for that year, and dealing a crippling economic blow to Kazakhstan.

KAZAKHSTAN AND THE INTERNATIONAL COMMUNITY

The difficulties in arranging for a new oil pipeline are a reflection not only of Kazakhstan's remote and landlocked geographical location, but also of Moscow's deliberate efforts to bind the country to Russia as a supplier of raw materials. Even the construction of the new Tengiz pipeline will not resolve all the problems of shipping Kazakhstan's oil and gas; additional pipelines will have to be constructed if the development of Kazakhstan's fossil-fuel resources is to be maximized. Of course, this reopens the question of routes, and since Kazakhstan has no direct access to the open seas, all freight—raw materials and finished products—will have to cross at least one other state before reaching ports. This places Kazakhstan at a considerable disadvantage in attempting to establish an independent economic policy.

Kazakhstan is under pressure from both Turkey and Iran to build pipelines that would favor their respective economic development plans, and one proposed Turkish pipeline would benefit both. The United States, meanwhile, is pressuring Kazakhstan to avoid taking any action that might possibly give economic or political advantage to Iran. The United States has many more ways of pressuring Kazakhstan than does either Iran or Turkey, both in terms of promises of direct assistance and through its influence in the international financial community.

The challenge of transporting goods to and from Kazakhstan provides a real incentive for Almaty to maintain especially good relations with Iran and China. Chinese efforts have recently resulted in the completion of a continuous rail line from Beijing through Almaty to Istanbul, thus providing a new major transit route, especially for Chinese goods. Since Kazakhstan's independence, China has become its largest non-CIS trading partner, accounting for 20 percent of Kazakhstan's exports and 42 percent of its imports in 1992; Chinese figures indicate that half of Kazakhstan's consumer imports come from China.[26] Although trade between the two states is said to have dropped by about one-third in 1994, the figures probably understate the actual volume of trade, since China has actively pursued barter deals, exchanging cheap consumer goods for raw materials; China has an insatiable market for metals.

China is also interested in providing Kazakhstan with eventual highway access to the Indian Ocean by helping construct spurs to the Karakoram Highway. While this project cannot become a reality until war in Afghanistan ends, Kazakhstan is anxious to maintain the possibility of Chinese assistance.

At the same time, though, Kazakhstan also fears China, both for historical reasons—the ancient struggles between Turkic nomads and Chinese emperors—and the more recent Sino-Soviet rift. Kazakhstan has watched nervously as Chinese traders move into the country, with as many as a half-million of them rumored to have taken up permanent residence. Thus Kazakhstan has attempted to keep a certain distance from its other giant neighbor, directing a large portion of its metals sales through Baltic ports, especially Estonia, rather than have them go to China. Kazakhstan's nervousness over China has also made it more willing to follow Russia's lead in establishing uniform trade policies. Nazarbaev marred an otherwise cordial visit to Beijing in October 1993 by informing his hosts that cash sales would have to replace China's preference for barter deals as part of Kazakhstan's general trade agreements with Russia. Moreover, Russia has kept pressure on Kazakhstan to limit barter trade even after the introduction of the tenge.

By contrast, Kazakhstan's relations with Iran began fairly coolly but have grown warmer, especially since mid-1993. President Rafsanjani visited Kazakhstan in October 1993, and a number of high-level delegations have visited since. Nazarbaev has also named a very senior Kazakh official, O. Dzholdosbekov, as ambassador to Iran.

Nazarbaev's insistence upon a secular identity for his country makes it obvious that Kazakhstan's interest in Iran is financial, not religious. Kazakhstan's geographical isolation gives the government very little choice in maintaining good relations with Iran if it wishes to have any realistic alternative transport routes outside of those going through Russia. However, it should not necessarily be inferred that Kazakhstan's relations with Iran run counter to Russia's interests; Russia too has maintained good relations with Iran. Rather, Kazakhstan's continued exploration of mutual interests with Iran may be as much to maintain a balance to the United States and other Western states as it is to provide an alternative to dependence on Russia.

Nazarbaev: Kazakhstan's "Unconventional Weapon"

For all the precariousness and weakness of Kazakhstan's present situation, the state enjoys one real advantage—its president, Nursultan Nazarbaev. Surprisingly, for a man whose entire career was spent in the republic, and who did not make his first unsupervised trips abroad until 1990, Nazarbaev has proven to have a real understanding of Kazakhstan's position in the realities of international politics. His careful forging of a special relationship with Russia, inevitable for two states that share so much common border and so much common history, has managed to keep a potentially explosive situation well within manageable limits. Nazarbaev's ability to balance the competing demands for Western-style democracy and Asia's model of state-directed economic development have permitted Kazakhstan to survive and even to begin to develop a post-Soviet identity far better than anyone might have expected.

It is certain that President Nazarbaev ranks Kazakhstan's good relations with the United States high among his foreign policy successes. However, it seems equally plain that he values these relations more for what they do to enhance his and his country's international stature and prestige than because of any innate desire to please the United States. Nazarbaev has been eager to accept offers of technical assistance from the United States, and has courted U.S. foreign investment assiduously. However, he will not compromise what he views as his country's sovereign rights to please the United States or any other non-CIS state.

The history of attempts by Western and Kazakh activists to widen the scope of democracy in Kazakhstan indicates that Nazarbaev's consideration for Western concerns is primarily pragmatic. The conduct of the 1994 parliamentary elections, the subsequent dissolution of the parliament, and Nazarbaev's decision to extend his term as president through a national referendum rather than through elections all demonstrate that Nazarbaev has a real ambivalence about democratic institutions in Kazakhstan, and also suggest that he is not overly concerned about U.S. reactions.

Nazarbaev intended the parliament that was elected in 1994 to be a malleable institution, easily subject to his manipulation. Election procedures were originally designed to make it very difficult for independent candidates to run, and also made it difficult for political groups to register, especially if they had a distinctly ethnic or local appeal. Local election officials were extremely strict about qualifying signatures on candidate petitions, so that candidates out of official favor found it all but impossible to get on the ballot; most of the few who did were defeated, and found election arbitration boards generally ill disposed to find in their favor. In addition, candidates were sharply limited in how much broadcast time they could receive and how many column-inches of newsprint could be devoted to their campaigns. There were also limitations placed on foreign election observers. The Western observers who did come noted enough voting irregularities to cause them to doubt the election's fairness. Even so, within months of the election, it was already clear that the new parliament was following its own agenda.

One year after the election, following a ruling by the republic's Constitutional Court, President Nazarbaev ordered that the legislature be disbanded, and announced plans for a future parliament to be elected in late 1995 whose electoral districts would be drawn up more democratically. Moreover, in light of the potential for instability in what was now a more fragile political environment, President Nazarbaev accepted "counsel" that his term be extended through popular referendum, which was held on April 29, 1995.

Nevertheless, President Nazarbaev and his government have managed to execute these "compromises" of democratic principles without greatly affecting the country's international prestige. This is probably due to Nazarbaev's shrewd assessment that international attention is primarily focused on Kazakhstan's economic potential, which is sufficiently large to allow him a certain pragmatic latitude in regard to other international concerns. Nazarbaev's independence in managing his country's internal political affairs has been matched by a flexibility in foreign policy as well, seeking to maintain good relations with virtually any state that shows an interest in this former Soviet republic. This strategy has created certain points of potential tension. Kazakhstan is accepting firm guidance from Western-dominated international financial institutions in its course of economic reform, while simultaneously trying to create a profitable intermeshing of the Kazakhstani and Russian economies.

For now, President Nazarbaev's approach to domestic and foreign policymaking seems to be working. Despite the country's unusual demographic mix, this new nation has been among the most stable of the Soviet successor states, and this stability in turn has encouraged foreign investment in Kazakhstan's rich and diverse economy. Kazakhstan's stability could prove fragile, though. Should Russia change its present policy and provide more active support to Russian nationalists in northern Kazakhstan, the country's political situation could spin out of control very quickly, as Nazarbaev has warned.[27]

Another possible change with less foreseeable consequences would be Nazarbaev's passing from Kazakhstan's political scene. Since the president is only fifty-four and in good health, a change in the country's political leadership does not seem likely in the immediate future. Nevertheless, for all the likelihood that Nazarbaev will remain Kazakhstan's president for the foreseeable future, the consequences of his passing must be considered. One of the reasons Nazarbaev has been able to retain the cooperation, if not the enthusiasm, of Kazakhstan's millions of Russians is that he achieved considerable political legitimacy during the Soviet era, when he was widely rumored to be a possible choice for posts as high as president of the Union, had Gorbachev succeeded in securing accession to the new Union Treaty.[28] There is no leader anywhere on Kazakhstan's political horizon who has managed to retain Nazarbaev's Soviet-era "internationalist" aura, suggesting that whoever eventually replaces him will inevitably be perceived as either pro-Russian or pro-Kazakh. Unless economic prosperity is by that time high enough—and equal enough—so that the country's major ethnic groups perceive that they have an interest in preserving the status quo, then the outlook for long-term political stability in Kazakhstan is dim.

5

KYRGYZSTAN

Surviving on Foreign Support

Kyrgyzstan's foreign policy is governed by two basic considerations. The first is that the country is too small and too poor to become economically viable without considerable outside assistance. The second is that it lies in a nervous and volatile corner of the globe, vulnerable to a number of unpleasant possibilities. Both of these considerations force Kyrgyzstan to play slightly different roles simultaneously in its relations with the outside world, which has sometimes made the country's foreign policy seem confused or contradictory.

President Askar Akaev and his advisers seem to be aware of the hurdles they face in trying to attract world attention—and aid—to their country; theirs is a small, relatively resource-poor, remote nation, which is more likely to be seeking help from the world community than contributing to it. As a result, President Akaev has consistently stressed Kyrgyzstan's intellectual and political potential, hoping to interest the world community in supporting the experiment in democracy that his "Silk Revolution" began. In return, world businesses would gain a stable and profitable beachhead deep in the vast potential market of Central Asia. Thus Akaev has spoken frequently of making his nation into an "Asian Switzerland" through a combination of international finance and a particular emphasis on "clean" industry, primarily electronic, in reaction to the heavily polluting Soviet-era industries in the republic.

President Akaev's strategy was designed to make potential investors emotionally committed to assisting this struggling democracy situated in a part of the world dominated by despots. The strategy's assumption that investors would flock to Kyrgyzstan to put their money into projects with both greater-than-ordinary risk and slower-than-ordinary return on investment may have been informed by wishful thinking from the beginning. It is hard to know whether President Akaev really thought this strategy would pay off or whether he simply believed he had little choice other than to try it, since by any traditional financial standard Kyrgyzstan presents a far-from-attractive investment prospect.

The nation has three main sources of potential income: gold, the mining of which will take years to develop fully; water, the sale of which is still largely regulated through regional agreements; and tourism, which is hard to promote despite the country's extraordinary beauty, since Kyrgyzstan is far away from virtually everywhere (in addition to which it has had little regular international air service for almost four years) and has no facilities to make it worth a tourist's while to visit, if one actually does manage to get there.

Certainly Akaev's personal charm and the diplomatic skill of Kyrgyzstan's ambassadors to the United States and elsewhere produced very little in the way of concrete results for the long-term development of Kyrgyzstan's economy in the first eighteen months of its independence. Some foreign aid came into the former Soviet republic, most of which the government chose to spend on food and medical supplies, and a few large, long-term projects were negotiated for the development of Kyrgyzstan's gold resources; the latter will take several years of development before they begin to yield any substantial revenue for the country.

A handful of other joint ventures were negotiated in the country's first eighteen months of freedom, but none of these seemed likely to produce substantial employment for Kyrgyzstan's small but increasingly idle working class, as shortages of fuel, customers, and spare parts (usually made in Russia) inexorably brought factories to a standstill. In addition to a decline in production of more than one-third, the country was also plagued with spiraling inflation, caused in large part by Kyrgyzstan's continued membership in the Russian-dominated ruble zone.

So bleak were Kyrgyzstan's immediate economic prospects that President Akaev is reported to have told the Japanese prime minister in May 1993 that if massive assistance did not come within six months, the country's economic downturn may prove to be irreversible.[1] Though the bleakness of Akaev's forecast was obviously intended in part to encourage the Japanese to implement the $60 million aid package they had promised more quickly than the proposed nine-month time period, Akaev's ingenuousness was confirmed by Kyrgyzstan's decision at about the same time to permit itself to become an experiment for the international monetary and aid community by agreeing to become the first Central Asian republic to have its own currency, the som, introduced in May 1993.

THE DIFFICULTIES OF DINING ON DEMOCRACY

Akaev's reputation and personality are the main reasons Western development economists and financiers became genuinely eager to assist this small nation of just over four million people. At the same time, the size of Kyrgyzstan's economy made such a financial experiment a manageable project. Thus Kyrgyzstan was offered an immediate fund of $40 million to stabilize the new currency, with a second $40 million deliverable only four months later. In addition, to help tide it through the first year of major economic reform, the republic was promised a further $350 million in international credits, with yet another $100 million earmarked by the Asian Bank for undertaking acceptable economic development projects.

The introduction of the som did not provide Kyrgyzstan with an easy solution to its economic difficulties, although the som itself has been Central Asia's most stable currency. Aided by strong international support, the som retained some 40 percent of its value over a two-year period. In addition, Kyrgyzstan's inflation rate is the lowest in the region, from a high of about 1,400 percent during 1992–93 to about 180 percent one year later. The government target for 1995 is 130–140 percent.

Support for the new currency was initially very weak, at least in part because the decision to introduce the som directly contradicted a resolution the country's legislature had adopted just one month before. The Kyrgyz were reluctant to convert their rubles into soms; initially only about 10 percent of the estimated ruble holdings in the republic were exchanged. This ruble "hangover" was a grave concern for the region's leaders, since rubles that could no longer be spent in Kyrgyzstan would almost surely find their way to neighboring Soviet successor states, further exacerbating inflation and shortages there. Kazakhstan and Uzbekistan hurriedly sealed their borders, instituting new monetary regulations and requiring that future payments for exported goods and services be made in dollars. In the early months of the som's existence, Kyrgyzstan was also forced to spend more than one-third of its stabilization fund to settle debts with fellow CIS members (primarily Uzbekistan and Kazakhstan, but Russia as well), while it also discovered that future imports of both energy and foodstuffs were going to be more costly than it had budgeted for. These additional expenses seem to have surprised the economists at the International Monetary Fund as well.

Six months after the som was introduced, Uzbekistan and Kazakhstan also left the ruble zone. This helped ease Kyrgyzstan's terms of trade with neighboring states, as will a proposed customs union among Uzbekistan, Kazakhstan, and Kyrgyzstan. However, this union is still far from functional, and as the most stable currency in the region, Kyrgyzstan's som is now draining away through the fluid commercial barriers of Osh oblast in the country's southern reaches and into Uzbekistan in particular. Kyrgyzstan's difficult trade relationships were also eased somewhat in late 1993, when both Russia and Kazakhstan rescheduled Kyrgyzstan's debt to them—Russia extending terms for seven years, and Kazakhstan for five. Uzbekistan agreed to wait only until 1995,[2] at which point it began to demand payment in dollars for natural gas and other crucial Kyrgyzstani imports.

Although just one of a myriad of other problems, the difficulties in introducing the som seem to have not only disenchanted President Akaev with the international community but fully convinced him of the severity of the country's economic crisis. Nor is Akaev the only Kyrgyz to have grown sadly wiser in the fourth year of independence. The republic's press, the least censored in the region despite increasing governmental pressure, still speaks of hope for a brighter future to come, but coverage of Kyrgyzstan's present is uniformly grim. Accounts of crime, demonstrations, and deteriorating public services are common, conveying a sense of general malaise about a widespread decline in the Kyrgyz standard of living and a breakdown of public order in general.

Nowhere is the sense of dissatisfaction stronger than among Kyrgyzstan's Russian population. The last Soviet census, in 1989, put their number at some 920,000; but if Russian accounts are to be believed, the country's Russian community has now dwindled to about 200,000.[3] Even the Kyrgyz nationalist opposition now agrees with the government that the future of the republic is in danger if this "brain drain" of the technically skilled Russian population is not arrested soon. The current dissatisfaction among members of the Russian and broader European communities in Kyrgyzstan is even greater than it is among the Kyrgyz themselves, for the non-Kyrgyz believe they have been stranded in the country by fate. Many of Kyrgyzstan's Russians came to the former Soviet republic for what they saw as a calmer and potentially fuller life. The introduction of the som and currency restrictions in both Kyrgyzstan and Russia make it impossible now for Russians to sell and move back, except at a considerable loss. To remain in Kyrgyzstan, though, is to accept a standard of living that is substantially lower than that of their conationals in Russia. Kyrgyzstani government officials privately estimated that at the height of the Russian out-migration, the real per capita income in the republic was $800 per year, compared to more than $3,400 in Russia.[4]

The Askar Akaev who looks out on the world in mid-1995 is far more skittish than the one who traveled to America bursting with optimism just two years before. His citizens are weary and growing hungrier—and more apprehensive: Russians are moving out, while Chinese appear to be moving in. Furthermore, just over the border in Tajikistan, Russian and CIS troops have battled for more than two years to restore civil order, without significant success. Meanwhile, growers, runners, and dealers from Afghanistan, Tajikistan, Uzbekistan, and Kyrgyzstan are turning the southern part of the republic into a major bazaar for opium and heroin.

At the same time, the outside world that the newborn Kyrgyzstani government rushed so enthusiastically to embrace appears to have few remedies for any of the country's problems, or at least none that would take effect with the speed the Kyrgyz desire. As a result, Akaev seems to be looking closer to home for answers and assistance, turning to Kyrgyzstan's oldest friend and its most dependable patron—Moscow. Yet it is uncertain whether Moscow's assistance will be sufficient to deal with Kyrgyzstan's problems, just as it is uncertain whether this apparent shift from the "far abroad" to the "near abroad" as a source of aid and assistance will encourage or threaten Kyrgyzstan's new and very immature democracy.

HOW DEMOCRATIC IS KYRGYZSTAN?

There are now signs that some of President Akaev's earlier enthusiasm for using democratic principles exclusively to govern Kyrgyzstan is beginning to wane. In August 1994, some of Akaev's advisers, apparently with his personal approval, effectively banned two "opposition" newspapers (one, *Svobodnye gory*, was actually the official newspaper of Kyrgyzstan's parliament) by refusing to let them be published by the country's sole publishing house, which is state-owned. Two weeks later, pro-Akaev parliamentarians walked out of the legislature, protesting the unprofessional behavior of their colleagues, whom they considered "relics" of the communist past. President Akaev then called for a new bicameral parliament to be elected in December 1994, after an October 1994 referendum to modify the republic's new post-independence constitution.

Elections to the new parliament did not begin until February 9, 1995, and only sixteen candidates in 105 constituencies managed to get clear mandates on the first round of balloting. When a second round of voting also proved indecisive, elections dragged on into May 1995, with widespread accusations of fraud, illegal voting, and government manipulation.

When the parliament finally convened, on March 28, 1995, there were still fifteen seats empty; no deputies had been chosen in two important oblasts (Naryn and Talas), fueling angry protests that regional interests were not being properly represented when the two houses elected their speakers. In mid-April 1995, there were still fourteen seats that remained vacant.

There are also real fears about how competent a legislative body the new parliament will be. Only six of the deputies have previous parliamentary experience, and a number of prominent political figures—including Medetkan Sherimkulov, speaker of the 1990–1994 parliament—failed to win what had been assumed were "safe" seats. Even more serious are concerns about the inchoate mandate of the new legislative system. The constitutional modifications voted on in the October 1994 referendum did not specify what the duties and limitations of the two houses would be. Not surprisingly, since its recent opening, the two houses of Kyrgyzstan's parliament have been preoccupied by procedural wranglings designed to delineate the respective rights of the legislative, executive, and judicial branches. In fact, so little substantive business has been conducted that several deputies have already threatened the "self-dissolution" of this parliament, and political observers speak of the parliament as already mired in deep crisis.

How President Akaev will respond to the efforts of the new and more docile legislature in its function as even a quasi-independent branch of government is difficult to predict. He was certainly quick to disband its predecessor, which had posed only an indirect threat to the Akaev program.

Akaev's squabbles with the country's parliamentary system have arguably damaged his image abroad, because for most of Kyrgyzstan's independent existence he has tried to present himself as one who is above politics. In spite of his international fame as a proponent of democratic reform, Akaev has been at best indifferent to Kyrgyzstan's democrats. The democratic opposition is informally headed by Topchubek Turgunaliev, the leader of Erkin Kyrgyzstan (Free Kyrgyzstan), the country's largest democratic opposition party and a major constituent of the loose affiliation of parties collectively known as the DDK, or Democratic Movement of Kyrgyzstan; in 1995, Turgunaliev was indicted on charges that he had diverted state funds for his own personal use.

Like democrats in other Soviet successor states, the democrats of Kyrgyzstan are disorganized and contentious. They are also virtually all Kyrgyz, who—conveniently for Akaev's supporters—are easy to portray outside of the republic as "Kyrgyz nationalists," and, since the August 1994 parliamentary revolt, even as "Kyrgyz fascists." Most foreign observers seem content to accept President Akaev's judgment about his opponents. The democrats' generally poor international image is in part a product of their own political inexperience, but it is also no less a product of the republic's politicians whose patronage they have accepted.

The democrats' first political hero was the former vice president Feliks Kulov (now *akim*, or head, of Chu oblast). Kulov, an ethnic Kyrgyz who speaks only Russian, was head of the republic's Ministry of Internal Affairs (MVD) at the time of the abortive August 1991 coup, when he vigorously defended Akaev and the republic's "Silk Revolution." Kulov's past as part of the Soviet security apparatus has made foreign audiences skeptical both of his motives and of the democrats who support him, despite the fact that Kulov has a reputation among most Kyrgyz as the "People's General." The relationship between Akaev and Kulov, while cordial, was always an uneasy one, since Kulov's popularity rivaled the president's. The problem of institutionalized political competition within the executive branch was resolved, first by Kulov's resignation in December 1993, and then by implementation of the country's constitution (adopted May 1993), which eliminated the post of vice president entirely.

After Kulov's resignation, the democrats' primary patron became Medetkan Sherimkulov, then speaker of the parliament and one of the republic's most skilled politicians. Though Sherimkulov repeatedly pledged his loyalty to Akaev, the floor of the parliament was the site for the greatest political assaults against the president, including the forced resignation of the government headed by Tursunbek Chyngyshev, and a move to withdraw from international agreements that had been concluded to develop the country's gold mining industry. (Government plans to develop the Kumtor gold field in conjunction with the Canadian firm Cameco narrowly averted being scrapped.) At the time of its dissolution in August 1994, the legislature was preparing to issue a report on the personal finances of several of President Akaev's key associates, some of whom have enriched themselves with the proceeds of privatization and other government policies. While Akaev must have breathed a sigh of relief over Sherimkulov's defeat in his reelection bid, most observers of Kyrgyzstan's political scene believe that the vote's outcome was never really in doubt, since the contest is widely described as having been rigged.

In addition to Akaev, another beneficiary of Sherimkulov's unexpected political demise is Kyrgyzstan's Communist Party. Though briefly banned following the August 1991 coup attempt, the Communist Party hurriedly embarked on the reform path, gradually becoming the best organized opposition in the republic. Three first secretaries of Kyrgyzstan's Soviet-era Communist Party (B. Amanbaev, A. Masaliev, and T. Usubaliev), representing thirty years of leadership in the Soviet republic (1961–1991), commanded substantial support as deputies in the 1990–1994 legislature, even though this was the same body that was responsible for Masaliev's ouster and Akaev's election. T. Usubaliev, the Brezhnev-era party boss, was elected to parliament in a by-election after spending nearly six years under virtual house arrest. Tarred by charges of corruption in the Gorbachev years, Usubaliev has made his political comeback by routing out political corruption among the Akaev people.[5] In fact, it was Usubaliev, acting as a member of a parliamentary commission investigating the government's sale of gold development rights, who was responsible for driving Akaev's prime minister, Tursunbek Chyngyshev, from office in December 1993. Usubaliev was prominent among the deputies who revealed that Chyngyshev was part of a joint-venture, private-stock company that was profiting from the sale of the republic's gold reserves, thus forcing Chyngyshev and his entire government to submit their resignations.

B. Amanbaev, who was head of the Communist Party when it was outlawed at the time of the August 1991 coup attempt, was ranked as the country's most popular party leader in a March 1994 government newspaper poll. Although he had placed himself in the anti-Akaev camp by supporting the 1991 putsch, Amanbaev was made deputy prime minister in charge of agriculture in the "unity" government that replaced Chyngyshev's cabinet in December 1993, and was reconfirmed to the same post by the succeeding government.

Even Masaliev, who was widely unpopular in the republic because of his handling of the 1990 Osh riots, has managed to remain politically active. Like Usubaliev, he played a part in exposing the government's gold concessions scandal, and was reelected as a member of the new parliament. As head of Kyrgyzstan's Communist Party, Masaliev will oppose Askar Akaev in the December 1995 presidential elections.

While not a party member, Prime Minister Apas Jumagulov is often associated with the Communists because of his long service in the same post during Usubaliev's rule. Appointed prime minister again after Chyngyshev's resignation in December 1993, Jumagulov has twice been reconfirmed as prime minister, first to head the caretaker government from September 1994 to March 1995, and then as head of the new government in March 1995. Polls consistently name Jumagulov as one of the most popular figures in the republic.

The Kyrgyz Communist Party, despite its name and the nationality of its leaders, is internationalist in ideology. As such, this remake of the old Soviet republic party organization still enjoys a lot of residual support among Kyrgyzstan's increasingly dissatisfied Russians, who are dramatically underrepresented in the political life of the republic. Unlike neighboring Kazakhstan, no party exists in Kyrgyzstan to represent the interests of its Russian community, even though Kyrgyzstan's current language laws will effectively bar the Russian minority from full participation in public life after 1996. As is the case in Kazakhstan and Uzbekistan, Kyrgyzstan's Russians are constitutionally barred from having dual citizenship. President Akaev has spoken vaguely of amending this, but introduction of dual citizenship would hurt his popularity across almost every segment of Kyrgyzstan's national electorate.

For all the political fragmentation within the republic since independence, President Akaev has always been and still remains Kyrgyzstan's most popular politician. Even so, the resignation of the Chyngyshev government was a considerable blow to the president, who publicly defended his prime minister just before the parliament forced Chyngyshev to resign. The whole issue of the republic's gold reserves has proven to be particularly sensitive, since it is generally recognized that gold is the only natural resource of value in Kyrgyzstan. When questions began to be raised about the authority under which mining concessions had been granted, the terms that had been agreed to, and, most importantly, where the money paid by foreign concessionaires was going, the interest surrounding the brewing scandal shifted to the country's Kenesh, or parliament. The answers provided by the Akaev government were inconclusive, leaving a climate of public opinion that, at its most charitable, viewed the government as incompetent, and at its most outraged, condemned the country's leadership as a cesspool of corruption.

The battering that Akaev received during the December 1993 legislative session was arguably one of the reasons he called for the January 1994 national referendum. The referendum was a vote of confidence over whether Akaev should finish out his term as president and also whether he should put the new constitution into effect immediately, rather than wait for it to go into effect after parliamentary elections, as the enabling legislation had stipulated when the constitution was accepted in 1993. With these sorts of issues at stake, Akaev, or those close to him, decided to take no chances with public opinion. In January 1994, the government staged a tightly controlled election campaign, resulting in a Soviet-style "yes" vote of nearly 99 percent, with a voter turnout of more than 95 percent. With the independent press silenced, the government-controlled press was little more than a tribune for presidential self-congratulation both before and after the event.

Because of the way it was conducted, though, the referendum actually weakened Akaev, since the government's obvious vote management demonstrated to an increasingly impoverished and dissatisfied electorate that Akaev requires the same sort of adulation as his communist-era predecessors. In the long run, the referendum is likely to do more for Akaev's chief opponents than it is for Akaev, as they hammer away at public confidence in the probity and fairness of the government, the process of privatization, and the government's overall conduct of policy. Moreover, political opponents will be able to attack Akaev for spending 4.5 million soms ($450,000) to buy his public vote of confidence, using public funds from a treasury that then had a deficit of 1.7 billion soms.[6]

Apparently, President Akaev and his political entourage considered their manipulation of the January 1994 referendum a practice run. The Akaev team was able to stage-manage the October 1994 referendum and 1995 legislative elections even more skillfully. They have also shown real skill in stage-managing the 1995 presidential elections as well, making it hard for potential candidates to get on the ballot, and using government auspices to advance the cause of Akaev's reelection.

For all the election fraud tainting its political environment, Kyrgyzstan remains the most outwardly democratic of the Central Asian states, for unlike Presidents Niyazov, Karimov, and Nazarbaev, Askar Akaev is at least willing to face Kyrgyzstan's electorate. While President Akaev will continue to receive kudos from his Western champions of democracy, it is much less clear whether he will be able to keep his country's economy afloat.

A FAILING ECONOMY

Kyrgyzstan is one of the smallest of the newly independent states, having an area of only 198.5 thousand square kilometers. It is bordered on the east by China, on the north and west by Kazakhstan, and on the south and west by Uzbekistan and Tajikistan. Although more than 40 percent of the population lives in rural areas, only 17 percent of the agricultural land in the republic is arable.

In 1990, when it was still a Soviet republic, Kyrgyzstan played a small but integrated role in the economy of the USSR. The republic contributed 1 percent or less of the USSR's total output of preserved vegetables, animal fats, plant oils, and meat; it supplied 3 percent of the Union's beet sugar. It also produced wine products and tobacco. It supplied 1–2 percent of the USSR's total output of cotton cloth, silk cloth, linen, and woolen cloth, and 1–2 percent of the Union's ready-made clothing and shoes. Soviet Kyrgyzstan had a full complement of industry, including machine-assembly plants, steel plants, motor-assembly plants, and other light industry, which contributed another 1 percent or less to the all-Union total. The only energy resources it contributed in any volume were coal (.5 percent of the all-Union total) and hydroelectric (.8 percent). Soviet Kyrgyzstan also had a small portion of the USSR's defense industry, including radio-assembly and other electronics plants; there was also a torpedo-assembly plant on the shores of Issyk Kul.

Kyrgyzstan's greatest role in the all-Union economy was in supplying minerals, especially antimony (in which Kyrgyzstan had a virtual monopoly), mercury, lead, and zinc. There are also deposits of wolfram, weismuth, iron ore, silver, tungsten, cesium, copper, uranium, and other mineral resources. The greatest asset of Kyrgyzstan's economy, however, is gold, of which the republic was the USSR's third-largest supplier. There are approximately 170 registered gold deposits in the republic, some with very large reserves. Talas may have as much as 200 tons of gold, Makmal 60 tons, and Chatkal 150 tons. Richest of all is Kumtor, the so-called Golden Mountain, which is reputed to be the seventh-largest gold deposit in the world, with a current value of about $5.5 billion. The right to develop this deposit was given to a joint venture between the state-owned Kyrgyzaltyn (Kyrgyz Gold) and the Canadian firm Cameco on the recommendation of Seabeco's Boris Birshtein.

Kyrgyzstan was also an important supplier of narcotics, both legal and illegal. Until 1974, when the USSR closed its plantations, Kyrgyzstan supplied 16 percent of the world's legal opium, which is said to be of an unusually high quality. The Chu Valley is a source of wild hemp and Indian marijuana, which flourish without cultivation. There has been talk in Kyrgyzstan of petitioning the World Health Organization to sanction the legal cultivation of opium again, an action the Akaev government opposes. In the meantime, illegal cultivation has flourished, as has the country's role in the transport and trade of narcotics, which typically flow from Afghanistan, through Tajikistan, to Osh—one of the major staging points for distribution throughout the CIS and elsewhere.

Since 1990, the economic decline in Kyrgyzstan has been steeper than anywhere else in the former Soviet Union, save Armenia. Kyrgyzstan's GNP, which the government put at 2.5 billion soms in 1994, is almost half of the government's figures for 1991. Most of the decline is in industry, which is now functioning at only about 40 percent of its 1991 level, with most of the republic's large industrial plants either completely idle or working at greatly reduced schedules. Agricultural output has also dropped by about 28 percent since 1991. Although vegetable production has remained essentially constant, grain and meat production—staples of the Kyrgyz diet—have decreased significantly. In 1994 alone, the republic's cattle herds were, on average, about 15 percent smaller, while the decline in sheep flocks was as high as 30 percent in some regions. The country's chicken flocks are now only 2 percent of what they were in 1991.

Unemployment in Kyrgyzstan is difficult to measure, since so much of it is agricultural; even much of the industrial unemployment is hidden, as nominally employed workers are either forced into unpaid vacations, paid in kind, or simply not paid for long periods. However, emigration of Russians and other non-Kyrgyz is also said to have created a shortage of highly skilled technical workers. In early 1995, the official number of unemployed in Kyrgyzstan was put at 42,400 people, with another 107,300 on forced vacations. Other sources claim that the work force had declined by about 25 percent in 1994. The biggest dislocations came in the industrialized areas, with jumps in their 1994 unemployment rates ranging from 370 percent in Osh to 1,020 percent in Talas— and even 1,580 percent in Jalalabad.

Needless to say, both the unemployed and employed alike have witnessed a sharp decline in their standard of living. Average monthly pay in Kyrgyzstan is 507.90 soms, while the government figures the minimal family budget to be 487 soms (500 in Bishkek). Food is said to require 61 percent of the average family budget.

Government officials speak of 1995 as a "make-or-break" year for Kyrgyzstan's economy. Government capital investment has fallen precipitously since independence, by 55 percent in 1994 alone. Tax collection is falling, with uncollected taxes accounting for almost one-fourth of state revenue in 1994 (when the budget deficit was 127.3 million soms). Prime Minister Jumagulov estimates that the 1995 budget deficit could be as high as 372 million soms.

Part of Kyrgyzstan's problem is the almost total decline of the country's defense industries, which had sent 98–99 percent of their output to Russia. With independence, these orders virtually ceased, ruining not only military-related industry but almost the entire industrial sector of the country, since defense industries had provided 27 percent of national employment.

Russian predominance in Kyrgyzstan's industrial work force meant that these declines hit Kyrgyzstan's Russians especially hard, providing part of the explanation of why more than 120,000 of them chose to leave the country in 1993. This emigration disturbs Russia almost as much as it does Kyrgyzstan, prompting Russia to attempt to stimulate Kyrgyzstan's defense industry by signing an agreement for the joint development and ownership of Kyrgyzstan's defense-sector industries. However, even if successfully implemented, this agreement is unlikely to staunch the outflow of Russians, who are fleeing not only the lack of general industrial jobs in Kyrgyzstan, but its relatively lower standard of living as well. According to the Russian Bureau of Statistics, Kyrgyzstan's national income in 1994 was 59.4 percent of the CIS average, while the country's per capita consumption of goods and services was 54.0 percent of the CIS average; Russia's average for the latter index registered at 118 percent.[7]

It is likely to prove extremely difficult to restart Kyrgyzstan's industrial economy, perhaps one reason Russia has so far failed to respond to Akaev's offer of majority ownership of the republic's twenty-nine largest industrial plants, in exchange for capital to keep them running. From the outset, Kyrgyzstan has been disadvantaged by its dependence on outside sources to meet its energy needs. Kyrgyzstan consumes 1.8 million tons of oil per year, but produces only 125,000 tons annually. The rest of the country's energy profile is similarly lopsided: It produces 2.6 million tons of coal per year, but consumes 4.3 million tons; and it annually produces 55 million cubic meters of natural gas, but consumes 2.1 billion cubic meters.

Even before Kyrgyzstan's decision in May 1993 to introduce its own currency, after which supplier states began to require payment in dollars, the effect of energy costs on the state was devastating. In 1991, oil and gas imports had taken 10 percent of the total state budget, and had swollen to 50 percent the following year. At the beginning of 1993, the year's energy costs were projected to be more than 80 percent of Kyrgyzstan's entire budget, even though a large portion of its natural gas was supplied by Turkmenistan at 60 percent of world price. In 1994, the situation grew worse still, forcing Kyrgyzstan into an agreement to purchase natural gas from Uzbekistan at 80 percent of world price. While Kyrgyzstan averted a potential energy crisis, it also amassed a significant debt to its larger neighbor. Even with this agreement, supplies were irregular through the winter of 1994–95. In March 1995, Uzbekistan began to demand payment in dollars for its natural gas.

Naturally, as energy prices have risen, demand has tapered off markedly, allowing the government to boast of energy surpluses. While industrial, commercial, and individual users have been increasingly unable to afford sufficient oil, gas, or coal to meet their needs, the republic's Ministry of Trade and Natural Resources was able to report in February 1994 that Kyrgyzstan's stockpile of coal was 8.6 times greater than it had been the previous year. The reason is simple: Factories simply do not have the additional capital on hand to purchase costlier fuel. For the same reason, many homes have gone unheated for the past two or even three winters; entire municipalities and cooperatives have been affected similarly. Even Kyrgyzstan's Ministry of Internal Affairs (MVD), the country's main law enforcement body, had its power temporarily cut off in April 1995 for nonpayment of its electric bill.

The higher energy prices have raised the pressure on the government to provide energy subsidies and impose price controls, but it has had great difficulty doing so. Under Soviet rule, the Kyrgyz republic had no budget deficit in 1990. In 1991, its deficit was 903.3 million rubles. In 1992, the deficit was estimated at 2.5 billion rubles. Two years later, the deficit was estimated at 1.7 billion soms ($170 million), and the country's foreign debt was estimated at $300 million.[8] By 1995, Kyrgyzstan's indebtedness had reached $400 million, while the government's budget shortfall was projected to be 127.3 million soms. One consequence of this growing indebtedness is the rising cost of debt service; interest payments of $13 million fell due in 1994, $54.3 million in 1995, and more than $100 million for 1996.

One reason for Kyrgyzstan's rising debt is the government's continued foreign borrowing, which seems limitless given the country's strong international support. Askar Sarygulov, head of the State Investment Committee, puts foreign assistance in the range of $250–300 million annually. In March 1995, the IMF approved Kyrgyzstan's progress on reform and released a tranche of $21.3 million in loans. The World Bank has promised a three-year loan of $1.5 billion, in addition to a $550 million loan for 1994–95 to cover the budget deficit and provide additional funding for social programs. More funding will be available to support other programs, including an upgrade of the country's telecommunications system, privatization of agriculture, and support of wage subsidies and the country's social welfare funds. Kyrgyzstan has no shortage of potential lenders. The Asian Development Bank has promised $40–60 million, Turkey has offered $75 million, and the European Union is offering $500 million over three years.

There are more fundamental reasons for Kyrgyzstan's growing debt, including the decline in production and the ineffectiveness of the government itself. For example, the government collected taxes on just one-third of the goods *legally* produced or sold in the country during 1993. In January 1994, tax collection dropped even further, falling to less than 20 percent. Things improved somewhat in 1995, although the government was still failing to collect nearly one-fourth of taxes. It is expected that tax and tariff reforms introduced in mid-1995 will bring in more revenue.

This shortfall in revenue drastically undermined government plans to provide agricultural subsidies for the spring 1994 planting, exacerbating shortages of seed, fertilizer, and equipment, and failing to bring down the high cost of fuel. Kyrgyzstan's agricultural sector can ill afford another bad season like the one in 1994, but it is hard to see how 1995 will be much better. Like energy costs, bread prices were freed in 1994;

the sharp price increases for these two basic commodities coming simultaneously led to repeated demonstrations in Kyrgyzstan's capital city of Bishkek throughout the winter and spring of 1994. Kyrgyzstan's need for generous terms on its grain purchases—in essence, subsidies—is yet another reason for Akaev's decision to reestablish a dependency relationship with Russia.

Theoretically, Kyrgyzstan possesses enough mineral wealth, especially gold, to support its first difficult years of state-building. Realizing this resource wealth, however, requires relatively sophisticated skills and knowledge, both of which seem to be in extremely short supply in Kyrgyzstan. Certainly, the development of the country's gold industry during the first two years of independence could have used some more skillful management. As was discussed in chapter 1, immediately after Kyrgyzstan's independence, the Akaev government entrusted Boris Birshtein and his Seabeco company to represent the republic in the search for a suitable foreign partner to develop the Kumtor site, as well as to oversee the sale of the republic's small reserve of gold bullion. A Lithuanian-born Jew who prided himself on his close relationships with members of the Communist Party of the Soviet Union's Central Committee, Birshtein emigrated to Israel in the 1970s, then became a Canadian citizen and businessman, with a number of Swiss-based companies to his name.

At the same time Birshtein was awarded the state contract, the government turned over the country's gold-mining operations to Kyrgyzaltyn. The management of this newly created state company was given to Dastan Sarygulov, who had no previous mining experience but was a close associate of President Akaev's wife. Also at about this same time, as noted in a subsequent report by the parliamentary Gold Commission in December 1993, several of the country's prominent politicians or members of their families had joined Birshtein in forming a company known as the Kyrgyzstan Development Corporation—a fact made public only with the release of the report.

Even without such information, considerable suspicion had surrounded the Akaev administration's plans for Kyrgyzstan's gold industry from the beginning. The unfairness that characterized the way development concessions had been awarded, followed by the discovery that nearly $20 million worth of gold had been sent to Switzerland by Seabeco, where it sat for nine months producing no income, led to the formation of the Gold Commission. Yet suspicions persisted even after

Prime Minister Chyngyshev was forced to resign in December 1993, and his successor, Apas Jumagulov, has approached issues even remotely connected with the country's gold development with painstaking probity. Although the government finally approved both Cameco's development of Kumtor in May 1994 and the large Jerui field, which is being mined by Morrison-Knudsen, the various delays in the former project's planning stages have meant that construction at Kumtor was effectively postponed until summer 1995; as such, the government will be unable to gain substantial income from its largest gold field until 1998. For similar reasons, Jerui will also not begin producing until nearly the end of the decade.

As bleak as Kyrgyzstan's economic situation now appears, independence has brought new opportunities for a very small segment of society to enrich itself. In some cases, this has been the result of spontaneous privatization of state assets; in others, it results from peddling influence (as is alleged to have happened in the awarding of gold concessions); in still others, it is the result of reselling at world prices metals purchased on old Soviet contracts. This last sort of enterprise often involves the smuggling of goods into or out of China.

Although fortunes have been made, most of the shady dealings occurred within a short period; as Chyngyshev himself declared just weeks before his own ouster, almost everything of any value in Kyrgyzstan has already been stolen. There is, however, another illegal but more productive second economy in the country that has even more serious foreign policy implications. Kyrgyzstan's borders, especially in the south, have become increasingly porous. Reports continue to surface noting the country's increase in smuggling, where larger and more frequent shipments of weapons and narcotics make their way through Kyrgyzstan and Tajikistan to Afghanistan and on to Pakistan. Instability in Afghanistan, and the tremendous quantities of weapons still available there after a decade of war, make the possible consequences of this essentially open southern border very worrisome to Kyrgyzstan's security officials.

Although the weapons trade in this area is serious, since it could further destabilize the situation near the country's borders with either Tajikistan or Uzbekistan, it is the narcotics industry that, in the long run, presents the greatest challenge to the internal security—and the capacity to destabilize the entire economy—of Kyrgyzstan. M. Isakov, head of Kyrgyzstan's state narcotics police in 1993, suggested that, for the moment at least, the fight against narcotics is very lopsided: The temptations and opportunity for cultivation are so great, and the means available to fight the illegal narcotics industry are so meager. Even the assistance the republic once received from Russia has now disappeared, allowing a full 80 percent of the drugs produced in Kyrgyzstan, by Isakov's estimation, to move freely out into world markets. Bakirdin Sudanbekov, head of the Osh oblast police, reported in March 1995 that more than 300 kilograms of opium were seized in his district the previous year; he estimates this quantity to be less than 10 percent of the total moving through his region. As Sudanbekov notes, the price of opium is dropping in Osh because there is so much passing through the country.

KYRGYZSTAN AND ITS CENTRAL ASIAN NEIGHBORS

While Kazakhstan's leaders view their country's long border with Russia as a mixed blessing at best, Kyrgyzstan's rulers are disturbed by how far away Russia is from their country's borders; unlike the Kazakhs, the Kyrgyz view the Russians as their only possible protectors in the region. Of Kyrgyzstan's four neighbors, only Kazakhstan commands any sort of trust among the Kyrgyz, but is unable to provide them with much protection. The Kyrgyz fear the imperialist ambitions of both the Uzbeks and the Chinese, just as they fear the possibility that the civil war in neighboring Tajikistan could spill over into their republic.

The Tajik civil war threatens the Kyrgyz directly, since the main road to the outside world runs from Gorno-Badakhshan, a center of opposition to Tajikistan's government, through the southern part of Osh oblast, thus serving as a conduit for the infiltration of guns, rebels, and "seditious" ideas. Like all the Stalin-era borders, this one bisects both Kyrgyz and Tajik communities, turning a section of southern Kyrgyzstan into a peninsula surrounded by its neighbor's civil war, while the rest of the southern border runs for hundreds of miles through rugged, sometimes impassable, mountain terrain.

Before the outbreak of the civil war, there were some thirty thousand Tajiks who lived on the Kyrgyz side of the border, and twice as many Kyrgyz who lived on the Tajik side. Since the war's outbreak, about a third of the Kyrgyz community has fled or tried to resettle in their home republic, burdening communities that have few resources to spare for them.

Concerned about the flow of refugees, and disturbed about the general disintegration of civil authority in a neighboring state, Akaev enlisted Vice President Kulov to mount a Central Asian peacemaking force in the summer and fall of 1992 that would have entered Tajikistan to ensure order and stability during the Islamic-Democratic coalition government of Akbarsho Iskandarov. This idea was dropped when Kyrgyzstan's parliament refused President Akaev permission to dispatch troops. Shortly afterward, Akaev joined his fellow Central Asian rulers in recognizing the government of Emomali Rahmonov, which forced out Iskandarov and seized power in November 1992.

However, the Rahmonov government did little to ease Kyrgyzstan's perceived security dilemma, and may have even increased its sense of risk. Now troops from Kyrgyzstan were joining Uzbekistani and Kazakhstani forces in Tajikistan to help guard the Tajik-Afghan border. Kyrgyzstan also set up military roadblocks in Osh, the major southern city, in an effort to stem the flow of contraband goods, people, and ideas into the country. These roadblocks are said to be increasingly ineffective. By late 1993, not only were arms and armed Tajiks reportedly slipping into Kyrgyzstan on a regular basis, but there were also reports of Kyrgyzstani soldiers based in the south selling their arms to Tajik insurgents.[9]

Relations with Uzbekistan are another, if less immediate, concern. Kyrgyzstan's Osh and Jalalabad oblasts, where 55 percent of the republic's population now resides, both border on Uzbekistan. More importantly, Osh oblast is about one-third Uzbek; about a half-million Uzbeks live in crowded proximity with some 1.2 million Kyrgyz. Living conditions in Osh oblast are entirely different from those in the Chu Valley, where most of the rest of the country's population lives, and where the capital is located; the southern oblast is much more traditionally Asian and Muslim than the north. The people of the Chu Valley are closely integrated with Kazakhstan (Bishkek is four hours from Almaty by car, a short distance by Central Asian standards) and, through it, with Russia. In both location and culture, Kyrgyzstan's south finds more affinity with Uzbekistan and, by extension, with the cultural life of the south Asian countries that lie beyond.

The breakup of the USSR, followed by the introduction of both the som in Kyrgyzstan and a different, nonconvertible som in Uzbekistan six months later, have all fractured what was traditionally a single, Uzbek-dominated economy in the Fergana Valley, at the nexus of Kyrgyzstan, Tajikistan, and Uzbekistan. Plans for a fully integrated economic union of Uzbekistan, Kazakhstan, and Kyrgyzstan indicate that these fissures could be closed again, but the full effect of the economic union agreement signed in winter 1994 will not be felt before early 1997. This may be too late to reestablish stability in Kyrgyzstan's south. Already, residents of Osh are demanding greater political autonomy. In November 1993, some local legislators even went so far as to introduce a new anthem for the territory,[10] in a broad hint at separatism.

President Akaev has had particular difficulty establishing control over the two southern oblasts. Several southern politicians, the most important of whom was Sheraly Sydykov (from an old Osh family that enjoyed great prominence in the Soviet era), have established themselves as leaders of national opposition against Akaev. It was Sydykov who headed the parliamentary corruption commission in 1994; significantly, he was also elected to the new parliament, where he is in charge of both the banking and investment committee and the ethics committee.

When the akim of Osh resigned to run for the new parliament in January 1995, Akaev appointed as his replacement Janysh Rustambekov, who had been state secretary. Rustambekov, the first northerner to hold this akimate, is considered to be Akaev's surrogate (a two-story-high portrait of Akaev hangs outside the akim's office) and to have little independence of mind. His appointment was highly controversial, as it was widely interpreted as an attempt to firm up Bishkek's control over the southern regions. Rustambekov has fired a large number of local administrators and is trying to counter the growing power of Bekamat Osmonov, one of the most skilled and influential politicians in the south.

Osmonov is the leader of the Osh *kenesh* (council) and is also a deputy in the lower house of the country's new bicameral legislature. Osmonov was an early Akaev appointment as akim of neighboring Jalal-abad, but in October 1992 Akaev forced him out of that post for financial abuses. Osmonov, whom many call the "Kyrgyz Escobar," is emerging as a consistent critic of Akaev in the parliament and may well run for president if Akaev is not able to prevent an election. Osmonov's growing power is particularly worrisome to Bishkek, since Osmonov is a *kipchak*, or scion of an elite warrior clan, which to some degree supersedes nationality and gives him clan connections to powerful figures in Kazakhstan and, especially, Uzbekistan.

A ubiquitous but unanswered question throughout the country is how much of Osh's growing discontent is being orchestrated by the Karimov government in Uzbekistan. Certainly, Karimov makes no secret of his interest in Osh and its environs, presenting himself as not only concerned about Kyrgyzstan's Uzbeks but also as their proper and fitting leader. Uzbekistani television, which is easily received in

Osh, made this point patently clear during its accounts of Karimov's visit to Kyrgyzstan in summer 1993 by broadcasting scenes of the Uzbek president lecturing Akaev on proper agricultural techniques and financial management.

The fear of Uzbek intervention has been a real one in Kyrgyzstan ever since the 1990 Osh riots. Akaev's determination to portray himself as a liberal democrat only serves to increase tension, since this contrasts sharply with Karimov's Soviet-style, strongman regime, which Karimov recently converted to a virtual presidency-for-life through a popular referendum.

One aspect of Karimov's growing personality cult is the widely shared fear that Uzbekistan's president will intervene where and when he sees fit, without troubling himself about respecting national borders. While the Akaev government would not want to provoke its neighbor by allowing pollsters to ask such a question formally, a sampling of public opinion would probably support the conviction among the Kyrgyz that it was the Uzbeks who not only installed Rahmonov in Tajikistan, but also supply the firepower that keeps him in place.

What is more frightening for the Kyrgyz is that Karimov has not been shy about flexing his muscles in their country as well. The first such demonstration occurred in December 1992, when Bishkek played host to the first-ever Central Asian human rights conference. Most speakers from Uzbekistan never reached Bishkek, but the three who did, including Abdumannob Pulatov, head of the Uzbekistan Society for Human Rights and a leader of the Uzbek independence movement Birlik, were arrested in front of the conference hall by Uzbekistani KGB officers. Subsequent official investigations found that even though the arrests and deportations precisely followed the *letter* of Kyrgyzstani law, public opinion held that the country's spirit of neutrality had been violated, and that part of the reason for the arrests had been to demonstrate contempt for Kyrgyzstan's pretensions to be a haven of democracy in Central Asia.

A few months later, in March 1993, the Uzbeks held military exercises in Osh, with the approval of the local akim, but apparently without Akaev's prior knowledge or permission. The pliant akim was sacked, but the two republics signed an agreement that summer allowing for military training on each other's territory. While Kyrgyzstan held a smaller exercise in Fergana in fall 1993, the subsequent announcement that the republic was being forced by lack of money and a shortage of officers to reduce its armed forces by 50 percent[11] suggests where the preponderance of benefit lies.

Another example of Karimov's influence that Kyrgyz observers point to is the Akaev government's refusal to license publication of an Uzbek-language religious journal in Osh, whose Uzbek Islamic community has always been well integrated into the Fergana Valley as a whole. Indeed, Suleiman's Mountain, Islam's main pilgrimage site for the Fergana Valley, is situated in Osh. Although the center of Central Asia's Islamic revival is in Uzbekistan, Osh's more politically tolerant climate has the potential to turn the region into a safe haven for Islamic revivalists suffering persecution in Uzbekistan; it was this possibility that the current Kyrgyzstani government felt necessary to forestall.

Nor has Karimov been shy about flexing his economic muscle either. Within days of introducing the Kyrgyz som, the country's natural gas shipments were suddenly terminated, to be restored only after Kyrgyzstan agreed to "stabilize" the Uzbek economy by using $13 million of its IMF money to pay off its debts to Uzbekistan and buy up "Kyrgyz" rubles that Uzbek authorities claimed had crossed the border. Gas was again cut off during the winter of 1993–94, when the Kyrgyz could no longer make payments even at the "fraternal" price (80 percent of the world price) Uzbekistan agreed to offer. Even with Uzbekistan's discount, Kyrgyzstan still found it difficult to make its payments; after all, the Uzbek price was approximately 8,000 percent of the price Kyrgyzstan had paid for gas just two years before. Even to get that 20 percent discount, Akaev had to devote considerable attention to flattering Karimov, including an elaborate ceremony staged in January 1994 by the Kyrgyz quasi-governmental society Rukhniyat (Spiritual Renewal) to honor Karimov as the society's "Man of the Year for 1994."[12] Karimov was said to have been angered when Nursultan Nazarbaev received the tribute for 1993 just one month before—the month when the tribute is usually made—hence making the premature presentation of the 1994 award necessary. The society's first award, conferred in December 1992, went to President Akaev himself.

IN CHINA'S SHADOW[13]

There is growing anxiety in Bishkek about President Islam Karimov's increasingly apparent ambitions to turn Uzbekistan into Central Asia's regional hegemon. For the moment at least, the Akaev government does not feel too directly threatened because of Uzbekistan's current entanglement in Tajikistan and its economic problems. Kyrgyzstan also believes that the CIS defense "umbrella" will afford it some protection against potential aggression by a fellow member-state.

However, the ambitions of Kyrgyzstan's fourth neighbor, China, will most likely fail to be sated by lavish ceremonies and medals bestowed by fawning Kyrgyzstani leaders. Chinese designs on Kyrgyz territory are centuries old, a fact that Soviet-era history courses never allowed the Kyrgyz to forget. With some 140,000 Kyrgyz of its own, most of whom live in the border region, China has an obvious interest in the affairs of its tiny neighbor. Beijing is not nearly as concerned about the Chinese Kyrgyz as it is about the Uighurs, for whom the Chinese border province is named. Kyrgyzstan has more than 35,000 Uighurs, but the Akaev government has been extremely cautious in dealing with this population, presumably out of deference to China. Attempts to register a Uighur nationalist party in Kyrgyzstan have been refused.

For their part, the Chinese have been quite proper in their dealings with Kyrgyzstan's government, which inherited from the Soviet regime eleven disputed border points with China. Border negotiations, most of which were conducted within a CIS framework, are said to have gone smoothly, and a preliminary document acceptable to all sides was produced during summer 1994.

More importantly, China is practically the only foreign trade partner both able and willing to develop barter trade with cash-poor Kyrgyzstan. In 1994, some 25 percent of Kyrgyzstan's official trade was with China, and this figure is likely to increase. There is already a link-up from Bishkek through Turugart to the Urumqi-Pakistan highway China was scheduled to open in summer 1995, and efforts are being made to upgrade the road from Osh through Sary-Tash to meet a route the Chinese are said to be cutting through to the border at Irkeshtam. It is nineteen hundred kilometers from Bishkek to Islamabad and thirty-five hundred kilometers from Bishkek to Karachi by this road; the Osh link-up will reduce travel by about two hundred kilometers.

Some of the Kyrgyzstan-China trade has developed along the lines of large state purchases, such as Beijing's extension of credits for grain purchases or barter deals for Kyrgyzstani hydroelectric power. In January 1993, the two countries reached agreement for the joint construction of a water conservation facility along the Horgos River, which forms part of their common border.

However, much more Chinese influence comes at less noticeable levels. China has been importing such industrial commodities as rolled metal, sheet steel, mineral fertilizer, and copper. Charges have appeared in the Russian media that many of these items were actually re-exports of commodities purchased elsewhere in the CIS at fixed prices and then sold to China at substantially higher, world market prices. Such trade has flooded Kyrgyzstan with Chinese consumer goods such as food, clothing, and simple electronic products. Chinese are also making considerable purchases of Kyrgyzstani real estate, especially in Bishkek and in the border region of Naryn, which attracts Chinese investors because of its status as a free-trade zone.

So great is the official and unofficial trade between the two countries that some observers in Kyrgyzstan fear if it is allowed to go unchecked, China will thoroughly dominate the republic's economy by the late 1990s. Naturally, such a prospect makes Kyrgyz politicians very nervous, further stimulating Kyrgyz nostalgia for the days of Moscow's control; the Kyrgyz themselves are quick to characterize this choice as being a case of "better the devil you know."

TURNING BACK TO MOSCOW FOR PROTECTION

It is quite clear that Kyrgyzstan is incapable of defending itself against a Chinese military threat, or indeed against a military threat from any quarter. For all that their folklore and oral histories are rich with the names and deeds of mighty Kyrgyz warriors of the past, present-day Kyrgyzstan is the least militarized of the Central Asian states.

In the early days of independence, Kyrgyzstan spoke of doing without an army entirely, relying instead on a national guard. The plans for such a guard were drafted in September 1991, immediately after independence from the USSR was declared; those plans were never realized. Instead, on June 1, 1992, Kyrgyzstan nationalized all troops and equipment then on its soil in response to Russia's announcement that it would no longer finance CIS troops. At that time there were approximately fifteen thousand soldiers in Kyrgyzstan, but what percentage of those were native Kyrgyz or troops from other former Soviet republics has not been published. While Kyrgyzstan did not immediately require a new oath of allegiance from these soldiers, the majority of the officer corps (most of which was ethnic Russian) refused to serve in a Kyrgyzstani army and have begun trying to repatriate to Russia. Desertion rates have also been relatively high (more than six thousand soldiers as of early 1993) but have been partially offset by the return of about two thousand Kyrgyz who transferred from CIS forces elsewhere in the former USSR.

In early 1993, there were said to be roughly three thousand to four thousand soldiers remaining in the country. The chairman of the Kyrgyzstan parliament's army commission, D. Umetaliev, has described plans for a standing conscripted army of about five thousand, with reserves of two to three times that number. However, the question of who would command these troops has been very troublesome. Throughout 1993 there were reports in the Kyrgyzstani and Russian press of Russian officers leaving Kyrgyzstan's army because of low pay and poor living conditions. These officers had until mid-1994 to decide which nation they would serve, but up until the February 1994 agreements between Kyrgyzstan and Russia, Moscow was encouraging the Russian officers to leave. Under the agreements, Russian officers who serve in Kyrgyzstan's army until 1999 will not only be entitled to free housing but will also be reassigned to Russia after their tour of duty ends.[14]

Russia has demanded a price for these agreements: Kyrgyzstan has agreed to abandon any thought of military neutrality, a goal that President Akaev had endorsed for his country on several occasions. Kyrgyzstan further agreed to let Russian border troops share the task of guarding Kyrgyzstan's border with China; Russia asserted that the continuing desertions by Kyrgyzstani border troops meant that the country was unable to patrol this border satisfactorily. Akaev has periodically dropped unsubtle hints that if Russia is not interested in reassuming control of the Soviet air bases in the republic, then perhaps others—such as the United States or NATO—might be. The fact that in early 1995 Kyrgyzstan gave the last remnants of its Soviet-era air fleet to Uzbekistan in a debt-swap suggests that such offers are not taken seriously, in either Moscow or Tashkent.

The government has also felt pressed to demand economic protection from Russia as well. The harsh reality of Kyrgyzstan's economic situation means that the nation will remain an international client state, at least for the foreseeable future. Despite concerted efforts to seek international "sponsors," Akaev has received much international goodwill, but not much else. The Kyrgyzstani president grudgingly realized where his country's economic salvation would come from. Having been surrounded by members of the old Soviet intelligentsia during his seventeen years in Russia, it is not hard to understand why economic necessity made President Akaev look toward Moscow.

During Akaev's February 1994 visit to the Russian capital, the leaders of the two countries signed a host of bilateral economic agreements. Having promised Kyrgyzstan a 75-billion-ruble line of credit (presumably for use in 1994) and some $65 million in trade agreements, Russia also promised to extend to Kyrgyzstan "most-favored" conditions for the purchase of oil and other fuels. For its part, Kyrgyzstan has agreed to the creation of a "Kyrgyz-Russian" investment company, which will purchase idle defense-related factories in Kyrgyzstan in order to provide employment for the country's increasingly dissatisfied Russian population. In early 1995, Prime Ministers Jumagulov and Chernomyrdin signed a series of agreements establishing bilateral coordination of economic reform in the two states, further binding Kyrgyzstan to Russia.

Kyrgyzstan appears to have little choice but to accept Russian "friendship" on whatever terms it is offered. For its part, Russia seems to be reaching out to its "little Kyrgyz brother" (the publicity photos of an ample Yeltsin embracing a diminutive Akaev make the metaphor particularly vivid) in order to create successful precedents in Russia's emerging policy towards the "near abroad." Russia does not want a massive in-migration of Russians, some two million of whom have returned since 1992.[15] Akaev also does not want to lose his Russian population, not just to placate Russia, but because their departure has left the country with a troubling dearth of doctors, teachers, and engineers.

This has made Akaev more compliant toward Yeltsin's demands than most of his fellow Central Asian rulers. In spite of opposition by Kyrgyz nationalists and even many moderate Kyrgyz politicians, Akaev has agreed with Yeltsin that Kyrgyzstan must re-examine its constitutional provisions that make Kyrgyz the sole state language and bar dual citizenship. As Kyrgyzstan grows hungrier, such re-examinations are likely to become constitutional amendments, which can then be held up as examples to Akaev's less hungry but more apprehensive fellow Central Asian leaders. Yet in the long run, the extent of Russia's willingness to help Kyrgyzstan is not at all clear. As Moscow's rulers become more assertive in demanding their due in the "near abroad," Russia is likely to dispense with such bilateral precedents. This in turn will make Kyrgyzstan even smaller in strategic importance.

6

UZBEKISTAN

Central Asia's Instinctive Imperialist

E ver since the bloody outburst of interethnic fighting in the Fergana Valley in June 1989, when Meshket Turks became the focus of local hatred, Uzbekistan has been a very quiet state. However, both outside observers and the republic's leadership itself fear that Uzbekistan could explode again at any time.

There are certainly grounds for thinking that this *might* be true. Before independence, Uzbeks were involved in bloody interethnic fighting in neighboring Kyrgyzstan's Osh oblast in 1990, and in a brief flare-up of student rioting in Tashkent soon after independence. Since assuming control of their country, Uzbekistan's leaders have been haunted by fears that their state could turn into a second, larger Tajikistan. The prospect of bloody civil war taking place in a country five times more populous is genuinely terrifying.

The risk of war's spillover from Tajikistan is more than theoretical. Nearly 1.2 million Uzbeks live in neighboring Tajikistan, and northern Afghanistan is home to another 1.3 million Uzbeks whose lives have also been disrupted by civil war. Communal violence between Uzbeks and Tajiks, or mass migration by Uzbeks returning to Uzbekistan, are both possibilities that are quite real and dangerous. More difficult to assess, but still a distinct possibility, is the risk of the ill-defined "Islamic threat," which is often cited as the cause of unrest in Tajikistan and the reason political Islam has been suppressed in Uzbekistan.

President Islam Karimov has repeatedly argued that, as "Asians," Uzbeks and Tajiks are prone to violent outbursts, and that their tempestuous character should be controlled by the strong hand of the state. Maintaining control has been the primary goal of Uzbekistan's government since the outbreak of the civil war in neighboring Tajikistan. As such, the republic's foreign policy opportunities, including those that hold the prospect of much-needed foreign investment, have been sacrificed if they threaten to interfere with President Karimov's "iron-fist" style of rule.

At no point in its recent history could Uzbekistan be considered a nascent democracy. During the Brezhnev era, Uzbekistan's Communist Party was probably the strongest in Central Asia. Even several years of ideological battering by Moscow reformers failed to destroy the memory and legacy of Uzbekistan's party boss during the Brezhnev era, Sharaf Rashidov, who turned this cotton-producing Soviet republic into a lucrative fiefdom. Karimov's appointment as the Uzbek Communist Party's first secretary, which came just after the June 1989 riots in the Fergana Valley, marked a partial return to power of the families that had run the republic's trade networks and cotton economy in Rashidov's day and in previous years.

However, events unfolding in Moscow in 1991 transformed Karimov's rule into something far different from a simple return to power of Uzbekistan's old guard. The banning of the Communist Party after the abortive 1991 Moscow coup allowed Karimov to institutionalize his version of one-man rule by confirming his assumption of the title "president" in March 1990 through popular election in December 1991; in 1995, a tightly orchestrated referendum extended Karimov's presidency to 2001.

In establishing his power, Karimov has been both aided and hobbled by the country's need for economic reform. Control of privatization is a powerful tool for meting out rewards and punishments, but the responsibility to meet the social welfare needs of a population that is overwhelmingly young and poor can win a ruler far more enemies than friends, at least in the context of Uzbekistan's economic transition.

Moreover, Karimov already had begun to develop enemies by the time of the USSR's collapse, encountering opposition from both religious and secular critics of Communist Party rule. More importantly, Karimov may have fallen into disfavor with some of the country's leading merchant families.

CONTROLLING SECULAR CRITICS

The best known among Uzbekistan's opposition groups is Birlik (Unity), which, at its height, claimed nearly half a million members, thousands of whom could be turned out at any given time for what were essentially illegal rallies. In the 1990 parliamentary elections, when it was all but impossible to place opposition candidates on the ballot, ten candidates with connections to Birlik succeeded in winning seats, demonstrating that the movement was a significant political force. Shortly afterwards, Birlik's impact was somewhat dissipated when one of its founders, Muhammad Salih, resigned to form a second party, Erk (Will), which shared a somewhat similar platform with Birlik, although it had a stronger position on independence.

When independence came in October 1991, President Karimov seemed willing to tolerate the activities of these opposition groups, including even the Islamic Renaissance Party, which was permitted to function publicly despite being denied legal registration as a political party. By the beginning of 1992, however, the illusion of tolerance was ending. Particularly since the May 1992 disturbances in Tajikistan, Karimov has moved relentlessly to extirpate political opposition in his republic; religious activists and secular opponents alike have fallen victim to his campaign. The leaders and most prominent members of Birlik and Erk have been arrested, jailed, and then either exiled or forced to live in the country as convicted felons who have been pardoned. Birlik's two founding cochairmen were badly beaten and then denied medical treatment. Moreover, the long arm of Uzbekistani law has extended as far as Moscow, where Birlik activists have been beaten up in their apartments, presumably with cooperation from some local Moscow officials.[1]

Erk's leader, Muhammad Salih, who ran against Karimov in the December 1991 presidential elections, has fled to Turkey in order to avoid facing a political trial. His supporters, however, remain under attack; those attempting to distribute Salih's writings are subject to beatings and arrests. Although it had been banned earlier, Erk was formally reorganized and renamed Istaqlal Yoli (the Path of Independence) in January 1994, with the goal of making it into "a party of positive opposition."[2] This move was done without the approval of Erk's founders and exiled leadership.

The formation of Uzbekistan's two other political parties was even more directly orchestrated by the Karimov government. The NDPU

(National Democratic Party of Uzbekistan) was organized in September 1991 as the successor to the Communist Party of Uzbekistan, whose property it partially inherited. Vatan Tarakieti (the Fatherland Progress Party) was organized in 1992 in celebration of Uzbekistan's independence, and is designed primarily to appeal to the country's younger generation. By late 1993, these were the only parties that had access to Uzbekistan's media, while the opportunity for independent groups to establish newspapers or journals was virtually eliminated.[3] Karimov's control grew to be so complete that distribution of various Moscow publications was periodically disrupted, while Russian Television lost its access to Uzbek airways entirely, and Moscow's Ostankino Television's broadcast time was cut back and its programs periodically censored. Karimov's harsh policies toward his secular opposition seem to have had their desired effect, leaving most of the supporters of Karimov's opponents too frightened to make any moves in public.

Karimov has also reportedly moved against many of the country's extensive, family-based patronage networks that dominate Uzbekistan's legal and illegal economies alike. Apparently, Karimov feared that Uzbekistan's transition to a market economy would permit the two economies to merge, empowering the partially obscured elite of the shadow economy at the same time.

In an effort to prevent this, Karimov tried to create a political climate that left no doubt about who was in charge of the nation. His first task was to punish Shahrulla Mirsaidov, the former mayor of Tashkent. Mirsaidov is often rumored to be at the top of the Tashkent family network, the existence of which has never been officially recognized. Handsome, intelligent, and wealthy, Mirsaidov served first as prime minister, and then as vice president in 1990–91. Believing himself to be the better ruler for Uzbekistan, Mirsaidov made his move against Karimov in October 1991, apparently with the support of both secular democrats and religious activists. This was two months before the scheduled presidential elections; probably more important, however, was that it was just one month after Rahmon Nabiev, the Brezhnev-era leader whom Gorbachev had sacked and disgraced, managed to return to power in neighboring Tajikistan by ousting Kakhar Makhkamov. Unlike his neighbor, however, Karimov rather easily defeated Mirsaidov's attempt at a parliamentary putsch, after which Mirsaidov was forced to resign in disgrace; subsequently the former vice president was arrested, beaten up, kept under house confinement, and finally tried and convicted of stealing state property.[4]

For all his firmness with Mirsaidov, however, Karimov has generally proceeded cautiously against the country's key families, punishing a few in each family network while lavishly rewarding others to demonstrate clearly that loyalty is preferable to opposition.

TAMING ISLAM

Karimov has been even more cautious in his treatment of Uzbekistan's Islamic groups, as his republic is home to Central Asia's largest and potentially most restive Muslim community. Equally important, Karimov's communist past leaves him open to criticism by Uzbekistan's clerics for hypocrisy and apostasy. In part to forestall such accusations, Karimov has made repeated public efforts to identify with Islam; he took his presidential oath of office on the Koran, made the *hajj* to Saudi Arabia on one of his first, post-independence trips abroad, and confided to the press that he and his family observe Muslim dietary laws.[5]

Nevertheless, following the country's declaration of independence, the Karimov regime found itself engaged in a losing battle with Uzbekistan's Islamic leaders, who no longer required the services of a sympathetic intermediary between themselves and the "godless" Soviet regime in Moscow. Mufti Muhammad Sadyk Muhammad Yusuf, Uzbekistan's then ranking Islamic leader and head of the state-sanctioned Central Asian Spiritual Directorate of Muslims (SADUM),[6] now began to make demands of the president rather than petitioning humbly as he had in the past, knowing that Karimov's legitimacy would be undermined if SADUM's clerics were to brand the president an enemy of Islam.

The Mufti was moving to end the Soviet-era rift between SADUM and the country's once-outlawed Islamic revivalists, thereby endorsing the latter's demands: that there be religious instruction in state schools, that religious figures be given more exposure in all media outlets, that Friday replace Sunday as the official closing day, and that Islam be declared the state religion. Such demands attracted supporters beyond the mere confines of Uzbekistan's clerical community. By the time of independence, hundreds of young men and women were getting advanced Islamic training in special, semiclandestine *madrasah.*[7]

Karimov took tentative steps to meet some of Mufti Muhammad Yusuf's demands. The Uzbek-language press began to explore religious themes on a routine basis,[8] and for a time, the Mufti himself was given a half-hour television show on Fridays. In April 1992, the state office of religious affairs was placed under the control of a SADUM official, the first time the office had been under clerical, rather than state, supervision. Shortly thereafter, the SADUM cleric in charge of the former state office announced plans to introduce Islamic instruction in state schools on an experimental basis.[9]

However, after Tajikistan's Rahmon Nabiev was forced to submit to a power-sharing relationship with Islamic and secular opposition groups in May 1992, Karimov began to back away from his support of such policies. Uzbekistan's mufti became a target of particular criticism, in part because he was an old friend and a public defender of Kazi-kolon Khojiakbar Turajonzada, the leader of Tajikistan's Islamic community. More notable was the mufti's February 1992 *kurultay*, or convocation, of SADUM leaders that was rumored to have offered tacit support for much of Kazi Turajonzada's program of increased Islamification in Tajikistan. Karimov's position against the clerics hardened still further after President Nabiev was forced to resign in September 1992.

Within days of Nabiev's resignation, the office of Uzbekistan's procurator-general formally charged SADUM with financial irregularities in its handling of foreign donations, including the sale (for considerable profit) of Korans and other religious books that had been donated for free distribution among Uzbekistan's believers.[10] On April 30, 1993, just before this investigation was concluded, it was announced that Mufti Yusuf had stepped down for "reasons of health," and that he was to be replaced by Muftarkhan Abdullaev, the rector of the Bukhara Madrasah and of Bukhara's main mosque. Muhammad Yusuf then let it be known publicly that he was, in fact, in perfect health. Shortly thereafter, the former mufti was formally charged with having sold Korans that had been donated by the Saudis. Rather than stand trial, Muhammad Yusuf escaped to Saudi Arabia with his family. The case against other SADUM members has continued, with charges brought in mid-1994 that some clerics had not only mishandled funds, but had also sold weapons to Tajik *mujahideen*.[11]

In November 1992, with substantial help from Uzbek and Russian troops, forces loyal to the speaker of the Tajik parliament, Emomali Rahmonov, ousted the coalition government of Akbarsho Iskandarov, intensifying Tajikistan's bloody civil war. Once Turajonzada and the pro-coalition Tajik Islamic leaders were forced into exile, all of their Uzbek supporters were viewed as potential traitors. President Karimov began an offensive against Uzbekistan's own Islamic revivalist community, which, in Karimov's estimation, included the Mufti as well as dissident seminarians in the Fergana Valley.

Ever since Yusuf's dismissal, Karimov has continued his assault against "extremists," not just in the Fergana Valley but, more recently, in Surkhan Darya and Kashka Darya as well, areas that border on Tajikistan and Afghanistan.[12] However, Karimov has worked to keep this campaign from appearing antireligious; though he may rail against Islamic extremism, Karimov continues to insist that he is for the spiritual purification of the Uzbek people.[13]

Whether Uzbekistan's large and increasingly more observant Islamic community will accept Karimov's position remains to be seen. It is quite likely that the answer rests with the ties among various elites that remain almost entirely beneath the surface of Uzbekistan's tradition-bound society, rendering definitive clues all but invisible to outsiders. Mufti Yusuf was known to have close ties to elites in several Arab nations as well as to powerful merchant families in the Fergana Valley, while the new mufti, a Naqshabandi sheikh for the past thirty years, has close ties to Turkey and to the merchant families of Bukhara. Whether the good relations that Karimov gains with the new mufti are sufficient compensation for the bad ones he incurred by ridding himself of the old mufti will become apparent only with the passage of time.

Certainly, it is too early to know whether Karimov's strategy will give him the period of political stability he requires to maximize the success of current economic reforms. Karimov's secular opposition seems to have been paralyzed, while enough members of the Islamic community have been given an economic stake in the current regime to dissuade any attempted threats to state security. With the introduction of privatization in 1994, Karimov has more than enough "goodies" to reward members of the country's important merchant families who remain loyal to him; it is probably no accident that Uzbekistan's first large property auction under privatization was held in Namangan, the heart of the Fergana Valley and the center of religious activism in Uzbekistan.

While Karimov's policies toward the secular democrats have sullied Uzbekistan's relations with the Western democracies, his treatment of local Muslims has caused little more than an occasional hiccup in Uzbekistan's otherwise smooth relations with the Muslim world. For the most part, leaders in the Muslim world consider what goes on within Uzbekistan, including the treatment of believers, to be largely an internal matter. For example, when Karimov was rumored to have strong objections to Saudi Arabia's funding of Islamic revivalist missionary groups who were working with "unsanctioned" Muslim groups in Uzbekistan, the Saudi royal family seems to have let the Uzbek leader's anger pass without comment. As demonstrated by the warm welcome he gave Iranian president Ali Akbar Hashemi Rafsanjani, Karimov's concerns about religious extremism are exclusively domestic. Consistent with this view, Uzbekistan's relations with Iran cooled in 1994, when the latter was seen to be actively supporting Tajik *mujahideen*. His preoccupation with and active participation in the affairs of Tajikistan indicate the length of the radius Karimov has determined for that sphere of domesticity, which essentially encompasses all of Islam in Central Asia.

TAJIKISTAN: "A FIRE ON THE NEIGHBOR'S ROOF"

Although it retains the trappings of formal independence, Tajikistan cannot really be called a state in the full sense of the term. More than four years of ongoing civil war have killed well more than fifty thousand people and have driven thousands more into exile, destroying most of what remnants of an economy the republic possessed before independence, and creating unemployment in excess of 50 percent. Government sources insist that it would take at least $7 billion to repair the nation's war damage and restart its economy.

With support from the IMF, Tajikistan established an independent currency in 1995; prior to that, the nation survived on specially marked rubles supplied by Moscow. At the end of 1993, when Russia withdrew Soviet-era rubles from circulation, Tajikistan's then-prime minister, Abdumalik Abdulojanov, confirmed that a full 70 percent of Tajikistan's income was coming from Moscow.[14] Ever since the Rahmonov government seized power in November 1992, considerable attention has been devoted to improving the country's self-defense capability, but it is troops from Russia and Uzbekistan, with token military assistance from Kazakhstan and Kyrgyzstan, that defend the country, patrol its air space, and guard its borders with Afghanistan and China.

Rahmonov, who had run the country as parliamentary speaker, became president in November 1994 with about 60 percent of the votes (against 35 percent for his main rival, former prime minister Abdulojanov), but the present government's authority is not well established. Gorno-Badakhshan oblast, a sparsely populated and geographically forbidding region that occupies about half the country's total area, has maintained since December 1991 that it is an autonomous republic. The Rahmonov government has attempted to invade the region on at least two occasions, each with little effect. Long stretches of the rugged border with Afghanistan are regularly crossed in both directions by people smuggling guns, money, and drugs, as well as by opposition fighters come to raid Russian border posts. Even in downtown Dushanbe, the nation's capital, public order seems tenuous, with assassinations of Russian soldiers, government officials, and prominent businessmen regular and unremarkable occurrences. In short, even after four years of concerted Russian, Uzbekistani, and Tajikistani efforts to hold it together, the country still seems to justify the remark of one Russian military observer that "Tajikistan will become a fully functional Afghanistan."[15]

Although Tajikistan's collapse as a state has been widely accepted as an object lesson of what could happen to the other Soviet successor states, it is far from clear whether Tajikistan could have envisioned any other possible, more stable future. Most sources on Tajikistan's history agree that the country has never been more than a bureaucratic catch-all. The origins of present-day Tajikistan go back to the early Soviet period, when a bit of Uzbekistan proper was tacked onto what had been an administrative subunit of Uzbekistan, which itself had been stitched together from various territories.

The north, Khojent, is essentially a political peninsula extending into the Fergana Valley, most of which is controlled by Uzbekistan. Indeed, until the final formation of Tajikistan in 1929, the Khojent region was an *okrug* of Uzbekistan. In addition to having most of Tajikistan's fertile land, and thus the bulk of its lucrative cotton crop, the Khojent region is tightly integrated both economically and culturally with Uzbekistan. As a consequence, the prominent families of the Khojent region were the wealthiest and most politically well connected in the republic, allowing them to dominate the government and economy of Tajikistan for most of its Soviet existence.

Most of the rest of the country is separated from Khojent by the Zaraf-shan Mountains. The southwestern portion of Tajikistan lies in a region that remained within the Emirate of Bukhara until it was conquered by the Red Army in 1920. Resistance to the Bolsheviks continued in this region until about 1924 or 1925, when the so-called Basmachi Rebellion was finally suppressed. Resistance was particularly strong in the extreme southwestern corner of the republic, in the region of Kurgan-Tiube. In 1924, the southern part of the republic was declared the Tajik Autonomous

Republic within Uzbekistan. It retained this status until 1929, when the present territory of Tajikistan received full republican status with the addition of Khojent.

The next region east is Kuliab, which claims to be the home of the "real" Tajik peasantry. This region has remained politically distinct in Tajikistan's recent history, apparently harboring resentments against both Kurgan-Tiube and Khojent, the economic and political supremacy of which it has always disputed.

Eastern Badakhshan nominally had been part of the Kokand khanate, which separated from Bukhara in the early nineteenth century and was then crushed by the Russians in 1876. However, the region is sparsely settled. Except for a few dark river valleys, the region consists of extremely high mountain plateaus that receive virtually no precipitation and are subject to frost year-round, with temperatures that can drop to –50°C in winter. The Badakhshani, or Pamiri, people are ethnically and linguistically distinct from the Tajiks, and are also distinct religiously by virtue of being Ismaili. This region, together with Garm, northeast of the capital, had little access to power for most of the Soviet period.

Although the capital, Dushanbe, is much nearer to the Kuliab region, Soviet Tajikistan was controlled and administered for most of its history by appointees from Khojent. Of necessity, this also provided Khojent with good ties to Moscow, especially since a large portion of the republic's economy was based on uranium, plutonium processing, and aluminum, all of which were under Moscow's control and supervision.

Khojent's nearly total grip on the republic's political and economic life was long contested by elements in Kuliab, the region southeast of Dushanbe. In 1988, Kuliab was joined with the southwestern oblast of Kurgan-Tiube to form a single oblast called Khatlon. There seems to have been a long history of tensions between these two neighboring oblasts, which separated in 1990 and then were forcibly rejoined (again as Khatlon) in December 1992 after troops loyal to Emomali Rahmonov, former head of the Kuliab executive committee, seized power in Dushanbe.

While the Kuliab factions seem to have been generally procommunist and pro-Soviet, Kurgan-Tiube was a place where traditional Islamic practices remained very strong, perhaps in part because it was a place to which people from other parts of Central Asia had been forcibly moved at various points in Soviet history. As early as 1976 there were public demonstrations in Kurgan-Tiube calling for the replacement of communist rule with Islamic rule;[16] in 1987, the arrest of a local religious figure, Mulla Abdullo Saidov, led to widespread demonstrations in the region.

Tajikistan began its current cycle of instability in 1985, when Mikhail Gorbachev forced the retirement of Tajik Communist Party leader Rahmon Nabiev, replacing him with Kakhar Makhkamov. Both are from Khojent, but Nabiev was better connected to the elites of the past.[17] Under Makhkamov, Khojent families continued to predominate in the republic's *apparat*, but they lost control of such lucrative posts as the agriculture, trade, and internal security ministries.

Makhkamov seems to have been typical of Gorbachev's early appointments to high-level positions in the outlying Soviet republics in that his ties with Moscow were better than those with local elites. There were distinct disadvantages in such a personnel policy, particularly in Tajikistan. Makhkamov's control of public order in the republic was challenged quite early; by 1989, protest rallies were a common occurrence in Dushanbe. Protest became violent in February 1990, when rumors spread that Armenians displaced by disturbances in Azerbaijan were to be given apartments in the city, which had long suffered an acute housing shortage. A state of emergency was declared after rioting left twenty-two people dead and more than seven hundred wounded, while downtown Dushanbe sustained extensive damage.[18]

The riots coincided with the elections to the republic's Supreme Soviet, which—like elsewhere in the Soviet Union under Gorbachev—were meant to be more open and representative than previous elections. Perhaps as a consequence, a number of new politicians emerged at the national level in Tajikistan, including Akbarsho Iskandarov, a Pamiri who had been a prominent official in Badakhshan; Iskandarov was now elected deputy chairman of the Tajik republic's Supreme Soviet. The new republic legislature also returned to political life some figures from the past, most notably Nabiev, who became a deputy.

As was true elsewhere in the Soviet Union, 1990 was a time of extraordinary political ferment in Tajikistan. Political groupings began to proliferate, with three gaining particular prominence: the Democratic Party (secular democrats), Rastokhez (or the "Renaissance Party" of secular nationalists), and the Islamic Renaissance Party (IRP). Although the local branch of the last group, which was originally formed in Astrakhan, was denied official registration, Islamic believers and clergy were becoming so active in the political process that Kazi-kolon Turajonzada, the highest-ranking official cleric in the republic, issued a warning to all clerics that they were forbidden to join political parties, including Islamic ones.[19] The same point was made more forcefully in September 1990, when the popular imam Sokidzhan Bedimogov was found guilty of fomenting the February riots and was sentenced to four years in prison.

One of the paradoxes of this time was that even as Makhkamov was jailing Bedimogov, he was also trying to court the republic's believers. Makhkamov permitted the opening of the Islamic Institute in Dushanbe in September 1990, freed religious practice in December 1990, and staged a large public ceremony in June 1991 to bid farewell to the republic's first five hundred *hajjis* as they set out for Mecca.

Muslims were not the only group Makhkamov attempted to control. In January 1991, charges related to the February 1990 riots were also brought against leaders of Rastokhez, and in May 1991, corruption charges were brought against S. Khasanov, the former head of Kuliab oblast.

Apparently, Makhkamov had never established good relations in the republic, which may be one reason he was so quick to endorse the leaders of the Soviet coup attempt during August 19–21, 1991. When the coup collapsed, Tajikistan's Supreme Soviet demanded Makhkamov's resignation, which he offered on August 31. The leadership of the republic passed to parliamentary speaker Kadriddin Aslonov (from Garm), and independence was declared on September 9, 1991.

Aslonov was acting president for all of one eventful month. Large crowds, many of them consisting of clerics and some waving banners with Islamic slogans, gathered around the monumental Lenin on what is now called Shohidon Square. Aslonov outlawed Tajikistan's Communist Party and permitted Dushanbe's mayor to have the statue of Lenin blown up. In reaction, the parliament demanded Aslonov's resignation and placed the rest of the country's Soviet monuments under police protection.

The parliament's response led to even greater demonstrations, with the Democratic Party, Rastokhez, and the IRP all mustering large numbers of supporters, who set up tent cities on the square in front of the government building. The leaders of these movements, together with Tajikistan's MVD chief Mamadaez Navdujanov (a Pamiri) and the parliament (under the control of its new speaker, Rahmon Nabiev), formed a coalition that would run the country until November 1991, when new presidential elections would be held.

Ironically, this political disarray produced the region's first truly contested, direct presidential election (even if there was also widespread fraud). The winner was Rahmon Nabiev, who received about 57 percent of the popular vote, outdistancing his rival from the Democrats, Dovlat Khudonazarov (a Pamiri who was head of the USSR Cinematographers Union at the time), who got about 31 percent.

The election of a president did not restore order in Tajikistan. The leader of the IRP, Sheikh Himmatzoda, announced in December that his party was going into passive opposition against Nabiev, followed soon afterward by Shodmon Iusuf's Democratic Party; at the same time, Gorno-Badakhshan oblast declared itself an autonomous republic.

Political positions continued to harden through early 1992. The Tajik parliament was under the control of Safarali Kenjaev, Nabiev's presidential campaign manager, who put a stamp on his legislative power early on by initiating a purge of senior officials who had opposed Nabiev. In March 1992, Nabiev fired Minister of Internal Affairs Navdujanov, the senior Pamiri in the government. The result was another outbreak of demonstrations by an unexpected coalition of Pamiris and Muslims, which led to the resignation of Speaker Kenjaev one month later.

Kenjaev appears to have had a power base in Kuliab, for soon after he was forced to resign, large numbers of demonstrators from the region appeared in Dushanbe's other large public square, Ozodi (Freedom) Square (less than a mile from Shohidon Square), and demanded Kenjaev's reinstatement. The parliament responded by imposing direct presidential rule.

In May, under circumstances that are not entirely clear, about twenty thousand of the Ozodi Square demonstrators got hold of government arms. Nabiev reinstated Kenjaev and vowed to clear Shohidon Square. Shots were fired, killing at least four demonstrators. The Shohidon Square crowd responded by seizing the city's television tower, airport, main rail terminal, and the presidential palace, although the president himself was in hiding. The Ozodi Square protesters responded by seizing parliament, demanding that appropriate measures be carried out.

With the situation spinning rapidly out of control, another compromise was hammered out, signed by government representatives and the leaders of Rastokhez, the Democratic Party, and the IRP, and witnessed by Kazi-kolon Turajonzada and others. Nabiev's appointment of Dovlat Usmon as deputy prime minister officially brought the IRP into the government. However, the figure who most disturbed leaders elsewhere in Central Asia and in Russia[20] was Kazi-kolon Khojiakbar Turajonzada, whose presence on the expanded Presidium of the parliament was taken as a signal that Tajikistan was about to "go Islamic." In a parallel move of equal importance, command of the local Russian garrison in Dushanbe was passed to General Ashurov, the first ethnic Tajik to hold such a high command.

Tensions were high throughout the summer and fall of 1992. In June, Nabiev legalized the formation of citizen militias, and released from prison a number of criminals who assisted in the creation of factional armies. The battles among the country's four main regions were becoming less bureaucratic and more deadly, as armed clashes became more common, particularly between Kurgan-Tiube and Kuliab irregulars. In what were presumed to be armory raids, attacks on the Russian garrisons in Dushanbe and Kurgan-Tiube also became frequent; prisons in Iavan and other cities were forced open.

In August, the parliament attempted to convene but was unable to muster a quorum, apparently because the Khojent delegation refused to participate. Even without a quorum, however, the parliament was able to dismiss speaker Kenjaev again and replace him with Akbarsho Iskandarov.

In September, order collapsed still further. A militia from Kuliab invaded Kurgan-Tiube, while a crowd in Dushanbe surrounded Nabiev's house and seized the government building, taking senior officials hostage. Nabiev once again went into hiding until parliamentary and public pressure forced him to resign on September 7, 1992.

Parliamentary speaker Iskandarov assumed power and began to cobble together a coalition government. Democratic Party founder Shodmon Iusuf and IRP leader Dovlat Usmon remained in power and were joined by Abdumalik Abdulojanov, a Soviet minister-turned-businessman from Khojent. By this time, though, the situation in Kuliab and Kurgan-Tiube was entirely out of control. A militia loyal to Nabiev seized the Nurek hydroelectric power station, southeast of Dushanbe, threatening to blow up the dam; attacks on Russian border posts and garrisons in Kurgan-Tiube, Lomonosovo, and even in the capital itself became common. The Kuliab militia was especially active under the command of Sangak "Bobo" Safarov, who had served twenty-three years in Soviet prisons for racketeering and murder before being released by President Nabiev.[21] In October, there was an attempted coup by former parliamentary speaker and Nabiev loyalist Kenjaev, who briefly installed himself as president before being driven from the capital with the assistance of the Russian garrison of the 201st Motor Rifles Division, headquartered in Dushanbe.

During its first year of independence, Tajikistan's neighbors and Russia remained largely aloof from the country's internal problems. By fall 1992, however, the battles were beginning to cause concern elsewhere. In September, Central Asian presidents Akaev, Nazarbaev, and Karimov issued a joint appeal to all sides in Tajikistan, urging them to end the conflict; in October, the first proposal was made to send CIS forces into Kurgan-Tiube to stop the fighting there. The Russian military detachments stationed in Tajikistan, both border guards and regular troops, were officially neutral, but there are scores of reports of soldiers deserting, sometimes with their tanks and other heavy weaponry, and of local commanders arming one side against another.

There are clear indications that by November 1992 the decision had been made elsewhere in the CIS to put an end to the fighting in Tajikistan. Russian Foreign Minister Andrei Kozyrev visited the region, conferring with government officials and the newly appointed head of Kuliab, Emomali Rahmonov. Speaker Iskandarov appointed a new governing State Council which briefly included General Ashurov, the ethnic Tajik who was commander of the Russian Army's 201st Motor Rifles Division in Dushanbe. Parliament was reconvened, although at Russia's insistence its venue was moved to Khojent, where it could be placed under Russian protection.[22] Fierce fighting erupted in the rest of the country, and communication with Dushanbe was cut off.

One of the first acts of the reconvened parliament was to remove Speaker Iskandarov from his post and to elect in his stead Rahmonov, whose militias had just entered Dushanbe, led by columns of tanks waving red Soviet flags. Once in power these militias, under the command of Safarov and the republic's new Minister of Internal Affairs Iakub Salimov (another amnestied convict), set about making good on Safarov's boast that they would cleanse the country of "democratic and Islamic filth."

The leaders of the Democratic Party, the IRP, and Rastokhez were all forced into exile, as was Kazi-kolon Turajonzada; many less prominent political figures were arrested or killed. Thousands of people fled to Badakhshan or Afghanistan.

The specter of an elected president being forced to resign more or less at gunpoint, as Nabiev had been, had galvanized the Central Asian leaders (save Turkmenistan's Saparmurad Niyazov) into trying to mount a joint intervention force. However, it took both Akaev and Nazarbaev several months to obtain the necessary permission from their respective legislatures, which meant that the guarantor of Rahmonov's victory was Uzbekistan's Karimov, who not only sent in troops, but also supplied air support and reconnaissance. One Uzbekistani official described his country's intervention in Tajikistan as similar to the natural concern a homeowner feels when a neighbor's roof catches fire.[23]

UZBEKISTAN'S INTEREST IN TAJIKISTAN

Besides his concern over Uzbekistan's proximity to the fighting, there were a number of interests Karimov was serving by intervening in Tajikistan's internal affairs. One of the less immediately obvious was the opportunity this presented to advance the interests of Tajikistan's Uzbeks. Historically, the ties between the Uzbek and Tajik Communist Party elites were extremely close. Indeed, given the ethnographic confusions between populations whose major distinctions were primarily linguistic, making credible the Uzbeks' claims that Tajiks were really Uzbeks (and vice-versa), the connections between the two sets of elites were all but familial. A case in point is the militia of Faizuli Saidov, who had been Sangak Safarov's chief deputy until the two had a falling out and killed each other in March 1993; Saidov was a Lakai Uzbek who had agitated for years to gain autonomy for his native region.[24]

The Russian Army, which had never left Tajikistan, did the bulk of the fighting to back up the anti-Iskandarov forces, but Uzbekistan's army played an even more significant role. Although it had informally undertaken the task as early as December 1992,[25] Uzbekistan accepted formal responsibility for the patrol and defense of Tajikistan's airspace in March 1993. Soldiers from Uzbekistan also remain in the country, helping Russia to maintain the fragile stalemate that has been in place since December 1992, when Rahmonov was recognized by Russia, the United States, and others as Tajikistan's legitimate head of state. Moreover, although official spokesmen from both Tajikistan and Uzbekistan have denied them, there are credible reports that Uzbekistani air support—both attack helicopters and SU-25 fighter-bombers from bases in Termez— have been used in attacks on Tajik "rebel" forces in Afghanistan.[26]

The flood of refugees into Afghanistan has further destabilized the situation there as well. There are persistent reports that Tajik opposition fighters are receiving military training and weapons, including advanced antihelicopter weapons systems, from Afghanistan and Pakistan, and that there have been attempts to establish a Tajik government-in-exile. For their part, Russia and Uzbekistan also have reached across the border, shelling and bombing "rebel targets" in Afghanistan. Although the allegations have been denied by government spokesmen, most observers believe that Karimov has supported Afghanistan's General Abdulrashid Dostum, an ethnic Uzbek, in his battle with President Burhanuddin Rabbani, a Tajik. The two had fought together against the various Soviet-backed regimes, but split into rival factions after the fall of President Najibullah. Karimov's connection to Dostum is literally familial: The Afghani General not only keeps his family in Tashkent but is said to have arranged the marriage of a son (or, in some accounts, a brother) into the Karimov family as well.[27]

However, when the Dostum-Rabbani alliance collapsed in winter 1993–94, so did Karimov's hopes of having his Afghani allies create a "buffer state" in northern Afghanistan that would insulate Uzbekistan and Tajikistan from Muslim fundamentalists and Tajik separatists further south. Ever the realist, Karimov seems to have let the public connection to Dostum cool at that point, making plain that his earlier claim of serving as the protector of all Uzbeks regardless of their state does not extend to the Uzbeks in Afghanistan. Yet wherever possible, Karimov still seems inclined to give Dostum covert assistance.

Karimov's involvement in Tajikistan remains active, although the neighboring republic is far from being an Uzbekistani puppet state. When Nabiev died, in April 1993, Karimov seems to have accepted the Kuliab-dominated Tajik political status quo, largely because Abdumalik Abdulojanov, a member of a powerful Khojent family, was named prime minister.

That Karimov remained interested in the well-being of Khojent's Uzbeks can be inferred from his reaction to Abdulojanov's sacking in autumn 1993, when Rahmonov was attempting to consolidate control of Tajikistan with members of his Kuliab power base; Karimov responded by shutting down the railroad between Uzbekistan and Tajikistan for several days. After this, Rahmonov appears to have abandoned efforts to usurp Khojenti commercial interests, and while Abdulojanov was not reappointed, several joint Tajik-Uzbek economic development initiatives were introduced in Khojent in the following months. Later, when bureaucratic tricks were preventing Abdulojanov from running against Rahmonov for Tajikistan's presidency, Karimov interfered again, persuading the parliament to postpone the elections from September until November 1994, to allow the former prime minister to mount a campaign.

UZBEKISTAN'S ARMY

Apart from his pliant parliament, one of the major reasons Karimov is able to carry out such an active foreign policy in the region is that, of all the new Central Asian nations, Uzbekistan has had the greatest success in creating its own standing army. The foundation on which that army has been built is the Soviet Army's Turkestan Military Command, which was headquartered in Tashkent. As the Soviet Union collapsed, the command seems to have been granted, or to have taken, considerable autonomy, including discretionary financial authority. As early as the beginning of 1992, officers of the command were reported to have established a commercial division, which among other things sold weapons and matériel. The transfer of Soviet troops and matériel to Uzbekistan's control was not universal. The military command at Termez, for example, initially refused to accept Uzbekistani control and attempted to remove some forty-five hundred combat vehicles (including T-72 and T-80 tanks) as well as some twenty-five hundred similar vehicles stationed in Samarkand.

In autumn 1992, when Uzbekistan's Ministry of Defense was created, with Rustam Akhmedov as its first minister, the military was slated to have between twenty-five thousand and thirty thousand soldiers, spread among ground forces, an air force, air defense forces, and a national guard. Universal military service was retained from the Soviet period, and a military training school for boys grade eight and up was opened in Fergana; the curriculum was to include, in addition to military subjects, mastery of Russian, English, and Arabic. At least sixty other Uzbek youth were sent to Turkey for military training. The bulk of military preparation for Uzbekistan's army is rumored still to take place in Russia.

Indications are that Uzbekistan's army is fully functional and may be considered a usable arm of state policy. Karimov spoke in March 1993 of the various armies of the CIS becoming like the armies of the former Warsaw Pact, which suggests that the forces under his control are already a functional, standing army. This does not mean, however, that Karimov's army can operate without constraint. Uzbekistan's army is dependent upon its overwhelmingly Russian officer corps, which officials in Tashkent realize cannot be "nativized" for at least another generation. There is strong evidence of coordination between Russian and Uzbekistani military commands. Uzbekistan's military leaders have signed two separate, bilateral security treaties with Russia (the most recent in 1994), both of which reaffirm the interdependence of the two countries in terms of military training and armaments, allow for mutual use of airfields and antiaircraft weapons systems, and prohibit either state from engaging in military actions that might be construed as hostile by the other.[28]

Karimov's immediate neighbors are fully, and anxiously, aware of his army's potential, particularly since Russia, which does not feel potentially at risk from Uzbekistan's army, seems content to allow Karimov a degree of discretion in developing his republic's security policy. Fortified by Russia's agreement to intervene in Tajikistan with Karimov, Uzbekistan's success in this theater of operations must look like a dangerous precedent to the other Central Asian leaders, particularly since Karimov claims the right of intervention to defend the interests of Uzbeks beyond his country's borders. However, unlike the claim Russia's leaders have made for "foreign" Russians, Karimov has not claimed the right of dual citizenship for Uzbeks living outside their home republic.[29]

Uzbekistan's role in Kyrgyzstan, which has already been detailed, increasingly unnerves the Kyrgyz, particularly since Karimov has claimed to be the guarantor of Kyrgyzstan's stability. A recent example came just after Akaev's resounding January 1994 referendum victory, when President Karimov announced that it was his support for Kyrgyzstan's president that had allowed Akaev to get 96 percent of the vote in Osh.[30]

So far, Karimov has not flexed his muscles so publicly in front of either Turkmen or Kazakh audiences, although he has barely concealed his contempt for Turkmenistan's president Saparmurad Niyazov, whom Karimov depicts as khan-like. Nursultan Nazarbaev of Kazakhstan presents a greater challenge to Karimov's ambitions for Uzbekistani hegemony in Central Asia; accordingly, Karimov treats him far more cautiously.

THE CHALLENGE OF ECONOMIC DEVELOPMENT

If the accounts of advisers close to Uzbekistan's president are to be believed, then there can be little doubt that Islam Karimov is quite jealous of the favorable international attention that his Kazakh colleague has received over the last few years. However, both Nazarbaev and Karimov understand that the only hope their states have of escaping complete dependence on Russia is to cooperate with each other. This is clearly the impetus for the economic union between these two states and Kyrgyzstan, which was signed in January 1994. In the beginning, at least, this union has been costlier for Kazakhstan than for the other members; the union agreement converts Uzbekistan's $39 million debt to Kazakhstan into a state credit.[31]

The agreement also makes it even easier for Uzbekistani commercial interests to invest in the southern part of Kazakhstan, home to most of Kazakhstan's more than three hundred thousand Uzbeks. This entire region, and especially Shymkent, Kazakhstan's second-most populous city, has traditionally traded with Tashkent, less than a two-hour drive away, rather than with Almaty, which is more than ten hours away by car. The removal of trade barriers between the two countries is certain to lead to the restoration of these traditional trade links.

However, free trade with Kazakhstan and Kyrgyzstan will not be sufficient to reverse Uzbekistan's economic decline. As the Karimov government clearly recognizes, such a reversal requires foreign investment. Even though Uzbekistan is abundantly endowed with natural resources that foreign partners could help develop profitably, the country has not been as successful in this sphere as its northern neighbor. This remains true even though Uzbekistan, like Kazakhstan, has introduced a sweeping privatization program, even providing more generous customs laws for locally owned and joint-venture firms than does Kazakhstan.[32]

One explanation for Uzbekistan's comparative lack of success is the difference in the personal style of the two leaders. Although Karimov's foreign advisers are as competent and reliable as Nazarbaev's, Karimov simply does not make the same strongly positive personal impression that Nazarbaev does. In part, this is the result of the bad media coverage Karimov has received for human rights abuses his political opponents have suffered. Karimov's human rights record has certainly been a factor in U.S.–Uzbek relations. Unlike Nazarbaev, Karimov has been refused an invitation to the United States as an official visitor; and unlike Akaev, Karimov was not received by the White House while he was in the United States on private visits.

The coldness the United States has expressed toward Karimov has also affected the willingness of U.S.-dominated international financial organizations, such as the IMF and the World Bank, to extend to Uzbekistan the same financial benefits the Kazakhs and the Kyrgyz have enjoyed. This reluctance to lend has undoubtedly increased the difficulty of Uzbekistan's introduction of its own currency, the som. Like the Kazakhs, the Uzbeks were unenthusiastic about the prospects of introducing their own currency, and so signed the October 1994 accord on the creation of the new ruble zone.

Karimov had chosen to stay in the ruble zone largely for economic reasons. Uzbekistan is Central Asia's most populous nation, with more than twenty-two million people who are overwhelmingly rural, young (more than 60 percent are under twenty-five), and poor. Karimov was therefore keen to reduce the economic stress of independence by maintaining substantial subsidies for basic foodstuffs and energy. State subsidies remained in place until late summer 1993, largely because Yeltsin kept Uzbekistan relatively well supplied with rubles, grain, and energy as a reward for Uzbekistan's support of Russian actions in Tajikistan. Uzbekistan was the only Central Asian country to enjoy such preferential Russian treatment.

However, when Russia once again redefined the terms for ruble-zone membership in November 1993, requiring member-nations to turn over their gold reserves, Uzbekistan finally balked. Home to a quarter of the proven gold reserves in the former USSR, Uzbekistan since its independence has been refining and depositing gold abroad to back the eventual introduction of its own currency.[33] Rather than turn over its gold reserves to Russia, Uzbekistan introduced the som instead, an action that nearly wrecked the country's young banking system and sent the Uzbekistani economy into an inflationary spiral.[34] Some of this inflation was to be expected; the Uzbeks used a som coupon for seven months before setting a rate for their som, in an effort to keep their money from costing more than the paper it was printed on. The som itself, introduced in July 1994, has also proved to be highly inflationary. Nevertheless, Karimov's economic advisers believed that Uzbekistan had no choice but to introduce a national currency, since control of the country's gold was the key to its economic independence.

Uzbekistan's gold also sparked the interest of the Europeans. Uzbekistan was the first Central Asian country to receive funds from the European Bank for Reconstruction and Development, which stepped in to fill the financial gap caused by Uzbekistan's initially bad relations with the United States. The funds allowed Uzbekistan to complete construction of a gold-mining site.

Despite his country's gold, Karimov was at first received with a certain condescension in western European capitals. In order to build foreign business confidence in his country, Karimov decided to honor his French and British hosts by depositing part of his republic's gold reserves in both countries' banks to serve as collateral for future joint ventures. However, at least in the French case, Karimov handled the issue so maladroitly that his hosts reportedly assumed that Karimov was carrying the gold in his suitcase. Matters went somewhat more smoothly in England, but Karimov is said to have taken personal offense when a parliamentary vote call nearly cleared the room of guests at an official luncheon.

The most formidable obstacle for Uzbekistan in the conduct of its foreign policy is the perception that it is a wholly "oriental" republic. Demographically resembling Tajikistan much more than it does "half-European" Kazakhstan, Uzbekistan is seen as potentially vulnerable to an ill-defined "Islamic threat." As independence progresses, however, Karimov is learning to turn this international reputation for "Asianness" into a certain virtue, particularly the iron-handed stability his rule guarantees. While in London, he confidently assured a group of British investors in a Kizil Kum gold-mining joint venture that they "need not be afraid of anything happening in our country in the next five years because Karimov will remain president.[35]

In fact, although they have had to renegotiate some of their contracts, neither this British consortium nor Newmont Mining, also at work in the republic, is likely to face the tortuous and expensive vacillations in government policy that Cameco has been forced to endure in trying to work with a fractious and publicity-sensitive Kyrgyzstani government and parliament. At the same time, however, no deal in Uzbekistan can be considered secure until it receives Karimov's personal blessing, and getting to Karimov is still no easy feat. The Ministry of Foreign Economic Relations, the Ministry of Foreign Affairs, the State Committee on Privatization, and various members of the president's in-house bureaucracy all compete vigorously with one another to control, and profit from, access to the president.

For all its well-publicized problems, Uzbekistan has real economic potential. While it lacks the energy wealth of Turkmenistan and Kazakhstan, Uzbekistan has more than enough oil and natural gas to meet its own energy needs. While the country suffers from an acute shortage of usable water, the import of Western technology has brought the Uzbeks both improved irrigation techniques and the prospect that they might be able to purify at least a part of their badly contaminated water supply. Both of these are improving living standards for large segments of the population, while also improving the long-term prospects of Uzbekistan's cotton industry.

In the next decade, Uzbekistan hopes to cut back its cotton production by about 25 percent in an effort to become more self-sufficient in food production, but cotton remains the country's principal export crop. Uzbekistan is the world's fourth-largest producer of cotton, now counting French, German, and Italian manufacturers among its customers. Most of Uzbekistan's cotton crop is still mortgaged to Russia, which views with alarm Uzbekistan's plans to develop a textile industry, since this could cut into the intended market for Russian industries Moscow is trying to revitalize. Undeterred, Uzbekistan continues to explore possibilities in this area, searching for foreign assistance; thus far, both India and Pakistan have responded with interest.

The industrial skills potential of Uzbekistan's population was never really tapped in the Soviet period. Some industry was located here, the best known of which may be the Chkalov aircraft plant in Tashkent. In the Soviet era, this production and assembly facility turned out the mainstay AWACS plane, the Midas tanker, and Candid transport crafts, as well as versions of the basic Il-76. Since independence, the Chkalov plant, in cooperation with Russia, has succeeded in bringing to production the Il-114, a short-haul, twin-turboprop plane designed for both civil and military purposes. Uzbekistan also had some truck and auto manufacturing facilities, both of which have been taken over by an Uzbek joint venture with Mercedes-Benz.

However, the expansion of Uzbekistan's industrial base is likely to be quite slow, primarily because of the outflow of Russians from the country, estimated by sources in Moscow to exceed a quarter of a million since 1990.[36] Although Uzbeks are generally well educated, especially by non-European standards, they have not had commensurate technical training, since technical subjects were traditionally taught in Russian.

The Karimov government is clearly disturbed by Russian out-migration and is looking for ways to keep this population in the country. Part of the answer, of course, would come with an improved economy. In Soviet days, the Russians of Uzbekistan, about 9 percent of the republic's population, enjoyed a generally higher standard of living than did their conationals in Russia. During the first year of Uzbekistan's independence, the Russians' standard of living remained relatively good, although "imported" goods, which included goods from Russia, became scarcer.

Since Uzbekistan's introduction of the som in November 1993, the sense of economic disadvantage among Uzbekistan's Russians has grown. Now they can no longer easily receive pension and other payments from Russia. The time required to complete ruble-to-som currency conversion, combined with the plunging value of the som, means that these Russians often lose half the value of the original draft. The som coupon was particularly unstable, losing more than 90 percent of its value in the first six months. As already noted, some of this was anticipated. However, as part of the som stabilization effort, all ruble trade in Uzbekistan has been banned as of April 15, 1994, and enterprises were forced to turn over 30 percent of their foreign currency earnings (up from the earlier 15 percent) to the Uzbekistan National Bank. This made the currency regime harsher than in neighboring Kazakhstan.

The current economic situation strengthens the perception of local Russians that they are "stranded" in Uzbekistan, a country that speaks a foreign language, observes an alien religion, and has an impenetrable family structure that controls much of the newly privatized economy. Formally and legally, Russians have the same economic rights as do the Uzbeks, but in reality there is a glass ceiling in the republic above which non-Uzbeks cannot advance.

Karimov has tried to make some concessions to appease his country's Russian population. Because more than three-fourths of the country's Russians do not speak Uzbek, Karimov is backpedaling on enforcement of a language law that effectively denies government employment to non-speakers of Uzbek. He has also ordered that Russian-language street signs be returned to Tashkent streets. However, Karimov has yet to compromise on what is arguably the most contentious issue for both local Russians and Moscow—the right of dual Russian-Uzbekistani citizenship.

SEEKING RUSSIA'S HELPING HAND

The citizenship issue points up many of the tensions in Uzbekistan's relationship with Russia, and in its foreign policy more broadly. Karimov is both clever enough to understand and blunt enough to state that the future of Central Asia will still be determined in Moscow. At the same time, though, independence has brought only mixed economic success to the country, and Karimov is not eager to surrender his sovereignty to Russia. Though a strong proponent of the CIS, and especially of the collective security guarantees the CIS structure is intended to provide, Karimov joined Turkmenistan's Saparmurad Niyazov in criticizing Nursultan Nazarbaev's plan to replace the CIS with a stronger Euro-Asian Union. Indeed, Uzbekistan's reaction was blunt: the tightly controlled press characterized Nazarbaev's proposal as one "for simpletons.[37] Still,

Karimov does recognize the fact that in order to maintain favorable trade relations with Russia, Uzbekistan will have to accept a CIS-based economic union that will limit some of his country's discretionary powers.

Karimov and the rest of Uzbekistan's elites understand that good economic relations with Russia are essential, and that Russia is also the key to the republic's security problems. Nevertheless, they want to reach out to other countries on their own terms.

The recent turn Russia is making toward greater authoritarianism has the paradoxical effect of strengthening Karimov, who has spoken with increasing frequency of the need for the Russian government to exercise stricter control at home in order to permit the proper functioning of the smaller sovereign entities that it dominates along its periphery. Karimov offers loyalty and obedience in exchange, as long as Russia does not interfere in the internal life of Uzbek society.

Yet with the passage of time, President Karimov appears to have become more fearful that Russian interference will develop. The regular breachings of the Afghan-Tajik border that have accompanied Tajikistan's lingering civil war make a Russian military buildup in the region a constant risk. As long as Russia has troops in the area, it retains the capacity to intervene in Uzbekistan with ease. The situation makes President Karimov nervous, so much so that by mid-1995 he had begun to reconsider some of the basic premises of his country's policy in Tajikistan. The idea of a military victory over the opposition to the Rahmonov government had been succeeded by a Karimov-sponsored initiative for reconciling with Tajikistan's Islamic "moderates" and democrats. The Uzbek president even went so far as to meet with Khojiakbar Turajonzada. In shifting policy on Tajikistan, much like his accommodation with Russia, Karimov has acknowledged that making friends with former as well as potential enemies may buy Uzbekistan the time needed to successfully launch Central Asia's most central and most populous state onto the international stage.

7

In Search of
Reunification

Today Central Asia's leaders look out at the world
beyond their borders far more soberly than they
did in the euphoric autumn of 1991, as they all
now understand both the expected and the unex-
pected burdens of independence. This is particularly true of the leaders
of the three states this book has considered at length, Islam Karimov of
Uzbekistan, Nursultan Nazarbaev of Kazakhstan, and Askar Akaev of
Kyrgyzstan.

Without question, the years since independence have been more
challenging than any of these leaders expected, and independence itself
has offered each of them opportunities that must have exceeded any of
their wildest imaginings as to what life in the post-Soviet period held in
store for them and for their new nations. Certainly it would have been
unthinkable just a few years ago that any of Central Asia's leaders would
address the United Nations, be feted by heads of state, or play host to
visiting captains of international commerce. The fact that all of the leaders have done these things, and more, must also excite their citizens
who preserved their ancestors' dreams of independence.

Yet it is equally true that everyone throughout the region now has a
new appreciation for the difficulty of making independence work. No
one has dwelled on this theme more insistently than Nursultan
Nazarbaev, who has used regional forums, CIS meetings, and his foreign
travels to reiterate that Kazakhstan and its fellow Soviet successor states

must find new ways to reintegrate in order to ensure their mutual security and even their survival.

Nazarbaev's preferred solution is to do away with the CIS and replace it with a Euro-Asian Union, a transnational body that would have a common currency, a multinational bank with an integrated economic policy, and a supranational parliament and President's Council.

Nazarbaev's proposal is a divisive one among Central Asia's leaders; only Askar Akaev has endorsed it, and even his initial enthusiasm has waned. By contrast, both Saparmurad Niyazov and Islam Karimov have viewed this proposal as an unacceptable surrender of sovereignty. Russia, too, seems uneasy with the proposed arrangement, at least on the terms called for by Nazarbaev, although at the spring 1994 meeting of CIS leaders, Yeltsin did endorse a substantial strengthening of the CIS and echoed this theme at subsequent meetings.

REINTEGRATION WITH RUSSIA?

Nevertheless, all of Central Asia's leaders accept some form of greater integration as inevitable. All have called for the strengthening of the CIS, although Niyazov wants only a minimal degree of reintegration. Russia, too, seems to want an expansion of CIS powers and responsibilities while also seeking a disproportionate share of authority within that body. Whether Russia can institutionalize a "first among equals" status remains to be seen, but it should come as no surprise that Moscow is finding little enthusiasm among the leaders of these newly sovereign states to return to institutionalized second-class status.

The greatest fear among Central Asia's leaders is that instead of developing into some sort of new multilateral organization, the CIS will gradually become a reincarnation of the old Warsaw Pact, in which the shared experiences and continuing linkages of the Soviet period substitute for Communist Party membership. For all the disagreements within the ruling elite, Russia's present and would-be rulers all share the conviction that their nation is heir to the USSR, and that Russia is a great power that should be free to exercise its influence as it sees best throughout the entire territory it ruled just a few short years ago.

Though all of the presidents in the former Soviet republics have privately accepted the continuation of Russian hegemony—and many even defer to Yeltsin and his wishes in much the same way that Communist Party first secretaries in the Soviet republics used to defer to Gorbachev—

in public the new presidents have objected to the baldness with which Russian leaders express neo-imperialist sentiments. Most take pains to avoid public demonstrations of their obsequiousness to Russia. However, as Russia's own problems have increased and as its stability has encountered more threats, Yeltsin has felt an increasing need to publicly demonstrate his position as the leader of a great power. The leaders of the new post-Soviet states have proven to be the best subjects for such demonstrations. Given the continued dependence of their states on Russia for economic support and security guarantees, the leaders of the Central Asian states have had little choice but to bend under Russia's pressure.

In an environment of growing economic uncertainty, even second-class status in the CIS may seem preferable to a wholesale ceding of sovereignty to Russia on a bilateral basis. This is a point the current rulers of Tajikistan have already reached, and it is far from clear if the deal they got from their acquiescence to Moscow is a good one. Tajikistan was the last to leave the ruble zone, but the rubles it received could be used only in Tajikistan. Russian troops keep Emomali Rahmonov in power, but Russian statesmen force him to send delegates to the negotiating table and make it patently clear that they can easily withdraw their support if the Tajik leadership proves too recalcitrant in its demands.

However, for all the obvious drawbacks to Tajikistan's dependency upon Russia, it no longer seems far-fetched to imagine the Kyrgyz willing to trade all but the trappings of sovereignty for desperately needed fuel and food. Unfortunately though, "cutting a deal" with the Russians is not such an easy thing for Central Asian rulers to do, especially since the Russian leadership is itself in at least partial disarray. What has become increasingly evident to all observers of Russia's political scene is that there is not one, but many Russias. This is especially true with regard to the "near abroad," a hopelessly tangled policy area in which geopolitics, ethnic politics, and economic self-interest send different policy-making constituencies off in different directions.

No one doubts that Russia will defend its Russian communities abroad. How this defense will be mounted, though, is still unclear. The Russian foreign ministry and the Russian parliament are both trying to draft formal institutional arrangements for the protection of "stranded Russians." How these will be implemented is an open question, since Russia has no formal hold over the other CIS states. However, everyone realizes that Russia has many effective methods of persuasion at its disposal, including cutting off energy shipments and restricting cross-border trade.

The great challenge for Central Asian leaders will be to find ways of accepting Russia's involvement in their internal affairs that does not diminish their own political legitimacy. This is a particularly acute problem for both Akaev and Nazarbaev. Public sentiment in both Kyrgyzstan and Kazakhstan has grown increasingly anti-Russian in the last few years, which means that any appearance of dancing to Moscow's tune could spark public unrest in these countries. Granting dual-citizenship rights to Russians (particularly if similar rights are not granted to Kyrgyz or Kazakhs living in Russia) would be just such a concession; another would be modifying existing constitutional provisions regarding the state language. In addition, if concessions are made to Russia, there is likely to be increased polarization in these societies, especially in Kazakhstan; such polarization would certainly lower the threshold for Russian intervention.

These kinds of issues are deeply troubling to Nursultan Nazarbaev, in particular, for nowhere in Central Asia other than in Kazakhstan is the balance between European and non-European societies so equal, while the gap between the two is really as wide as that in any of the states where Asians are more predominant. Interethnic tensions in his country help explain Nazarbaev's desire for the creation of a Euro-Asian Union, which would take autonomy away from Kazakhstan but would still leave it in equal standing with the other union members. Nazarbaev undoubtedly fears that, absent such a union, Kazakhstan will have to pay a disproportionate "tribute" to Russia over time in the effort to preserve its independence, or that Kazakhstan may even risk losing its independence entirely.

Direct Russian intervention is something the Kazakhs in particular live in constant fear of, even if there are no indications that Russia has any concrete plans to change its present borders—notwithstanding Vladimir Zhirinovsky's unwieldy tongue and the broad dissemination of Aleksandr Solzhenitsyn's Slavophile musings. Even so, it is not difficult to understand why Kazakhs become apprehensive over such things as the publication of a map in the April 8, 1994 issue of *Nezavisimaia gazeta*, which depicted Kazakhstan's northern oblasts as part of Russia.

When the situation is viewed objectively, there is little immediate risk to Central Asia's current borders. Changes in political and territorial boundaries have been very difficult to execute: Witness the ongoing conflict over Chechnya, the struggle for Crimean autonomy, and the ambiguous status of the "Trans-Dniestr Republic" in Moldova. Incorporating any of these territories into Russia proper would be far easier to accomplish, both physically and in terms of the potential international repercussions, than would be the annexation of northern Kazakhstan.

Even more important, though, is the question of how enthusiastic most influential Russian policymakers would be about taking up the reins of empire once again. A neo-imperial Russia would immediately return to the dilemma that prompted it to sever its direct ties to Central Asia in the first place: Even the most exploitative form of neo-imperialism would require that Russia provide Central Asia some level of social welfare, which Russia neither can afford nor wishes to provide. The social needs of Uzbekistan and Kazakhstan are enormous and growing, while Tajikistan is reminding Russia of the lesson it should have learned in Afghanistan: that military support for a factional regime in this part of the world is both financially draining and endless.

Moscow's dilemma will remain what it has always been in the region—how to extract benefits without incurring greater costs. The sentiment to rid Russia of Central Asia began in the mid-1980s, when the Central Asians' growing concerns about water shortages and environmental devastation led them to propose gigantic construction projects to reverse the flow of the Ob and Irtysh Rivers. Thinly disguised as a discussion of ecology and the preservation of historical monuments, the public debate grew surprisingly rancorous during those years of censorship, with the prevailing Russian sentiment concluding that Central Asia was costing Russia far more than it was contributing to the USSR as a whole. The same sentiment informed the collective position of Belarus's Shushkevich, Ukraine's Kravchuk, and Russia's Yeltsin, who engineered their December 1991 meeting to create the Commonwealth of Independent States in such a way that Nazarbaev would either have to sign documents he had not previously read or not sign them at all, and so permit the formation of a post-Soviet union dominated by overwhelmingly Slavic countries.[1]

Since independence, a countersentiment has clearly entered Russia's debate over the region: Central Asia is too rich a source of raw materials and cheap labor to lose; the region also remains what it was to the tsars, a captive market for Russian manufactured goods, which are too low-quality to compete elsewhere in the world. Thus in 1993, Russia began to drift back into the Central Asian states, especially in the form of joint-venture companies that are exerting increasing control over important industries and extraction sites. Now, as it did in the nineteenth century,

Russia is seeking to tap Central Asia's natural resources, while assuming little or no responsibility for the region's growing welfare needs.

Nevertheless, Russia is unwilling to abandon the twenty-five million Russians who live just beyond its borders, about half of whom live in Central Asia. These "diaspora" communities add yet another imponderable dimension to an already complex Russian foreign policy, further complicating efforts to predict its course, particularly since the various Central Asian leaders weigh Russia's threat to their sovereignty in different ways. One of the many cruel paradoxes of Central Asian history is the often highly disparate perceptions of power and advantage among the region's leaders. Given Kazakhstan's long border with Russia, when Nazarbaev submits to Moscow's demands he is palpably diminishing his authority within his own state. By contrast, Uzbekistan is far enough away from Russia that Karimov can make similar concessions with little consequence, much in the tradition of a medieval khan who accepted the suzerainty of a strong but distant master in return for the security guarantees necessary to rule his land as he wished.

The emirates of Bukhara and Khiva managed to survive intact under the tsars this way, as did Sharaf Rashidov, who managed to make Uzbekistan a sort of "Red Emirate" under Brezhnev. It is no accident that Karimov has rehabilitated the memory of Rashidov, renaming Tashkent's main street and central square in his honor. Interestingly, the other leader whose reputation has recently re-entered Uzbek lore is Timur (Tamerlane), Central Asia's most famous conqueror, who is now acclaimed as founder of the Uzbek nation (which, in fact, he was not).

Thus the question of Russia's proper role in Central Asia finds no generally agreed-upon answer. The regime in Tajikistan needs Russia for its survival on the political and economic fronts alike, while the Kyrgyz teeter on the brink of full economic dependence on Russia. Turkmenistan claims to be fully independent of Russia, but its actions belie President Niyazov's words. Most importantly, while Presidents Nazarbaev and Karimov currently enjoy a satisfactory working relationship, the issue of Russia's role is one that may well drive an immovable wedge between the two, just as Moscow may have intended.

REGIONAL INITIATIVES: TURKMENISTAN THE SPOILER

Since independence, Central Asia's leaders have found it difficult to make foreign policy decisions that do not have adverse consequences throughout the region without some degree of mutual consultation. Obviously, one defense the Central Asian leaders have against Russia's erosion of their sovereignty is the power provided by their membership in overlapping international and regional organizations. All are members of the United Nations; however, the UN tacitly grants Russia special privilege throughout the CIS, even if it has denied Russian soldiers the right to wear the UN's blue helmets in actions Russia unilaterally defines as "peacekeeping operations." All the Central Asian states are also members of the Organization for Security and Cooperation in Europe (OSCE), but none is an active participant in that organization.

The only real possibility for Central Asia to counterbalance Russian or CIS influence lies with more regionally based organizations. Should the Economic Cooperation Organization (ECO) acquire more powers, it could serve such a role for the Central Asian states. However, the strengthening of this organization seems unlikely, given the present climate of mutual suspicion between Turkey and Iran. Another mitigating factor is the relatively poor economic prospects all of the original ECO members presently face.

Perhaps Central Asia's most realistic hope in this regard lies in a strong regional confederation within Central Asia itself. For many reasons, the prospect of establishing such an organization seems relatively remote. The framework of a Central Asian regional organization does currently exist, and the five heads of state do gather several times a year for discussions. In addition, the economic union of Kazakhstan, Uzbekistan, and Kyrgyzstan draws the presidents of the three countries together in working sessions on an even more periodic basis.

However, it is quite clear that no Central Asian unity will develop if Russia works to impede it. As has been mentioned, Nursultan Nazarbaev and Islam Karimov have a highly competitive working relationship, a rivalry that Russia's leaders seem adept in manipulating.

More troubling is the question of Turkmenistan, the one country not examined in depth in this volume. One reason for this is the veil that shrouds the political life and economic relations of the country for all but those with close ties to the country's president, Saparmurad Niyazov. While relations among Turkmenistan's political elite are said to be dominated by interclan rivalries, it has been difficult for outsiders to predict political shake-ups in advance, though hard to miss them afterwards. For example, independent Turkmenistan's first foreign minister, Avdy Kuliev, is now living in political exile in Moscow, reportedly fearing for his life.

Certainly it is true that President Niyazov has little interest in tolerating any form of political opposition. Nor is Niyazov, who now prefers the name Saparmurad Turkmenbashi (or Saparmurad, the Head of the Turkmen), comfortable accepting the role of an equal among his fellow Central Asian rulers. Turkmenistan has refused to join any Central Asian economic union, although Niyazov seems to be moving toward accepting a form of observer status for himself. Niyazov has also been reluctant to endorse the strengthening of economic ties within the CIS, even though Russia favors such a policy. In spite of this apparent independence, bilateral economic relations between Russia and Turkmenistan remain relatively good. As Turkmenistan's economy has deteriorated, ties between the two states have grown closer still. A series of agreements signed in April 1995 provided for the exchange of Turkmenistan's cotton for Russia's liquid gas, rolled metal, and grain; Turkmenistan also agreed to Russian participation in the construction of various gas pipeline projects.

More importantly, security relations between these two states were initially the closest in the region and, hence, originally served as Russia's model for the rest of Central Asia. At the time of independence, there was a considerable Soviet military presence in Turkmenistan, with Russia's 36th Army performing border guard duties. There were also a number of forward strategic air bases, as might be expected in the Soviet republic closest to the Middle East and Persian Gulf regions. Originally, President Niyazov wanted to convert this military legacy into a joint Turkmenistani-Russian force under combined command. However, Marshal Pavel Grachev, Russia's defense minister, made clear in a May 1992 visit that such an army could only be under sole Russian command. It was then agreed that the air bases would come under Russian command. Turkmenistan was also the first state in the region to request that its borders be guarded jointly by its army and Russian border troops. This arrangement gave Russia much desired de facto control of the Turkmen-Iranian border. With Turkmenistan's "invitation" in hand, Marshal Grachev then went to Kazakhstan and Kyrgyzstan and eventually forced both states to accept a similar arrangement for their borders with China. By early 1995, Russia began to demand that Turkmenistan turn over full control of its border to Russian authorities, and Turkmenistan appears prepared to accede to this request.

Turkmenistan is also the only Central Asian state that has unconditionally agreed to honor Russia's demand that its ethnic Russians be granted rights of dual citizenship. Since enlisting Turkmenistan's endorsement, Russia has used this agreement to press the other Central Asian states for similar concessions. To date, only the Kyrgyz have shown any willingness to bend on this volatile issue, and then only tentatively.

Turkmenistan has always been something of an anomaly in Central Asia. While the country can boast of its vast natural resource wealth, its population's standard of living, measured in terms of wages and access to health care and other social services, ranked Turkmenistan as perhaps the poorest of the Soviet republics, probably because most of its oil and gas was being marshaled as part of the USSR's reserves for the next century. The republic was probably also the most prone to opposing Moscow's policies during the Soviet period.[2] The Turkmen were always adamant in their refusal to adopt Soviet ways, particularly on issues concerning the observation of traditional customs, especially those surrounding Islam. However, Turkmen resistance never transformed into pro-independence or pro-democracy movements.

Niyazov was an early Gorbachev appointee who managed to avoid introducing *perestroika* and *glasnost* into his large but sparsely populated republic. If anything, Niyazov used the Gorbachev years to tighten his control on political power, making concessions only in the one area that seems to matter to the Turkmens—the observance of Islam.

While Turkmenistan remains a secular state, Niyazov has fully legalized religious observation and has permitted the flourishing of religious schools throughout the country. The huge statue of "Hajji Turkmenbashi" that has replaced the statue of Lenin in downtown Ashgebat leaves little ambiguity about Niyazov's stand on religion's role in the state. Any remaining doubt is dispelled by the erection of an enormous new mosque in the village of Niyazov's birth (which the Turkmen president has modestly permitted to be renamed in his honor).

Niyazov's political style has nearly turned Turkmenistan into a caricature of one-man rule in a newly independent state. Adulation of Niyazov has become an art form in a cult of personality that may even outdo Stalin's. Even Stalin never put his own likeness on the ruble, while Saparmurad Turkmenbashi's visage is on every manat bill, regardless of denomination. Not only has Niyazov's name been given to scores of streets, towns, and institutions, but it was recently announced that a new division of Turkmenistan's state historical society would be devoted to research on Niyazov's ancestors. The state has even introduced a new and peculiar form of censorship, limiting the number of photos of

Niyazov that may be printed, since most of the country's presses are not of high enough quality to do justice to Turkmenbashi's face.

To be fair, a considerable part of the adulation for the Turkmenbashi may be genuine, for Niyazov has introduced some revolutionary changes in this previously poverty-stricken republic. Alone among all the former Soviet republics, Turkmenistan has grown quite wealthy since independence. While the republic's officials have not always managed this wealth to the nation's best advantage, state treasuries have profited handsomely from the sale of development rights for its oil and, particularly, natural gas deposits. Yet much of this money has been put to questionable use; for example, a string of small five-star hotels has been erected outside of Ashgebat, each controlled by a different ministry or state office.

Turkmenistan ranks as the fourth-largest producer of natural gas, after Russia, the United States, and Canada. Unlike the three leaders, Turkmenistan has a population of less than four million, upon whom Niyazov has been happy to shower the benefits of economic development. Income from sales of natural gas should bring the country $5.5 billion annually (or about $1,500 per person).[3] Turkmenistan's revenues are intended (as of 1994) to provide gas, water, and electricity to its citizens free of charge. As of 1996, Turkmen citizens will not only receive two months of paid vacation each year during the hottest summer months, but will also receive bread without charge.[4]

Yet many of these goals are amounting to little more than wishful thinking, as Turkmenistan has found it quite difficult to collect payment for its gas from CIS partners, either in the hard currency its contracts stipulate, or even in the form of barter. By early 1995, for example, Ukraine owed Turkmenistan more than $1 billion. The delay in making such a large payment, compounded by the instability of the manat, has created rising inflation and a shortage of goods in the country. The introduction of the manat in November 1993 has proven far more destabilizing than any Turkmenistani official anticipated. Without the backing of any international financial organization, the manat's street value a year later was only about a hundredth of its official exchange value. As a result, real commerce in Turkmenistan is conducted almost entirely in rubles or dollars; the general population's access to all but the most basic commodities is declining. The situation may begin to reverse itself somewhat by late 1995, as Turkmenistan finally reached a comprehensive agreement with Ukraine in March 1995, in which part of Ukraine's debt to Turkmenistan was converted to long-term loans in a barter arrangement that also involves improved Turkmenistani access to a new oil terminal in Odessa.

Russia's position in these developments is a curious one. Unlike what it has done in Kazakhstan and Azerbaijan, the Russian government has been slow to demand a share of Turkmenistan's oil. Turkmenistan is also not being pressured to ship its oil and gas exclusively through Russia; plans for a pipeline through Iran are going on undisturbed. Russia also seems unperturbed by Japanese proposals to build a thirty-seven-hundred-mile natural gas pipeline from Turkmenistan through Central Asia and China to a terminal complex on China's east coast. Russia could easily exert pressure to stop any of these plans if it wanted to, since most of Turkmenistan's leading economic officials, including almost all of the second- and third-tier officials in the energy sector, are Russians. Indeed, if the frequency of rumors is any measure of their accuracy, then the development of Turkmenistan's natural gas and oil industries has proceeded from the outset with at least some under-the-table involvement of old USSR Ministry of Oil and Gas personnel.

Significantly, the protection afforded the Turkmen through these connections to the old Soviet energy ministries appears to have real limits. As already noted, Turkmenistan has generally been left on its own to collect debts for gas it has already shipped. Moreover, after Turkmenistan refused to join the new ruble zone announced in September 1993, trade with Russia, its largest partner, has been substantially disrupted. Trade with other Central Asian states has also been disrupted, but Turkmenistan still refuses to enter a Central Asian currency or trade union despite the fact that the failure of the manat can only work to the benefit of Russia, since the introduction of centralized banking would make Moscow the clearinghouse for Ashgebat's hard currency reserves.

The weakness of the manat, combined with Turkmenistan's inability to collect payment for its natural gas sales, finally led President Niyazov to reevaluate Turkmenistan's formal relations with Russia. Faced with the choice of closer integration with other Central Asian states or reestablishing intimate ties with Moscow, President Niyazov chose the latter—much to the chagrin of his Central Asian colleagues. In May 1995, Turkmenistan and Russia signed a series of bilateral agreements calling for strengthened economic and security relations, including joint development of Turkmenistan's energy resources.

Turkmenistan's close ties with Iran, which to some degree disturb the equilibrium of relations within the region, also do not seem to cause the

Russians much concern. Turkmenistan is the only Central Asian country that shares a border with Iran; there are also significant cultural and tribal connections between the peoples on either side of the border. Indeed, there are about 1.2 million Turkmen who live on the Iranian side of the border, which is especially significant given that the number of Turkmen in Turkmenistan is only about 4 million. Many of these Turkmen are Sunnis, but there is a pro-Khomeini Shi'ia clergy among them in Iran. However, as it is elsewhere, Iran's primary interest in Turkmenistan appears to be commercial. Iran has made major investments in Turkmenistan's oil and gas development, in its petroleum transport infrastructure, in its road and railroad construction, and in improving its cotton industry. Iran has also made a major commitment to build a modern air transport facility in Ashgebat, and has assisted with improvements in communications facilities. Iranians and Turkmen are cooperating on environmental projects as well, most notably a joint investigation of the rising water level in the Caspian; Iran has also been responsive to Turkmen concerns about the placement of a proposed nuclear reactor near the Turkmen border. As a result of all these initiatives, the border between the two nations has essentially been thrown open to citizens of both countries; only an internal passport is required for crossing.

From the Iranian point of view, access to Turkmenistan will open up the rest of Central Asia to Teheran. With the completion of the Beijing-Teheran rail link in 1995, a new shipping route to Europe and the Middle East will be open. The Iranians are using the Turkmen pipeline accord to pressure Kazakhstan to agree to use this route as well. Much to the displeasure of the United States, Turkmenistan's special relationship with Iran is contributing to Teheran's increased visibility throughout the region. President Rafsanjani's autumn 1993 tour of the region seems by all accounts to have been a successful one, which further strengthened the already strong Iranian belief that they have a historic mission to fulfill in the region. For the Iranians, history is a relative concept, and they expect to be in Central Asia long after American interest in the region subsides.

U.S. pressure on the Central Asians not to do business with Iran has the capacity to backfire. What Iran apparently inspires among Central Asians is respect for that country's independence and its willingness to attempt to develop and control its own resources—as well as its distinct national culture—in spite of tremendous pressure from international agencies and Western governments to conform to their dictates. It is not impossible that Iran may ultimately provide a model for some of the Central Asian states to emulate. If it does, it will have less to do with Islamic issues than with the Central Asian nations' attempts to participate in the world community on terms that preclude their continued humiliation and impoverishment.

Turkmenistan's special friendship with Iran may well be one that Moscow sees as ultimately redounding to Russia's benefit as well, since independent Turkmenistan, which receives virtually no U.S. assistance, is free to act as Russia's surrogate and set up bilateral relations with Teheran. While such an overture might prove embarrassing to Russia if done directly, diplomats in Moscow are fully skilled at the use of surrogates, and they do not consider the Iranian government to be an "outlaw" regime. Rather, they maintain full trade relations with Teheran and have been regularly selling the Iranians advanced military equipment and nuclear technology.

Niyazov's policies on Afghanistan have left him out of step with his fellow Central Asian leaders. Turkmenistan has made a real effort to maintain good relations with Afghanistan, since having Afghanistan as a neighbor makes the Turkmen leader nervous. Niyazov has developed a close personal relationship with the local "warlord" who rules the neighboring Herat region, and Turkmenistan has agreed to cooperate in the construction of a rail spur from Chardzhou to Kerki, which will free Turkmenistan from having to move freight from the south through Uzbekistan.

From the standpoint of Central Asian unity, however, Turkmenistan's greatest apostasy is the refusal to join the CIS peacemaking force deployed in Tajikistan and on the Tajik-Afghan border. Declaring a policy of "positive neutrality," Niyazov has deemed the Tajik war to be an "internal affair." For Niyazov, regional solidarity matters less than the prospect of raising his neighbor's wrath.

Although Turkmenistan has a model army on paper, the reality is that it is still fully dependent upon Russia for its defense, and will continue to be for the foreseeable future. In 1995, Yeltsin announced that Russia would not complete the final ratification of the 1992 agreement creating a joint Russian-Turkmenistani force. Turkmenistan's army is little more than a renamed Russian 36th Army; its commander, Lt. Gen. Kormiltsev, resigned to become head of Turkmenistan's army in September 1992, and fourteen thousand of his troops were commissioned along with him. However, these Russian officers have been increasingly unhappy in their new service. Kormiltsev himself resigned as head of the army in April 1993, reportedly to take a new position in Moscow. Unconfirmed rumors, however, suggest that the general resigned because 180 of his officers had been arrested by Turkmenistani security forces on charges of selling weapons and other matériel.

Turkmenistan's place in Central Asia highlights the chimera of greater regional cooperation. Certainly, Niyazov's determination to carve out his own path for Turkmenistan's economic and foreign policies has made the prospect of regional cooperation less likely. So too has the ferocity and duration of Tajikistan's civil war. None of the region's leaders really believes the situation in Tajikistan to be unique; each requires only a few moments of contemplation to see elements of Tajikistan's society mirrored in parts of his own. The horror of that war seems only to confirm what all of these men were taught as students in Soviet schools: Left alone in their traditional societies, the Central Asians will be violent by nature.

The Central Asians don't really trust one another; more importantly, they don't fully trust themselves. These states are all new, and all still fragile. None is capable of withstanding outside aggression without outside support, and for the moment at least the only realistic source of such support remains Russia.

THE INSTABILITY AHEAD

Current events in Central Asia are difficult enough for U.S. analysts and policymakers to comprehend, let alone to attempt the far more difficult task of prediction. Central Asia, as is the case with every other part of the former Soviet Union, is still in a state of flux. Mere weeks before the collapse of the USSR, world leaders and their advisers scoffed at the idea that the republics of Soviet Central Asia would soon become internationally recognized independent states. Today it is considered equally unimaginable that current borders—or entire states—in Central Asia or elsewhere in the former Soviet Union could be changed.

In fact, this second conviction could prove as false as the first, and perhaps just as rapidly. If events since 1989 teach us anything about the pace of change, then U.S. policymakers should probably prepare to witness a state-building process in Central Asia (and elsewhere in the former Soviet Union) that will more closely resemble a roller-coaster ride than a smooth, steady incline.

The collapse of the USSR has obscured the fact that the changes yet to come in Central Asia are part of development crises these societies were already facing before the Soviet Union fell apart. These crises, which began to appear in declining standards of living and growing unemployment, were undoubtedly compounded by the suddenness of the USSR's collapse, even though the independence that Central Asia so unexpectedly obtained may provide solutions to these crises. What must be kept firmly in mind now is that declarations of independence and international recognition provide only a de jure basis for statehood; de facto statehood, if it develops at all, does so only with the passage of time.

For nearly two hundred years the political and economic future of Central Asia has been shaped by events and decisions made outside the region; such a historical pattern will not change overnight. Without question, independence has broadened the range of decision-making options available to Central Asia's leaders, but it has not entirely transformed them from dependent political actors into adventurous leaders of independent states.

The Central Asian states are at the first stage of their transition to becoming responsible, independent members of the world community, as indeed Russia is itself. The major feature of this period is reintegration of the various constituent parts of the former USSR in a way that acknowledges Russia's hegemony while preserving the independence of the other new states. However, none of the new states, Russia included, has figured out just how tight it wants this reintegration to be, or whether such a reintegration should be a permanent one.

How long this first period of transition will last is difficult to say. Shaped by their Soviet careers, the leaders of Central Asia still instinctively think in five-year periods, but the status quo of the moment may change drastically before a half-decade passes. Post-Soviet reintegration is a tentative process that can be destabilized easily by two factors: the need of the Soviet-era leaders who now head these states to gain enough economic autonomy to preserve statehood, and the mutability of Russia's interest in continuing its self-proclaimed role of regional hegemon. Regarding economic issues, the enormous difficulties of elaborating stable institutional structures for this reintegration have been exemplified by the fight over the ruble and by how the new states attempt to balance their need to maintain the networks and volume of Soviet interrepublican trade and the need to protect their newly acquired sovereignty.

Russia's desire to remain a hegemon is brought home to the new states' leaders every day, if only by turning on the CIS-wide broadcast of Ostankino Television's evening news and its stories of how difficult life is for the Russians "stranded" in the other former Soviet republics.

The situation in all of the new states, but especially in Central Asia, is intrinsically unstable. Russia is unlikely to view the fate of the region's large Russian population with detachment, and the current regimes in Central Asia will almost certainly be forced to make political compromises that jeopardize their legitimacy in the view of their countries' nationalists. At the same time, though, Russia is also likely to remain too closely tied to Central Asia's current oligarchs, who will inevitably have to leave the political scene one way or another to make room for a new generation of elites who will have received their political education almost entirely in their own country.

The process of elite succession in Central Asia could very well be destabilizing; but if we have failed to learn from other experiences with decolonization that such a succession process is inevitable, then we will only serve to compound the problems associated with a generational change of leadership. The Russians and the other current oligarchs alike share an understandable tendency to both overstate threats to these current regimes and overestimate the advantages of stability over democracy.

Inevitably the current period of transition will come to an end, just as a new post-Soviet generation comes to power. When that happens, the Central Asian states—which may not necessarily be the current five—will then begin a new phase in the creation of national identities, and may begin to elaborate a new regional identity as well. It is uncertain how quickly this will occur, particularly since both Moscow and the current Central Asian elites, all former members of the Soviet *nomenklatura*, will try to stave off this second period of transition as long as possible. This has been amply demonstrated by the extension of presidential terms to 2001 in Uzbekistan and Kazakhstan, and the debate on this issue in Kyrgyzstan as well. At the same time, however, it is certain that exercises in returning the old guard to power after new elites have attempted to take control—the first examples of which were the ousters of both the Iskandarov coalition government in Tajikistan and the National Front government in Azerbaijan—are going to become even costlier, bloodier, and harder to achieve in the future as opposition groups and alternative elites become more politically seasoned. Nor should it be forgotten that even these first leadership "successes" were purchased at shockingly high costs.

Whatever the pace, though, it seems certain that by the beginning of the new century, Central Asian societies will have advanced to this second stage, as all of the region's current rulers will most likely have left, or be preparing to leave, the political scene. If it is sufficiently secure in its economic realm, then Russia will continue to try to direct this second stage of the transition as well. This is particularly true in situations like Kazakhstan's, where Russia feels its own national interest is potentially challenged. Given Kazakhstan's enormous common border and large Russian population, it is very difficult to imagine Russia tolerating Nazarbaev's succession by a Kazakh nationalist regime. Should such a change seem even remotely likely, Moscow is almost certain to support and encourage Russian separatists in Kazakhstan's northern regions.

Russia is by no means alone in devising such worse-case scenarios. Should Kazakhstan begin to split up, then Uzbekistan may also lay claim to part or all of Kazakhstan's three southern oblasts. The Uzbeks could also choose to move into southern Kyrgyzstan (Osh oblast), which is nearly half Uzbek, especially if Kyrgyzstan's plummeting economy does not improve. Uzbekistan could also lay claim to the western part of Turkmenistan, which was once the Khivan outlands.

Transition in the more autocratic states will be a more difficult process. Whether Turkmenistan will survive Niyazov remains to be seen, for Niyazov is president of not so much a nation as a tribal confederation; even the new state flag reproduces the symbols of the five main clans. Niyazov has been able to succeed as president in large part because he portrays himself as "non-tribal"; although nominally of the Tekke clan, Niyazov is an orphan, and grew up in Soviet institutions. His inability to name his "seven fathers," a custom by which Turkic nomads establish social position, is a significant weakness in this tradition-bound society, as is his failure to produce a son of his own. (Curiously enough for this patrilineal part of the world, only Kyrgyzstan's Akaev is the father of sons.) Thus there will quite likely be some form of interclan struggle in Turkmenistan's elite succession.

The second phase of Uzbekistan's transition could also take the form of a particularly violent succession. Although for now Karimov seems to have stifled the major sources of opposition within the country, he too is heirless, both genealogically and politically. Thus it is inevitable that

Uzbekistan's dominant political groups, most of which are regionally based, will reassert themselves in some form of active competition. If one group easily establishes dominance, the succession could be an orderly one. If this does not occur, Uzbekistan could also find itself transformed into a patchwork of warring fiefdoms.

FEAR OF THE FUTURE

While it is certainly true that none of these doomsday scenarios may necessarily come about, the fear of these possible futures makes the Central Asians, despite their anger over past colonial abuses, eager to have Russia remain in the region as the guarantor of regional security. While history has provided Russia's leaders with a rough guide for their involvement in the region, it seems inevitable that as the Russian regime becomes more routinized it will begin to further distinguish between primary and secondary security interests in Central Asia.

Enthusiasm for military engagement has a tendency to evaporate over time, especially in situations that have no clear objectives and that require both a long-term presence and ongoing expenditures. The Soviet military eventually agreed to pull out of Afghanistan, which was a much greater, direct security interest to the USSR than Tajikistan is to Russia. It seems unlikely that five years hence, Russia will continue to be willing to serve as the primary guarantor of security in Tajikistan, just as it would seem increasingly unlikely during that same period that Russia would be willing to serve the same role in Uzbekistan should the Karimov regime find itself unable to contain domestic turmoil. While unforeseen events abroad and new political exigencies at home may alter Russia's calculus of interests in this part of the "near abroad," Russia's leaders will continue to rely on historical precedent for differentiating between primary and secondary security interests in the region. Since imperial times, Russia has distinguished "the Steppe" of the north from Central Asia further south. Thus it is likely to pursue a different policy in Kazakhstan than in the rest of the region.

At the same time, politics in Tajikistan, Turkmenistan, and Uzbekistan are likely to evolve in a very different way than they will in Kazakhstan and, perhaps, Kyrgyzstan. Like Ukraine, Kazakhstan must either develop its statehood in a way that is acceptable to Russia or expect to be crushed, either by direct or indirect means. Russia does not appear to have this same level of interest for any of the other Central Asian states;

so, as time goes on and as more Russians continue to emigrate from the area, Russia's direct interest in most of the Central Asian states will likely continue to wane.

For all of recorded history, save the last hundred years, those who live south of the Syr Darya River—in what is today southern Kyrgyzstan, southern Kazakhstan, Uzbekistan, Tajikistan, and Turkmenistan—have been integrated into, or at least oriented toward, the countries of the Near East and South Asia. This has been a Muslim region for a millennium, and it is the point of intersection between Turkic and Persian cultures. It has also served as the corridor joining China with the Middle East.

As the Central Asian states begin fully to assume their new statehood, such ancient connections are assuming a new importance. Li Peng's April 1994 trek through Central Asia, the first trip the Chinese leader had made abroad in more than a year, is a vivid reminder of these historical connections.

The current period of reintegration with the other Soviet successor states reaffirms that forty years of tsarist colonization and seventy years of Soviet rule have left imprints that cannot be erased overnight. Even so, the Russian presence on Central Asia's borders is almost certain to diminish over time.

Already, the economic linkages among the Central Asian states and Russia are undergoing a certain transformation; in five years' time, even greater change seems assured. Economically irrational linkages, such as the current practice of Kazakhstan and Russia refining each other's oil exports, or Tajikistan processing Azerbaijan's plutonium while Russia processes Tajikistan's plutonium, are rapidly disintegrating. Others, such as the practice of air-freighting Arctic fish to Kazakhstan for processing in factories left idle by the evaporation of the Aral Sea, are already history.

To be sure, Russia is the major trade partner of all the Central Asian states, and it is likely to remain so for some time. To suddenly sever these ties would be disastrous for all concerned. Allowing these ties to atrophy slowly will not endanger either Russia or the Central Asian states, or at least those among them that are economically viable. For now, Uzbekistan's economy depends upon Russia to buy cotton and sell grain. Ten years from now, however, Uzbekistan's plans to diversify its economy may be a success, ending its need for preferential trade with Russia to meet its food and energy needs. By the same token, a decade may also give Russia's industrial sector plenty of time to compensate for the loss of Uzbekistan's cotton.

Energy and precious metals are of much greater concern to Russia, which is not eager to have Kazakhstan, Turkmenistan, or Azerbaijan flood the world market with oil any more than it wants Uzbekistan or Kyrgyzstan to destabilize the world gold market by a rapid sell-off of its gold reserves. The latter possibility is relatively remote, while in the case of oil, Russia's continuing role as provider of Central Asia's major transportation links gives Moscow considerable influence over the development of Central Asia's energy resources.

As development plans begin to be realized, and Russia has secured its vital interests, the necessary transport links are likely to be put on a contractual basis. The tendency everywhere is to try to develop joint ventures with a number of countries simultaneously. This partially explains why the Central Asian states are eager to explore new transport routes toward China, Iran, and Pakistan. At the same time, none of these routes is likely to be selected for development at the exclusion of all others. Central Asia's exploration of new trade and transportation links always raises fears of Iranian domination of the area, or of some kind of Turkish-Iranian struggle for influence in the region. If the Central Asian leaders prove able to do so, the roles played by Turkey, Iran, Russia, and China in the region will all be varied but restricted. Central Asians are not about to trade one colonial power for another, and they see Turkish and Persian paternalism as uncomfortably reminiscent of Russian-dominated Soviet ideology. Central Asia's leaders also view Russia and China with distrust, in the way that new states intuitively fear great powers.

Yet for now, as Tajikistan's civil war clearly illustrates, the threats to stability in Central Asia are likely to come from within. Foreign actors will become involved only when final defeat for one side or another seems imminent, as occurred in Tajikistan when the opposition fled to Afghanistan to avoid arrest or worse.

No matter how many of these "mujahideen" are now receiving guerrilla training in Afghanistan, Russia remains the "foreign" actor that is most likely to intervene in Central Asia. Even so, it is unlikely that Russia would decide in favor of a heavy military presence to shore up pro-Moscow regimes in Central Asia, especially if such a commitment were for an extended period of time. Only in Kazakhstan is there any real possibility of Russian military intervention, and only in the areas of Russian settlement, which are both contiguous to Russia and unique to Central Asia for being majority Russian.

Had Uzbekistan's Karimov faltered two years ago, Russia might have intervened to prop him up. However, Karimov seems to be in no immediate danger, just as the country's Russian population faces no particular danger while he is in power. The longer Karimov is in charge, the more likely it becomes that Russia would solve a threat to the country's Russian community through evacuation rather than invasion.

Russian expansionism—Kazakhstan excepted—is not a very likely prospect in the region. Uzbek expansionism, however, could well become a reality by the end of the decade, particularly if Tashkent's rulers perceive the existence of power vacuums across their borders. The potential for such expansion exists whether or not an Islamic regime comes to power in Uzbekistan. Historically, whoever controls the lands between the Amu Darya and Syr Darya also dominates Central Asia; it is precisely this territory that now lies largely under Uzbek control.

Whoever rules Uzbekistan will have a natural inclination to fortify the country's position in the region, particularly if neighboring states are crumbling. This may happen in the name of Islam, or of a greater Uzbekistan, or of Central Asian unity. The assumption should not be made that a non-Islamic regime, should one come to power in Uzbekistan, would be less aggressive than a hypothetical Islamic regime. Even the republic's democrats, should they come to power, cannot be counted on to renounce expansionism; just like Russian democrats, who look at Ukraine every bit as possessively as do Russian autocrats, Uzbekistan's democrats and autocrats alike are subject to the same historical motives.

The risk to the United States will come only if it employs a zero-sum definition of its interests in the region, requiring the victory of one side or the defeat of the other. The most effective way it can influence events in the region is through a strong, continuous economic presence. However, American firms require stable governments before they will consider doing business in their countries, and none of the current regimes in Central Asia is likely to prove sufficiently stable in the long run. All the current regimes represent the pro-Soviet past more than they do a post-Soviet future; as such, they all face a high likelihood of being pushed aside.

Short-term trends in Central Asia will favor the current, Sovietized elites, who are secularists to be sure, but long-term developments will eventually make them superfluous. The process of elite transformation may or may not be orderly, but at its end—within a decade at most— Central Asia will be dominated by leaders who conduct business in their native languages, practice their traditional religion, and seek primarily to aid their citizens rather than to appease an outside power. Ten years from now, the current borders that define the Central Asian states may have undergone changes; and some of the current Central Asian states may not even exist. In ten years' time, Russia could still be the regional hegemon, but if so, it will be struggling hard to preserve its influence. As their familiarity with independence grows, the Central Asian states will become less willing to be Russian client states, just as Russia will become more aware of the unaffordable costs of trying to control clients that are so remote, culturally and geographically. In ten years' time, the Central Asian states, in whatever configuration they assume, will still be working to escape from Russia's influence and beginning to define themselves just beyond the edge of Russia's shadow.

There are only a few points in this relationship between Moscow and the new states where outside actors, especially the United States, might exert some influence. Obviously, U.S. assistance can help these states develop their economies in ways that will make them less dependent on Russia. Such assistance can also take the form of political consulting (i.e., assisting local political elites in their efforts to widen their power bases so that they are better prepared for the political shocks that lie ahead). The United States can also apply pressure on Russia to be even-handed in its treatment of these new and fragile states. Beyond this, the United States can do little more than watch from the sidelines and hope that the consequences of change in this region do not spread beyond their present confines and destabilize a much broader international setting.

8

PEACEFUL BRIDGES
TO THE FUTURE?

entral Asia's transition to independence has been far more peaceful than expected, especially given the outbursts of violence in the region during 1989 and 1990. The course of this transition makes it possible to hope that the process of state-building in Central Asia will proceed as smoothly as did the movement toward independence among all the Central Asian states, save Tajikistan.

Yet the prospect remains that the process of state-building in this region will not be a smooth one. Tajikistan remains a fractured nation, and the continued fighting in the republic continues to pose risks for neighboring states, as do waves of refugees fleeing the civil war there. Gun-runners and drug-traders have filtered into Kyrgyzstan's Osh oblast, along with the Tajik and Kyrgyz refugees who have been displaced by fighting just over the Tajik border. This contributes to the growing political separation of northern and southern Kyrgyzstan, a division that is further exacerbated by the political fractures in the increasingly impoverished country.

Political stability in Uzbekistan is also at risk. Karimov is a gambler who has staked his political future on being able to neutralize and disarm political Islam in Tajikistan. Tajikistan's prolonged civil war is inevitably destabilizing for Uzbekistan, if only because of the 1.2 million Uzbeks in Tajikistan who might be tempted to return "home" in the wake of continued fighting there. Uzbekistan must also treat with care the roughly one million Tajiks within its borders. However, as much as Uzbekistan's president wants peace in his neighboring nation, he does not want to achieve it at the cost of politically empowering Tajikistan's Islamic opposition, because of their close ties to Uzbekistan's own religious opposition. A partial solution, the physical eradication of the most volatile elements among Tajikistan's Islamic population, appears to have been one goal of Uzbekistan's policy on Afghanistan. Karimov simply shifted his priorities: from supporting Afghanistan's General Dostam to carrying out aerial bombardment of Tajik refugee camps across the Afghan border.[1]

Of course, such "solutions" become even more destabilizing to Uzbekistan if the "wrong people" come to power in Tajikistan. It is difficult to know approximately where the political breaking point lies in Uzbekistan. If history is any guide, strongman regimes are usually overthrown in uprisings led by subjects who have grown too angry and too hungry to care about the consequences of their actions. A smooth transfer of power seems possible, though not guaranteed, if a serious threat to Karimov were to emerge from within Uzbekistan's current elite. However, if such a threat were to come from outside, such as an Islamic opposition, then a violent struggle for power in Uzbekistan would be virtually inevitable; such a struggle could also draw in Russia, which has an interest in supporting the current power-holders.

There is no shortage of struggles among factions of the Kazakh community, but the most likely agent of political instability in Kazakhstan remains Russia. Interethnic rivalries in the country are far more bitter than the divisions within Kazakhstan's main ethnic groups. Kazakhstan's Cossacks have very close ties to their fellow Cossacks across the Russian border, even serving in the Russian Cossack militias. Kazakhstan's Russian nationalist groups look to support from Russia, whose policy for the "near abroad" roughly corresponds to the main points in their own political agendas. Kazakhstan's responses to the demands of its Russian citizens have been negative on the whole, which only further increases the possibility that Russia may resort to pressure, either overt or covert, to help Kazakhstan's Russians get their way.

Russia is also key to Turkmenistan's stability, and Niyazov explicitly recognizes the hegemonic nature of the Russian-Turkmenistani relationship. If an obstacle were placed in the way of Turkmenistan's oil and gas exports, Niyazov would become another of history's short-lived dictators. As various leaders of Azerbaijan have now learned, at considerable cost to their state, Russia retains a close interest in the sale of all energy resources within the territory of the former Soviet Union, and has considerable means by which to ensure that its wishes are taken into account.

Iran has fewer levers by which to control Turkmenistan, but even so, Turkmenistan's stability could be disrupted by shifts in Iranian policy. As we have seen, Iran has also defined a role for itself in Tajikistan, where Teheran could choose to play the role of either spoiler or savior of the country.

China is another potential source of destabilization in Central Asia, particularly in Kyrgyzstan and Kazakhstan. Beijing may be counted on to intervene in either state if events seem likely to upset China's policies for dealing with its own large populations of Kazakhs, Kyrgyz, and Uighurs.

Disputes between the Central Asian states themselves, or between Kazakhstan and Russia, are another source of possible conflict. Although Yeltsin and Nazarbaev agreed in 1991 to accept as final the existing border between their countries, recurring public debates suggest that the issue is far from resolved. What price Moscow might be willing to pay in order to change the border in its favor is unclear, just as it is unclear what advantage Russia would derive from such a change.

Should the Russian-Kazakh border be changed, there would be immediate pressure to change a number of other borders in the region, particularly from Uzbekistan, which would see its interests served by expanding its borders in almost all directions.

For the moment, these border issues are in abeyance precisely because they are seen as so volatile. None of the Central Asian leaders trusts any of the others, or indeed themselves, to place the interests of regional security above the national interest. In addition to distrusting one another, Central Asia's leaders also do not trust Russia, although all accept the inevitability of Russia continuing to act as a regional hegemon. After its military operations in Chechnya, there can be little doubt of the callousness with which Russia will pursue its aims. This mistrust of Russia in particular has pushed Central Asia's leaders to sponsor or support the many initiatives to create new regional organizations, including periodic attempts to restore vitality and legitimacy to the Commonwealth of Independent States.

The fear of Russia and of wider instability is also the principal reason the Central Asian states have joined virtually every international body that offers them membership. Whether any of these international organizations would be prepared to intervene in a Central Asian political crisis—or indeed whether any of them could—is uncertain. Although international agencies might be mobilized to deal with absolute disaster once it arrives, it is far less clear whether international agencies would, or could, intervene earlier, while most of the incipient crises outlined above are still in their early stages. There are a number of international actors and organizations already or potentially active in Central Asia that might serve to mitigate a crisis by early intervention, but it is difficult to know which of these might see its mandate requiring a more direct involvement in these countries.

Russia Learns from Tajikistan

The best guide to predicting how states and other actors in Central Asia might react to increasing instability is the response to the continuing civil war in Tajikistan. Not only is this the first intractable conflict in the region, but it also has served to educate most of the actors about the various dimensions of any future Central Asian conflict, thus shaping their possible future responses.

Russian involvement in Tajikistan has produced conflicting reactions among the Russian public and Russian policymakers. Its length, cost, and complexity, compounded by its very remoteness, have revived memories of Russia's endless and costly involvement in Afghanistan. Russian military planners in particular remember how little public support exists in Russia for shedding Russian blood in attempts to settle disputes between Muslims. Moreover, divided public opinion on the use of troops in Chechnya is likely to make Russian officials cautious in considering any subsequent deployments of troops in combat. At the same time, however, the media's regular display of dead or wounded Russians in Tajikistan created a strong current of sentiment in the country for the deployment of Russian troops in the region. In the new, post-Soviet era of popular empowerment, Russians also feel the right to demand even more of their politicians, such as the development of a foreign policy that would protect other Russians who live in the "near abroad" against the sort of danger Russians living in Tajikistan endured.

Russian public opinion, though, only reaffirmed the inclinations of Russia's foreign policy establishment. By mid-1993, Foreign Minister Andrei Kozyrev and his staff had articulated a foreign policy doctrine that emphasized the special relationship between Russia and the other former Soviet republics, explicitly stating Russia's claim of responsibility to protect ethnic Russians wherever they live. Russian defense doctrine was evolving along similar lines. In 1993, as battles along the Tajik-Afghan border became more frequent and more serious, Russian military strategists became more convinced in the correctness of their predisposition to see Russia's security zone extending as far as the borders of the former USSR; Russian policymakers' commitment to this doctrine has only hardened over time.

To Russia's national security officials, it is simple logic that governs these newly articulated foreign policy doctrines. Given the absence of fortified borders within the CIS, as well as the universally weak development of new national armies, Russian security could indeed be put at risk by unrestricted traffic across any of the USSR's old internal and external borders. If those borders remain undefended against an invader, Russia would have only the age-old defense of its enormous size on which to rely. Yet, vast stretches of geography pose little resistance to increasingly sophisticated weapons systems, which is undoubtedly what pushed the Russian leaders to strong-arm the other CIS governments in 1994 into allowing Russian troops once again to patrol their "external" international borders. When Azerbaijan balked at Russia's "request," Russia responded by closing its border with Azerbaijan, effectively stranding the former Soviet republic.

Not satisfied with establishing security rights over the old Soviet borders, Russia's leaders have also used the absence of defensible borders within the CIS as justification for their self-declared right to intervene in intra- and interstate conflicts that they define as posing a risk to Russian security. Such a definition is extremely broad, extending well beyond the basic goal of protecting ethnic Russians in the "near abroad." Russia's reluctance to take sides in the Tajik civil war until summer 1992, when the participation of Islamic elements in the Iskandarov government became obvious, makes it clear that Russia also includes in its definition of national security threats the rise of a potential Islamic state within the borders of the old USSR.

Since the present leaders of Kazakhstan, Uzbekistan, and Kyrgyzstan agreed that such a possibility posed similar security threats to their own states, Russia had little difficulty in gaining the agreements necessary to launch a CIS military operation in Tajikistan, thus enlisting the other Central Asian states to share both the responsibility and the cost for this attempted peacemaking operation. However, both President Boris Yeltsin and Foreign Minister Andrei Kozyrev have made it plain that Russia will not wait for such assistance in the event of a perceived threat to a CIS state with which Russia has a "blood relationship," a term that was invoked for the first time at the UN in autumn 1994.[2] Indeed, now that Russia's determination to intervene has been unambiguously stated, it seems likely that any future Russian military action will come more quickly than it did in Tajikistan, where delay and dithering only increased the financial and human costs of Russia's "police action."

RUSSIA AND THE CIS

Despite Russia's apparent reaffirmation of its right to respond unilaterally in conflicts throughout its expansive security realm, the conflict in Tajikistan has demonstrated that Russia prefers to secure CIS approval for interventions in the "near abroad," as well as to use Russian-dominated multinational (as opposed to exclusively Russian) forces whenever possible. CIS military operations will always be Russian-dominated, given the imbalance in military capabilities of the various CIS states. This is particularly true of military operations in Central Asia, where it would be almost impossible to gain Ukrainian participation; Ukraine is the only other CIS state that has a large, well-trained military whose members have significant international experience.

At present, military operations under CIS sponsorship are planned and staffed on an ad hoc basis, which greatly limits the capacity of the CIS, in its present configuration, to serve as an effective peacemaking or peacekeeping organization. From the moment the CIS was created, the newly independent former Soviet republics have viewed the current structure of their commonwealth arrangement as temporary, with frequent expressions of support for further strengthening CIS institutions.

However, there are great differences of opinion among the various CIS member-states about what should be strengthened and how. In the first days of independence, Moscow could count on Central Asian officials to support virtually any attempt to reintegrate the ex-Soviet states, but this is no longer the case. None of the Central Asian leaders will permit the Russians a carte blanche to redefine the CIS exclusively according to Russian desires, but neither do the region's leaders agree among themselves about the shape and functions of an ideal commonwealth.

Karimov and Niyazov would surrender very little of their states' sovereignty to the CIS. Their philosophy, best articulated by Karimov, is that the integration of the CIS states should not be achieved through formal mechanisms; rather, new CIS institutions should develop as they are required, and only the types of integration that emerge as the new states pursue their various economic and strategic interests should be formalized.[3]

By contrast, Nazarbaev's vision is of a new union of former Soviet republics, tightly bound together by a series of formal institutions designed to coordinate foreign and domestic policies. Nazarbaev's proposed Euro-Asian Union would essentially create a confederation of nominally independent states, each of which would be equally represented, but whose freedom of action would be substantially limited by the new supragovernmental legislative and financial bodies to which the member-states have ceded authority.[4]

Russia's preferences seem to lie somewhere between these two extremes. President Yeltsin's advisers in charge of CIS issues vow that in the near future the CIS will be redefined, linking the economies, foreign policies, and armies of the member-states in new institutions designed to ensure Russian domination; yet, it is not clear how this will be achieved.[5] Russia may issue a preemptory warning to the United States and other Western powers not to risk incurring Russia's anger by opposing these changes,[6] but for such a warning to be fully effective, Russia will have to convince the world that the CIS member-states are voluntarily relinquishing a portion of their own sovereignty, which has not been the case to date.

While there is great reluctance among most CIS leaders, including those in Central Asia, to create institutional mechanisms that permit Russian hegemony within the CIS, many of them, including all of the Central Asian states save Turkmenistan, are participating in the newly created Interrepublic Economic Council (IEC), the first formal Commonwealth institution. Russia possesses 50 percent of the votes in this council, which requires an 80 percent majority to approve most decisions, making the IEC a model for further institutional development within the CIS.

However, the IEC is still far from operational. Most significantly, no formula has been agreed upon to permit the convertibility of currency within the CIS. By summer 1995, Russia no longer seemed eager to find one, preferring that Russia's banks fulfill all the clearinghouse functions for its trade with CIS members.

If the IEC should become fully functional according to its current institutional guidelines, Russian economic domination of the CIS would still be ensured, as would the long-term viability of a single trade bloc encompassing much of the former USSR. However, even if the IEC fails to thrive, Russia is unlikely to abandon its efforts to control and coordinate the development of all strategic resources within the former USSR.

Russian intentions are already clear in the energy sector, where Russia has effectively demanded veto power throughout the CIS. While agreeing up to a point that the former Soviet republics are sovereign states that are free to develop and profit from their energy reserves, Russia clearly feels that its status as the heir of the USSR, which mapped, explored, and began development of these reserves, gives it proprietary rights and interests in perpetuity. Russia asserts the right to help set priorities in the development of energy resources throughout the former Soviet Union, and demands minority ownership of all major oil and gas deposits. Its geographic position makes transportation routes Russia's strongest card, and by trying to determine the location of new pipelines, refineries, and oil terminals, it demonstrates its desire to maintain control over this sector's development; Russia also pursues this goal in a more economically rational way by working to become a substantial shareholder in such projects.

The role of economic hegemon that Russia has claimed for itself naturally makes the other CIS members nervous. The former Soviet republics are all sovereign states and, as such, are free to leave the CIS; even as member-states, all are formally free to refuse membership in new, Russian-sponsored CIS institutions. However, no CIS member-state failed to notice the fates of Georgia's Zviad Gamsakhurdia and Azerbaijan's Abulfaz Elchibey, both of whom refused to join the CIS. Russia is widely believed to have had a large hand in these leaders' ouster and the accompanying political destabilization of their countries. The other CIS leaders also recall the curious timeliness with which the tiny Abkhazian separatist forces discovered the requisite amount of military weapons and supplies to rout Georgian troops soon after President Shevardnadze refused to join a Russian-sponsored CIS collective security arrangement. A similar unexpected turn of events occurred in the armed dispute over Nagorno-Karabakh: Armenian forces swiftly captured Azerbaijan strongholds while the latter state was trying to cut itself free of Russia and the CIS.

The present leaders of the CIS member-states have too much Soviet experience to believe that any of these events were coincidences, even if some truly were. These leaders know that the price of their refusal either to join the IEC or to accept the conditions of a CIS-wide customs union is to suffer much more adverse terms of trade with Russia. In Central Asia, only the oil- and gas-rich Turkmen can even contemplate the effects of having to pay real-world prices in hard currency for their trade with the Russians. The Turkmen are aware, though, that their rejection also has limits, since Russia could wreak havoc on their country's economy should the policymakers in Moscow decide to do so.

CENTRAL ASIAN REGIONAL COOPERATION

How could the Central Asian states protect themselves against a Russia that chooses to expand its hegemony in the region? An obvious strategy would be to seek protection in numbers. As already noted, the Central Asians have banded together in a loose regional association, and three of these states have gone the next step of creating a formal economic union. However, the potential benefits of regional unions among CIS member-states are relatively small. Even fully functional, the new economic union joining Kazakhstan, Kyrgyzstan, and Uzbekistan could serve only as a buffer against Russian indifference; no such union would ever be strong enough to be a counterweight against Russian aggression, economic or otherwise.

The primary goal of the new tripartite economic union is to facilitate trade within the region. For more than seventy years, the Central Asians were able to trade freely among themselves, so trade patterns within Soviet Central Asia ignored republic borders. Tashkent was a trade hub for southern Kazakhstan and for Tajikistan's Khojent. Khorezm oblast, in Uzbekistan, supplied most of western Turkmenistan, just as the economy of Kyrgyzstan's Osh oblast was closely intermeshed with that of neighboring Andizhan in Uzbekistan. Almaty served Bishkek as an airport and transportation center, just as Petropavlovsk and the other cities of Kazakhstan's north served and were served by Omsk and other cities in Russia's Siberia.

Now this once economically integrated region uses five separate currencies (in addition to the Russian ruble), each unstable in some basic way, while the universal currency of dollars (or other hard currency) is in short supply for governments and private citizens alike. This disruption of traditional trade patterns has reduced the standard of living for all who live in border areas, which increases the likelihood that traditional rivalries and irredentist land claims may be aggravated. The most obvious case is the Kyrgyz-Uzbek border, but there are many others in each of the five Central Asian states.

The tripartite union is an effort to ease the impact of new trade barriers by creating an interrepublic bank and a tariff-free trade zone. Each country has already pledged $3 million towards the establishment of a clearinghouse for intraregional trade. If the union is successful, the potential for border conflicts should be lessened, while regularizing interstate and enterprise-level trade among these three states should help the region's economies more generally. However, even if these three states should begin to function as a single economic unit, they will be only slightly less economically dependent upon Russia as a single unit than each one is individually. Such a union also fails to address the severe trading problems that Kazakhstan presently suffers along all the three thousand miles of its border with Russia.

More importantly, although diplomatic relations among these three states have been very good, no state in the region would rely solely on the security guarantees that the Central Asian states offer one another. What makes the Central Asian intraregional security arrangements acceptable to the various signatories is the bilateral military agreements each has made with Russia. For its part, Russia has no objection to Central Asian regional economic and political cooperation as long as this does not substitute for close bilateral ties with Russia or interferes with the participation of the Central Asian states in the CIS.

CENTRAL ASIA AND ITS NEIGHBORS

The Central Asian states also have begun participating in a variety of regional organizations with non-CIS nations. As noted, all have participated in meetings of both the ECO (the Economic Cooperation Organization, formed by Turkey, Iran, and Pakistan) and the Organization of the Islamic Conference (OIC). In the long run, either or both organizations may develop a well-defined collective identity and exert a strong international presence. For now, neither is particularly active in the region, and Central Asian participation has brought little benefit to the new states as they attempt to carve out collective and individual identities that distance them from their Soviet pasts.

The founding nations of both the ECO and the OIC have been almost as eager as the Central Asians are themselves for these new states to distance themselves from Russia. This is particularly true of Turkey and

Iran, both of which now include in their own national interests a leadership role among the former Soviet Central Asian republics.

Turkey has tried to do so by holding itself up as a model for all of the Turkic countries to emulate, reminding the Central Asian states that it is an industrialized society in which secular forces predominate but live in harmony with Islamic groups. The Turkish government has also tried to forge an active Central Asian partnership in order to permit Turkish political leaders and economic interests to prosper among five new Turkic states (the four Central Asian states of Turkic heritage, plus Azerbaijan).

Highlighting mutual benefit was the intent of the first Turkic summit, convened in Ankara in 1992 by Turgut Ozal; the theme was repeated at the 1994 meeting in Istanbul, hosted by Suleiman Demirel. A concrete example of such mutual benefit was provided in a resolution adopted at the 1994 meeting, which called for the construction of a new pipeline through Turkey to facilitate the further expansion of oil production in Central Asia.

However, that same resolution also illustrates the tentative quality of such meetings as long as Russia is not represented. The resolution approves a pipeline but does not specify a route, thereby avoiding the issue of the legitimacy of Russia's claims to oil on the Caspian shelf. In much the same way, the Istanbul declaration applauds the independence of the Central Asian states and their right to behave as sovereign actors, but takes great care to stress that Turkic unity is intended only to augment, and not to usurp, the traditional friendship between Central Asians and Russians.[7]

The Ankara and Istanbul declarations confine themselves largely to questions of economic and political cooperation, making only the vaguest promises of cooperation in regional security matters. This reflects the understanding among Turkey's leaders that to challenge Russia's special security relationship with all the CIS states is to risk a sharp deterioration in their own relations with Russia. Any illusions Turkey may have had otherwise quickly evaporated when Russia vigorously opposed Turkey's fairly tentative efforts to serve as Azerbaijan's protector on security questions during Abulfaz Elchibey's rule.

If Turkey's relations with Azerbaijan and its efforts to mediate the Nagorno-Karabakh conflict are any guide, Turkey is unlikely to be an effective mediator in Central Asia. At the same time, it is equally unlikely that Turkey would want such a role. Azerbaijan and Nagorno-Karabakh are far closer to Turkey's vital interests than would be any potential dispute in Central Asia. Moreover, if Russia fails to see a legitimate role for Turkey in Nagorno-Karabakh, then it is even less likely to accept Turkish intervention in Central Asia, where many of the potential security crises are far closer to Russian security interests. While it is possible to imagine scenarios where Central Asian leaders might wish Turkey to arbitrate or intervene, it is very hard to imagine any situation in which either Russia might call in Turkey or the Turks choose to involve themselves. The only conceivable case for possible Turkish intervention is if the United States strongly urged Turkey to play such a role and also agreed to compensate Turkey for the losses it would suffer in the inevitable souring of Russo-Turkish relations. Yet, such a scenario seems highly unlikely. The United States has on occasion given formal support to the idea of a Turkish "bridge" to Central Asia in matters of trade and technical assistance, but there has been no indication that it has ever considered using Turkey as a surrogate or agent for U.S. strategic interests.

By contrast, although it is far less able than Turkey to use Central Asian independence as a means to advance broader international goals, Iran has enjoyed some success as a mediator in the region, in part because it has been able to synchronize its efforts with Russia. The most notable diplomatic achievement to date has been the preliminary peace accords, signed at a September 1994 meeting in Teheran, in which all sides in Tajikistan's civil war agreed to a six-month cease-fire. While Iranian negotiators hope that this temporary accord can become the basis of a wider agreement, the latter is proving to be very elusive.

The cease-fire, which has not led to a cessation of hostilities, came about in part through a broader international negotiation effort. As already noted, Tajikistan's civil war by 1994 had spread into wider South Asian regional problems, now directly affecting the security interests of Pakistan and Iran, as well as those of Afghanistan, Russia, and the other Central Asian states. Representatives of all these states were granted some degree of participation when all of the parties to Tajikistan's dispute were first brought together in Moscow in summer 1994 with full support from the United Nations.

However, when the second round of talks, held in Teheran, failed to produce even a tentative agreement, the Iranians set up smaller, less formal talks, with substantial Russian participation along with some from the UN. These unofficial talks yielded the temporary accord and became the basis for discussions at the third set of meetings, held in Islamabad in October 1994. However, there has been little progress at subsequent meetings held in winter and spring 1995.

One reason for Iran's temporary success is the country's special relationship with Islamic opposition forces in the region. How much financial and military support Central Asia's Islamic revivalists get from Iran is a subject of great debate; there is no question, however, that Iran provides Central Asia's Islamic revivalists with considerable moral support. Iranian success as a negotiator in Tajikistan should make Iran even more credible in Central Asia, demonstrating that the Islamic Republic is more interested in regional stability than in taking sides.

Russia at least has shown no displeasure with this Iranian role, and might well seek similar Iranian assistance in the future. Given the broader international community's attitude toward the Islamic Republic of Iran, to involve Teheran in a peace process is to move it beyond U.S. involvement in particular, while also distancing it from Western involvement more generally. From the Russian viewpoint, such alienation is not undesirable, making the point that Central Asia and environs are in Russia's backyard, where the Americans are not able to play an effective role. Iranian involvement in negotiations also helps minimize the role of other international organizations, suggesting that conventional peacemaking operations are doomed to fail since Tajikistan's conflict is an unconventional problem, requiring unconventional solutions.

THE ROLE OF INTERNATIONAL ORGANIZATIONS

As discussed previously, the five Central Asian nations are all members of a number of international organizations including, most prominently, the United Nations and the OSCE. They joined these organizations for a variety of reasons, not the least of which was the international respectability that membership in these bodies brings them. Of greater importance, though, was the hope that their membership in both these organizations would help to guarantee their sovereignty and independence. Both of these organizations rank peacemaking and peacekeeping high among their list of responsibilities; however, it is unclear how effective either the UN or the OSCE might be in undertaking peacekeeping missions within the CIS.

Once the USSR was disbanded, membership in the United Nations for the new states was more or less automatic. That was not the case, however, with the decision to expand the membership of the OSCE's predecessor to include all of the Soviet successor states; this was a more calculated move, designed to encourage the new states to behave in a more "European" manner, at least in regard to both human rights and the organization's culture of negotiation rather than confrontation.

That calculation has been a success, at least in the case of the Baltic states, where OSCE membership has been of great value in controlling and channeling tensions with Russia regarding ethnic Russians in these new states. It is difficult to imagine, though, that OSCE membership will ever confer the same benefits in similar disputes involving Central Asian states.

The issue of human rights in Central Asia is complex. Local Russians have been offered full rights of citizenship in all five republics, while the dual citizenship Russia's government is demanding for Central Asia's ethnic Russians is neither common nor widely accepted in the international community. As a consequence, Russian efforts to involve the OSCE High Commissioner of National Minorities in the plight of Russians in Central Asia in general, and in Kazakhstan in particular, have had only limited success. If current plans go forward in modifying existing national language laws in Kazakhstan and Kyrgyzstan to give the Russian language a wider role, there will be even less formal justification for Russian complaints, and fewer grounds for potential OSCE mediation. At the same time, though, local Russians are likely to continue to feel that they are second-class citizens in Central Asia, which will still make it possible that Russia will feel the need to undertake some sort of action to redress perceived wrongs.

In the event of aggressive action on the part of Russia, it would certainly be within the mandate of the OSCE to respond on the side of the aggrieved Central Asian states. Realistically, though, it is difficult to imagine that any of the Central Asian states would have sufficient diplomatic representation at the OSCE to be able to make a successful formal complaint; it is also difficult to imagine their leaders would choose such a public forum for airing their countries' grievances against Russia. This is particularly true since none of the Central Asian states has done an especially good job of living up to the various OSCE guidelines. However, even if such a protest is given notice, it is very difficult to imagine conditions in which the OSCE might feel competent to undertake action against Russia.

Russia seeks to protect itself against even this remote eventuality by recommending a change in the OSCE charter to create a ten-member executive council in which five countries, including Russia, would have veto powers.[8] This proposal is unlikely to be adopted since it is strongly opposed by the OSCE member-nations that also belong to NATO. In any event, reorganization of the OSCE would seem to be an unnecessary formality since Russia will exercise its own effective veto power over all peacekeeping missions in the CIS. This was certainly the case with the OSCE mission to negotiate the Nagorno-Karabakh dispute. After several months of undermining the OSCE position through its own unilateral efforts at peacemaking, Russia finally demanded in October 1994 that it be granted a formal OSCE mandate to become the primary agent for reaching and maintaining a peace agreement in the Armenian-Azerbaijani territorial dispute, while the CIS negotiating team would be relegated to a secondary role.[9]

It is quite likely that, if the situation warrants, Russia would demand a similar arrangement from the OSCE in Tajikistan. Russia has already essentially demanded this from the United Nations, repeatedly asking that Russian and CIS troops in Tajikistan be allowed to don the UN's blue helmets; it has also asked that the United Nations pay for such peacekeeping missions as well.

What Russia would ideally like to achieve is a blanket mandate (and funding) from the United Nations for CIS troops to act as UN peacekeepers throughout the CIS. With its military resources sorely stretched and resources generally in short supply, the UN has had little inclination to provide such a broad sanction. To date the UN Security Council has limited its sponsorship to specific operations, such as supervising the resettlement of refugees in Georgia's separatist conflict. However, the UN leadership recognizes that Russia has a special de facto role within the CIS; as such, it is difficult to imagine the UN ever taking an active role in mediating a conflict within the CIS without Russia's approval. It goes without saying that Russia's veto in the Security Council makes it impossible for the UN to undertake independent military action anywhere within the CIS.

Is There A Role for the United States?

What should be the appropriate reaction of the international community to Russia's self-proclaimed hegemony in the former Soviet Union? More to the point, does the international community have much choice in the matter? Russia sees itself as a superpower, even if a comparatively dormant one at the moment; given Russia's vast nuclear arsenal and long-term economic prospects, this is a difficult claim to dispute.

Initially Russian leaders justified their assumption of hegemonic power in the CIS region as consistent with democracy-building, claiming that Russia was the logical choice to lead their more benighted ex-Soviet brethren along the path toward democratization and market reform. Now, the Russians defend their actions in more pragmatic terms, asserting that the CIS is their sphere of influence, and assuring the international community that it will behave responsibly as it seeks to protect its strategic interests.

The United States and other Western powers have been reluctant to accept Russia's claim in regard to the Baltic states, but the international community, and the United States in particular, have granted Russia enormous leeway for its actions in the CIS. Given the history of the region, as well as its distance from the United States, Russia's claims take on an irrefutable logic. It is not unnatural for a "mother country" that is contiguous and has the capacity to protect its fellow ethnics easily to take an interest in the welfare of people it considers to be conationals. After centuries of migration and settlement during Russia's imperial and Soviet periods, ethnic Russians in the "near abroad" must now cope with massive dislocation in the period of independence. In addition, Russia is itself a new state, with new and wholly unfortified international borders that are nearly as long as the Soviet Union's. Thus from a strategic standpoint, common sense governs Russian military officials' definition of their country's geopolitical interests as extending to the former USSR's borders, which are already fortified.

While the West spent decades trying to vanquish its ideological foundation, the USSR's breakup was not something the international community sought or desired, since the "rebirth" of the Soviet republics as independent states was viewed as potentially destabilizing to both the region and the much wider arena of international security. At most, the CIS states had only a year or so to prepare for independence, not enough time for them to consider their own solutions to the region's new, large irredentist populations, created when internal administrative boundaries became inviolable international borders upon independence. To the international community, these new states appear potentially very unstable. Although Russia, too, is a new state, at least it has a mature state administration that it inherited from the USSR, which should allow Russia to understand that it has more to lose from regional instability than has anyone else, and so should encourage Russia to include in its definition of national interest the goal of maximizing order rather than disorder in the region.

In ceding so much regional authority to Russia, the United States and the international community at large should accept the responsibility of trying to make this goal a reality. For moral as well as for geopolitical reasons, the world must try to ensure that Russia behaves as a "good" hegemon rather than as a bully toward these new and fragile neighboring states. It is not enough simply to insist that Russia not violate the sovereignty and independence of these states, if only because there is no accepted international standard by which to define sovereignty or independence, except to agree that one state may not be under formal and involuntary occupation by another.

The case of Tajikistan illustrates the complexity of this point. It is difficult to say whether or not Tajikistan is now a sovereign country; the current government does not control the security or the economy of the country, nor did it come to power through any exercise of popular choice. The current government is in place only because Russia, with the support of Tajikistan's neighbors in the CIS, serves as its guarantor. Nevertheless, Tajikistan and its current government are both "recognized" as sovereign and independent by the United States and virtually all of the international community. Indeed, the U.S. decision to recognize the Rahmonov government as legitimate seems to have come largely as a result of Russian pressure.

This poses a quandary for U.S. foreign policy: U.S. *opposition* to a continuing Russian military presence in Tajikistan, or an American refusal to recognize the Rahmonov government, would not have kept the Russians from pursuing what they define as their national interest in the area, but U.S. *support* of Russia's actions does have serious implications for both Russian foreign policy and U.S. long-term interests in the region.

Tajikistan was already at war in October 1992 when Russia intervened; decisions had to be made quickly by all parties, including the United States. Yet, the United States has not used the subsequent two years to elaborate any criteria by which to judge the legitimacy of possible future Russian interventions. In fact, U.S. policymakers have actively avoided considering any such criteria out of concern for doing anything that might weaken the position of Russia's "democratic" forces, who are frequently, usually erroneously, understood to be the captives of Russian nationalists and former communists on questions of policy toward the

new states. In fact, virtually all key actors and advisors in Russia's foreign policy community are unanimous in their opinion that Russia has
the right to act unilaterally within the CIS and throughout the territorial
expanse of the former Soviet Union.

The U.S. decision to treat dependent states as if they were wholly
sovereign, combined with its reluctance to take up the question of Russia's relationship to the other CIS states, will certainly hamper any
future attempt by the United States to criticize or prevent Russia's
actions toward the CIS. Russia's growing inclination to see itself as having proprietary rights to the "near abroad" will eventually thwart the
American commitment to see all of the Soviet successor states transformed into market-based democracies, making future clashes between
Russia and America on this issue all but inevitable.

Already the United States and Russia are on opposite sides of the question of developing the Caspian Sea's oil reserves. U.S. firms are already
losing substantial amounts of money in seemingly endless rounds of
negotiations and renegotiations. Chevron's losses mount each day while
the torturous and convoluted discussions drag on about building a new
pipeline for the export of oil from Kazakhstan's Tengiz fields. Perhaps
most important, however, is that after six years of effort and investment,
none of this oil is headed west. If the current battles over Tengiz and the
Caspian shelf are any guide, the prospect of the West's ability to ensure
secure sources of fossil fuel from anywhere within the former USSR
seems very dim indeed.

Can the West really afford the present state of ambiguity in Russia's
relations with the Central Asian states? Is ceding Russia control in the
former Soviet republics, without clear limits, really in the interests of
either international or regional security? Current conditions very strongly
suggest that the answer to both questions is no, which means that eventually the West is likely to regret its decision to grant Russia an effective
carte blanche within the CIS.

Future Russian regimes may well be less democratic and more
aggressive than the current one. With the precedent of Russian control
already firmly established, it is hard to believe that these future regimes
would even give a second through to Western or U.S. objections over
their violations of their neighbors' sovereignty.

Of course, if Russia is successful in its efforts to transform the CIS
into a thoroughly institutionalized, integrated alliance system, then the
West would have little occasion to complain. Given current conditions,

however, it is difficult to imagine such a transformation occurring through the voluntary surrender of sovereignty by all the CIS member-states. If such reintegration involves these states' *involuntary* loss of sovereignty, then the United States and the West will find themselves trapped in the very corner they are currently trying so hard to avoid.

Of course, it is difficult to set up informal standards of accountability for Russia's actions in the "near abroad." A delicate balance must be struck between respecting Russia's security concerns and protecting the rights of the other new nations. All the same, Russia should not be granted special rights in the "near abroad." If the international community permits Russia to behave with less than full respect for the states closest to it—nations with which it has the closest and most long-standing ties—then the world ought not be surprised when Russia fails to show proper respect for more distant neighbors.

The United States should be no more tolerant of abusive Russian behavior in the Central Asian republics than it is of such behavior toward the former Soviet Union's European republics. Central Asia may be far from Europe's and America's other zones of primary security; however, the world grows ever smaller, while its peoples and resources become ever more interconnected. Not only will Central Asia's energy resources become increasingly important in the decades to come, but events in this part of the world are already having a direct impact on at least one important U.S. ally, Turkey, as well as on the South Asian security system more generally.

Russia is now and will always be more important than Central Asia to U.S. security concerns at a time when the West's long-term security interests include integrating Russia into the Western alliance as a full and responsible partner. However, Russia will never become such a partner if it is permitted to be a whimsical and capricious bully among its weaker immediate neighbors. Russia's "police actions" in the "near abroad" should be scrutinized closely by the international community, even if this means that U.S. "police actions" come under the same type of scrutiny. America bases its international involvement on a respect for democratic principles and the rights of sovereign states. If Russia is admitted into the community of democratic nations on any terms other than these, then its membership would make a mockery of the very institutions of international cooperation in which Russia seeks acceptance.

NOTES

1. A PREMATURE BIRTH

1. Personal accounts of members of Kazakhstan's delegation to the United States on February 14, 1994.

2. Even in the late 1980s, the leaders of Uzbekistan and Tajikistan were complaining that the majority of their populations lived below the poverty level.

3. *Literaturnaia gazeta*, no. 40 (1991): 2.

4. For an assessment, see Gregory Gleason, "The Struggle for Control over Water in Central Asia: Republican Sovereignty and Collective Action," *Radio Liberty Report on the USSR* (21 June 1991): 11–14.

5. Only Kyrgyzstan's Askar Akaev immediately came out against the coup. *Slovo Kyrgyzstana*, 19 August 1991.

6. Islam Karimov, press conference, Uzbekistan television, 20 September 1991.

7. *Izvestiia*, 19 October 1991.

8. *Izvestiia*, 4 October 1991.

9. An oft-quoted piece in this regard was the two-part essay by Igor Beliaev that appeared in *Literaturnaia gazeta* in May 1987.

10. *Moskovskiye novosti*, no. 22 (1991).

11. *Kazakhstanskaia pravda*, 21 September 1991.

12. Ankara Domestic Service, 16 March 1991, as printed in *FBIS Daily Report: Soviet Union*, FBIS-SOV-91-052, 18 March 1991, p. 74.

13. *Kazakhstanskaia pravda*, 25 September 1991.

14. *FBIS Daily Report: Soviet Union*, FBIS-SOV-233, 4 December 1991, pp. 81–83.

15. *Ibid.*

16. Postfaktum, 28 January 1991, as translated in *FBIS Daily Report: Central Eurasia*, FBIS-SOV-92-023, 4 February 1992, p. 70.

17. *Nezavisimaia gazeta*, 25 December 1991, as translated in *FBIS Daily Report: Central Eurasia, Baltic and Eurasian States*, FBIS-USR-92-004, 14 January 1992, p. 88.

18. *FBIS Daily Report: Soviet Union*, FBIS-SOV-91-100, 23 May 1991, p. 16.

19. *Kazakhstanskaia pravda*, 16 July 1991.

20. *Izvestiia*, 21 September 1991.

21. *Kyrgyz tuusu*, 3 December 1993.

22. Interfax, 6 November 1991, as printed in *FBIS Daily Report: Soviet Union*, FBIS-SOV-91-215, 6 November 1991, p. 74.

23. Interfax, 1 February 1992, as printed in *FBIS Daily Report: Central Eurasia*, FBIS-SOV-92-023, 4 February 1992, p. 68.

24. Radio Mayak, 28 January 1992, as printed in *FBIS Daily Report: Central Eurasia*, FBIS-SOV-92-023, 4 February 1992, p. 68.

2. FAILED ETHNIC CARDS

1. A very early version of some of the material in this chapter appears in my article, "Nation Building and Ethnicity in the Foreign Policies of the New Central Asian States," in Roman Szporluk, ed., *The International Politics of Eurasia, Vol. 2: The Influence of National Identity* (Armonk, N.Y.: M.E. Sharpe, 1994): 209–229.

2. Interfax, 4 February 1992, as printed in *FBIS Daily Report: Central Eurasia*, FBIS-SOV-92-025, 6 February 1993, p. 70.

3. *Izvestiia*, 6 February 1992.

4. *Slovo Kyrgyzstana*, 11 December 1992.

5. *Kazakhstanskaia pravda*, 15 May 1992.

6. *Daily Report: Western Europe*, FBIS-WEU-220, 20 November 1991, p. 60.

7. *Daily Report: Western Europe*, FBIS-WEU-235, 6 December 1991, p. 40.

8. *Izvestiia*, 20 December 1991.

9. Interfax, 4 March 1992, as printed in *FBIS Daily Report: Central Eurasia*, FBIS-SOV-92-045, 6 March 1992, p. 57.

10. Ankara television, September 30, 1992, as reported in *FBIS Daily Report: Central Eurasia*, FBIS-SOV-92-192, 2 October 1992, p. 32.

11. Address of Prime Minister Tansu Ciller to the Turkish-American Business Council, Istanbul, November 1992.

12. On Iranian credits to Turkmenistan, see Postfaktum, 5 March 1992, as printed in *FBIS Daily Report: Central Eurasia*, FBIS-SOV-92-045, 6 March 1992, p. 57.

13. Tehran IRNA service, February 6, 1992, as printed in *FBIS Daily Report: Central Eurasia*, FBIS-SOV-92-027, 10 February 1992, p. 78.

14. *Izvestiia*, 13 October 1992.

15. *Izvestiia*, 3 December 1991.

16. Radio Tashkent, 11 April 1992, as reported in *FBIS Daily Report: Central Eurasia*, 14 April 1992, p. 60.

17. Radio Tashkent, 20 February 1992, as reported in *FBIS Daily Report: Central Eurasia*, FBIS-SOV-92-037, 25 February 1992.

18. *Nezavisimaia gazeta*, 7 January 1992. *Halal* meat comes from animals slaughtered according to dietary restrictions of Muslim *Shari'a*.

19. *Izvestiia*, 24 February 1992.

20. Riyadh SPA, 21 February 1992, as reported in *FBIS Daily Report: Central Eurasia*, FBIS-SOV-92-037, 25 February 1992, p. 71.

21. *Izvestiia*, 21 September 1991.

22. *Komsomol'skaia pravda*, 26 August 1993.

23. *Panorama* (Bishkek), 15 August 1992.

24. *Erkin Too*, 30 June 1993.

3. False Hopes of Cooperation

1. *Nezavisimaia gazeta*, 8 October 1992. In October 1992, General Shaposhnikov claimed that he and Yeltsin were already in control of the "briefcase" containing the launch codes for all of the former USSR's nuclear weapons.

2. ITAR-TASS, 16 April 1993, as quoted in *FBIS Daily Report: Central Eurasia*, FBIS-SOV-93-073, 19 April 1993, p. 1.

3. Interfax, 8 October 1992, as quoted in *FBIS Daily Report: Central Eurasia*, FBIS-SOV-92-197, 9 October 1992. President Karimov calls Russia the guarantor of stability in Central Asia, and says Russia has to look after its own interests there, as it has for centuries.

4. *Kazakhstanskaia pravda*, 25 June 1990.

5. *Kazakhstanskaia pravda*, 23 June 1990.

6. *Kazakhstanskaia pravda*, 17 August 1991.

7. *Slovo Kyrgyzstana*, 18 December 1992.

8. Broadcast of "Vremiia," 10 December 1991.

9. This interpretation is consistent with Nazarbaev's later reflections on those days; see *Nezavisimaia gazeta*, 28 July 1993.

10. Turkmenistan declared independence on October 27, 1991. Kyrgyzstan and Uzbekistan both declared independence on August 31, 1991.

11. *Izvestiia*, 25 April 1992.

12. *Izvestiia*, 7 January 1993.

4. Kazakhstan: Living with a Hegemon

1. Martha Brill Olcott, *The Kazakhs* (Stanford: Hoover Institution Press, 1987). See especially pp. 224–247.

2. *Komsomol'skaia pravda*, 18 September 1990.

3. *Izvestiia*, 4 May 1994. In this article, Solzhenitsyn called for Russia to take back oblasts in Ukraine, Belarus, and Kazakhstan that were predominantly Russian.

4. *Kazakhstanskaia pravda*, 11 August 1992.

5. *Rossiiskaia gazeta*, 3 January 1992, p. 7.

6. *Kazakhstan: Ekonomika i zhizn'*, no. 9 (1993): 58.

7. *ABV*, 18 February 1994.

8. *Panorama*, 26 February 1994.

9. *Kazakhstanskaia pravda*, 16 May 1992.

10. *Nezavisimaia gazeta*, 8 September 1993, p. 1.

11. *Kommersant*, 18 September 1993, p. 6.

12. *Izvestiia*, 13 September 1993, p. 4.

13. For details, see *Trends in the Southern Tier* (Philadelphia: Foreign Policy Research Institute, November 1993), a report prepared for the Office of Net Assessment, U.S. Department of Defense.

14. *Izvestiia*, 2 March 1995, p. 4.

15. *Karavan*, 7 April 1995, p. 2.

16. *Nezavisimaia gazeta*, 16 March 1994.

17. Victor Kianitsa, "Test Anxiety," *The Bulletin of the Atomic Scientists* (October 1993): 37–38.

18. Julian Cooper, *The Soviet Defence Industry: Conversion and Reform* (London: Royal Institute of International Affairs, September 1991), p. 23; calculations were made from information revealed in *Pravda*, 11 January 1991.

19. For details, see the World Bank, *Trends in Developing Countries, 1993* (Washington, DC: World Bank, 1994).

20. See Nazarbaev's plan for the economic development of the republic, as outlined in *Ogni Alatau*, 19 May 1992, unpaginated insert.

21. *Birlesu*, no. 1 (1994).

22. Interfax, 1 March 1993, as reported in *FBIS Daily Report: Central Eurasia*, FBIS-SOV-93-038, 1 March 1993, p. 3.

23. The best Chernomyrdin could manage by then was a Caspian-wide agreement advocating that the Caspian should be treated as "a single ecological complex," the development of which should "respect each state's sovereignty and [adhere] to the goals and principles of dynamic and harmonious development of their economies." ITAR-TASS, 14 October 1993, as reported in *FBIS Daily Report: Central Eurasia*, FBIS-SOV-93-198, 15 October 1993, p. 1.

24. The total profit is to be divided in the following way: 85 percent for Kazakhstan and 15 percent for the contractors. The latter will split three ways: 15 percent to Gazprom and 42.5 percent each to British Gas and Agip.

25. Russia owns 34 percent of the stock of the Trans-Caspian Consortium (the holder of Tengiz pipeline rights), Kazakhstan 34 percent, and the Omani Oil Company 31 percent.

26. Xinhua, 27 October 1992, as quoted in *FBIS Daily Report: China*, FBIS-CHI-92-210, 29 October 1992.

27. In Nazarbaev's words, "God grant that no one should stir up Kazakhstan on ethnic grounds. It would be far worse than Yugoslavia." *Kazakhstanskaia pravda*, 23 November 1991, p. 1.

28. *FBIS Daily Report. Central Eurasia*, FBIS-USR-92-140, 31 October 1992, p. 84. Other rumors say Nazarbaev was slated for a vice-presidency, presumably behind Gorbachev; still others say he was to become prime minister.

5. KYRGYZSTAN: SURVIVING ON FOREIGN SUPPORT

1. Informal communications to the author by a senior member of the Japanese Ministry of Foreign Affairs who wished to remain anonymous.

2. *Vechernyi Bishkek*, 12 July 1993, p. 3.

3. *Delovoi mir*, 14–20 March 1994.

4. Personal interviews by the author in January 1994.

5. *Svobodnye gory*, no. 22 (April 1993).

6. *Slovo Kyrgyzstana*, 5 March 1994.

7. *Delovoi mir*, 14–20 March 1994.

8. *Slovo Kyrgyzstana*, 26 February 1994.

9. *Slovo Kyrgyzstana*, 28 December 1994.

10. *Rossiiskaia gazeta*, 11 November 1993.

11. ITAR-TASS, 16 October 1993, as reported in *FBIS Daily Report: Central Eurasia*, FBIS-SOV-93-199, 18 October 1993, pp. 85–86.

12. *Moscow News*, 16–23 January 1994.

13. I am especially indebted to Ross Munro of the Foreign Policy Research Institute for access to his unpublished manuscripts in the preparation of this section.

14. *Trud*, 15 March 1994, as reported in *FBIS Daily Report: Central Eurasia*, FBIS-SOV-94-051, 16 March 1994, p. 45.

15. *Delovoi mir*, 14–20 March 1994.

6. UZBEKISTAN: CENTRAL ASIA'S INSTINCTIVE IMPERIALIST

1. *Nezavisimaia gazeta*, 11 December 1993.

2. *Radio Liberty Daily Report*, 14 January 1994.

3. *Segodnya*, 11 January 1994, as translated in *FBIS Daily Report: Central Eurasia*, FBIS-SOV-94-008, 12 January 1994, p. 79.

4. In August 1993, a bomb also exploded in Mirsaidov's apartment, although no one was home at the time. *Ekspress*, 24 August 1993, p. 1.

5. *Nezavisimaia gazeta*, 7 January 1992.

6. Established in 1943, SADUM was the USSR's official religious organization that licensed state-recognized clerics, mosques, and religious schools, and supervised Islam in the five Central Asian republics. In 1989, Kazakhstan split off and formed its own religious directorate. After independence, the other Central Asian states gradually severed ties as well.

7. Abdujabar Abduvakhitov, "Islamic Revivalism in Uzbekistan," in Dale F. Eickelman, ed., *Russia's Muslim Frontiers* (Bloomington, Ind.: Indiana University Press, 1993), p. 88.

8. For an example, see *Kashkadarinskaia pravda* (in Uzbek), 14 November 1992.

9. *Nezavisimaia gazeta*, 3 April 1992.

10. *FBIS Daily Report: Central Eurasia*, FBIS-SOV-92-180, 16 September 1992, p. 50.

11. *Nezavisimaia gazeta*, 30 March 1994, p. 6.

12. *Khorezmskaia pravda*, 17 April 1993.

13. *FBIS Daily Report: Central Eurasia*, FBIS-USR-93-070, 7 June 1993, p. 69.

14. *Izvestiia*, 30 November 1993, p. 3.

15. *Nezavisimaia gazeta*, 9 July 1993, p. 3.

16. *Sovetskaia Rossiia*, 29 July 1993, pp. 1, 3, and 4.

17. Nabiev had been appointed First Secretary of the Communist Party only in 1982, when death had created a vacancy in this position. Nabiev, however, was the number two Tajik in the party hierarchy at the time of his appointment.

18. *Vechernii Dushanbe*, 20 February 1990.

19. *Al'-Vakhdat*, no. 1 (9 January 1991): 4.

20. There have been persistent reports that the United States was also sufficiently disturbed by Turajonzada's apparent ascension that it helped fly Uzbek troops and equipment into Tajikistan in October–November 1992. *Al-Hayah* (London), 3 March 1993, as reported in *FBIS Daily Report: Central Eurasia*, FBIS-SOV-93-048, 15 March 1993, pp. 90–91. See also *Izvestiia*, 7 August 1993, p. 7.

21. *Nezavisimaia gazeta*, 9 September 1993.

22. *Nezavisimaia gazeta*, 29 July 1993, p. 1.

23. Embassy First Secretary Fahreddin Parpiev as quoted in *Manchester Guardian Weekly*, 23 April 1995, p. 4.

24. *Nezavisimaia gazeta*, 1 April 1993, p. 3.

25. Interfax, 23 December 1992, as reported in *FBIS Daily Report: Central Eurasia*, FBIS-SOV-92-247, 23 December 1992, p. 73.

26. *Nezavisimaia gazeta*, 23 February 1993, p. 3. See also *Al-Sharq al-Awsat*, 22 December 1992, p. 7, as reported in *FBIS Daily Report: Central Eurasia*, FBIS-SOV-93-005, 8 January 1993, p. 34.

27. *Novaia ezhednevnaia gazeta*, no. 6 (14–20 May 1993), p. 4, as reported in *FBIS Daily Report: Central Eurasia*, FBIS-SOV-93-095, 19 May 1993, p. 68.

28. *Narodnoe slovo,* 10 March 1994, as translated in *FBIS Daily Report: Central Eurasia,* FBIS-SOV-94-050, 15 March 1994, p. 40.

29. *Izvestiia,* 15 April 1994.

30. *Obshchaia gazeta,* 11 March 1994, as reported in *FBIS Daily Report: Central Eurasia,* FBIS-SOV-94-031, 30 March 1994, p. 105.

31. Interfax, 11 January 1994, as reported in *FBIS Daily Report: Central Eurasia,* FBIS-SOV-94-008, 12 January 1994.

32. *Moskovskaia pravda,* 3 March 1994, as translated in *FBIS Daily Report: Central Eurasia,* FBIS-USR-94-031, 30 March 1994, p. 109.

33. *FBIS Daily Report: Central Eurasia,* FBIS-SOV-93-017, 28 January 1993, p. 47.

34. *Delovoy mir,* 4 December 1993.

35. Interfax, 25 November 1993, as reported in *FBIS Daily Report: Central Eurasia,* FBIS-SOV-93-226, 26 November 1993, p. 62.

36. *Delovoy mir,* 14–20 March 1994.

37. *Narodnoe slovo* quoted by Interfax, 2 April 1994, as reported in *FBIS Daily Report: Central Eurasia,* FBIS-SOV-94-065, 5 April 1994, p. 48.

7. IN SEARCH OF REUNIFICATION

1. *Argumenty i fakty,* no. 2 (1993), p. 2.

2. *Nezavisimaia gazeta,* 21 January 1993, p. 5.

3. *Moskovskie novosti,* no. 4 (1992), p. 9.

4. *Izvestiia,* 24 June 1993, p. 2.

8. PEACEFUL BRIDGES TO THE FUTURE?

1. *Al-Sharq Al-Awsat* (London), 2 October 1994, p. 4, as quoted in *FBIS Daily Report: Near East and South Asia,* FBIS-NES-94-192, 4 October 1994, p. 62.

2. *RFE/RL Daily Bulletin,* 27 September 1994.

3. *Nezavisimaia gazeta,* 21 June 1994.

4. *Nezavisimaia gazeta,* 8 June 1994.

5. Interview with Anatoly Adamshin, *Rossiya,* no. 26 (13–19 July 1994), as translated in *FBIS Report: Central Eurasia,* FBIS-USR-94-088, 15 August 1994, p. 64.

6. *Financial Times* (London), 21 September 1994.

7. Ankara TRT television broadcast, 19 October 1994, as printed in *FBIS Daily Report: West Europe,* FBIS-WEU-94-203, 20 October 1994, p. 54.

8. *RFE/RL Daily Bulletin,* 16 September 1994.

9. *RFE/RL Daily Bulletin,* 24 October 1994.

GLOSSARY

Akim (head). A ruler, governor, or judge; the leader of an oblast-sized administrative unit.

Akimate. An administrative unit, roughly equal in size to an oblast.

Apparat. Body of officials who administer Communist Party organizations.

Hajj. The pilgrimage to Mecca prescribed as a religious duty for all Muslims.

Hajji. One who has made a pilgrimage to Mecca; often used as a title.

Hakim. Variant of *akim.*

Khanate. The state or jurisdiction of a local chieftain or man of rank in some countries of Central Asia.

Madrasah. Muslim secondary school.

Mujahideen (warriors). Beginning in the early 1980s, a term used to define regionally based guerrilla fighters who resisted the Soviet invasion of Afghanistan as well as the Soviet-backed Afghani army.

Nomenklatura. Soviet-era list of acceptable candidates slated to fill mid- and high-level state and party positions under control of the Communist Party.

Oblast. Major administrative subdivision of a republic.

Okrug. Administrative region, larger than an oblast.

Rayon. Administrative unit consisting of an urban district or a group of rural villages; usually constitutes part of an oblast.

Shari'a. Islamic law.

INDEX

Organization for Security and Cooperation in Europe *(cont.)*
future prospects, 174–175
OSCE. *See* Organization for Security and Cooperation in Europe
Osh
demands for greater autonomy, 106
drug trading, 98, 104, 161
ethnic makeup, 105
ethnic unrest, 42–43, 53, 113
military roadblocks, 105
potential as haven for Islamic revivalists, 108
Uzbekistan's interest in, 106–108
weapons trading, 161
Otunbaeva, Roza, 23
Ozal, Turgut, 15, 25–26, 171

Pakistan
relations with Central Asian states, 17
relations with Uzbekistan, 135
Tajikistan's civil war and, 129, 172
transport routes, 158
Palestinians, 33
Persian nationalism, 25, 27–31
Press
Kyrgyzstan, 90, 92, 96
Uzbekistan, 116
Pulatov, Abdumannob, 107

Rabbani, Burhanuddin, 129
Rafsanjani, Ali Akbar Hashemi, 27, 82–83, 120, 150
Rahmonov, Emomali
Central Asian leaders' views of, 56, 105
CIS role in supporting, 51, 56, 127–128, 141
Karimov's interference, 129–130
opposition figures in Afghanistan, 29
rise to power, 29, 51, 118, 120, 127–128

Rashidov, Sharaf, 114, 144
Rastokhez, 123, 124–125, 127
"Ruble zone" negotiations, 6, 47–48, 63–64, 133
Russia
as arbiter of disputes, 50–51
CIS dominance, 44–45, 47–52, 166–169, 174–175
coup attempt, August 1991, 10, 54, 124
energy resources, 78–79, 163, 168
future role in Central Asia, 144, 156–160
intervention in Tajikistan, 55, 144, 177–178
nuclear weapons, 45–46, 176
OSCE and, 174–175
reintegration efforts, 140–144, 153–154
relations with Central Asian states, 6, 7–8, 21–22, 36–37, 47–52
relations with Iran, 173
relations with Kazakhstan, 21, 36–37, 48, 49, 51, 57–59, 62–70, 143, 144, 163
relations with Kyrgyzstan, 21–22, 36–37, 49, 91, 110–112, 144
relations with Turkmenistan, 36–37, 49, 144, 146–147, 149, 151, 164
relations with Uzbekistan, 136–137, 144, 163
security issues, 45–47, 164–169
support of ethnic Russians in Central Asian states, 8, 144, 174
Tajikistan civil war as object lesson for, 143, 164–166

SADUM. *See* Central Asian Spiritual Directorate of Muslims
Safarov, Sangak, 126, 127, 128
Salih, Muhammad, 115
Saudi Arabia, 31, 32, 33, 120

CENTRAL ASIA'S NEW STATES

This book is set in Slimbach Book; the display type is Arrow. Hasten Design Studio, Inc. designed the book's cover, and Joan Engelhardt and Day W. Dosch designed the interior. Helene Y. Redmond of HYR Graphics did the page makeup. Kenneth Allen was in charge of computer cartography, and Andrew Robarts provided research for the map and the glossary. Peter Pavilionis was the book's editor. Copyediting, proofreading, and indexing were done by Joyce Peterson, Sarah B. Forman, and Lee Ann Regan, respectively, of Editorial Experts, Inc.